The Book of the Jaguar Priest

The Book

of the Jaguar

Priest

HENRY SCHUMAN

NEW YORK

a translation of

the Book of Chilam

Balam of Tizimin,

with commentary

Maud Worcester Makemson

Vassar College

Acknowledgments

WITH DEEP GRATITUDE I ACKNOWLEDGE MY DEBT TO President Sarah Gibson Blanding and the Trustees of Vassar College for granting me a year's release from teaching duties in order to pursue my research in Maya astronomy by translating the Book of Chilam Balam of Tizimin. I am also grateful to the Salmon Fund Committee of Vassar College for a generous grant in aid of publication.

To Mr. Julian Yonge, director of the P. K. Yonge Library of Florida History of the University of Florida, special thanks are due for the use of a table and the microfilm reader of the library during the fall semester of 1948. And I am most grateful for being given the privileges of the University of California Library at Berkeley during the spring of 1949.

I should also like to express appreciation of my debt to Linton Satterthwaite, Jr., of the University of Pennsylvania Museum for calling my attention to the valuable information regarding the Maya calendar locked away in the Tizimin manuscript and for making a microfilm copy available to me for study. Warm thanks are also due to Miss Louise Howe Evans, Vassar '51, for her patient assistance in checking the microfilm transcription, verifying the vocabulary, and other valuable aid.

Maud Worcester Makemson

Vassar College, September 1950.

Contents

Foreword

CORDOBA, GRIJALVA, CORTES, AVILA, THE ADELANTADO de Montejo and his son Don Francisco—one after another the Conquistadores in their winged ships were borne on the winds to the shores of Yucatan. From 1517 onward, the Maya provinces were seldom free from the bearded adventurers, the "strutting turkey-cocks," to quote the Jaguar Priest. By 1546 the military conquest of upper Yucatan was complete.

Then began the long and bitter struggle between those Spaniards whose purpose was merely to plunder the material possessions and exploit the labor of the hapless Yucatecans and the single-minded friars who sought to snatch their souls from the tenacious grasp of Satan.

Among those who received the early invaders in a peaceable and friendly manner were the Xiu and Chel tribes of northern Yucatan. If they expected by this agency to secure deliverance from their native oppressors whom they call only by the name *Itza*, "wise or skilled ones," in the Tizimin manuscript, these gentle and cultured people suffered one bitter disillusionment after another. In the course of time their smoldering resentment burst into flame and they rebelled against their oppressors. Their story is recorded in the Book of the Jaguar Priest.

Their leaders were imprisoned, tortured to death or hanged. Their precious books, which they valued above their own lives for the ancient learning they embodied, were burned before their eyes. Their people were enslaved. Their women were enticed away with tawdry gifts. Their children were taken captive to the monasteries and taught to read and write in a new language and to worship the white god whose signal was the roar of the arquebus.

The nobles who had gained a precarious immunity at the price of outward adherence to the new form of worship saw with mounting dismay that the ancient Maya learning was doomed to oblivion. Already by 1593, the date of the opening pages of the Book of Chilam Balam of Tizimin, there must have been left only a few men who could decipher the ancient hieroglyphs. They were forbidden to teach the hereditary lore to their sons and, herded into towns as they were, they found little opportunity to do so. It was then that they decided to record in the new European characters what they could remember of the ancient ceremonies and prophecies. Such were the books of Chilam Balam.

The present translation of the Book of Chilam Balam of Tizimin was made from a microfilm, obtained from a photostatic copy in the possession of the University Museum, University of Pennsylvania. The original manuscript is said to be in the National Museum of Anthropology and History in Mexico City, and it is doubtless one of a succession of copies of still older documents. The Motul Maya-Spanish Dictionary, as represented by a photostatic copy of the manuscript in the John Carter Brown Library of Providence, and the Maya-Spanish vocabulary of Pio Perez were used in making the translation, in conjunction with the Maya grammars of Tozzer and Gates.

It is extremely unlikely that two individuals of differing backgrounds would agree exactly in a translation of such a manuscript. Aside from the usual mechanics of deciphering the handwriting and supplying partly obliterated portions, questions must arise as to the piecing together of words which have been separated into syllables. It is generally agreed that the punctuation is arbitrary.

The principal source of perplexity, however, comes from the fact that Maya homonyms have a great variety of unrelated meanings. In speech it is doubtless possible to distinguish one from another, but in dealing with the written word the translator must make a selection without benefit of accent or intonation. The diffi-

culty of making an appropriate choice of meanings is not ameliorated
by the fact that each Maya word must first be rendered into Spanish
and the Spanish word then translated into English. My own method
was to find all the possible meanings of the words in several lines and
then study them to find relationships among them that "made sense."
It seemed advisable to select the fundamental rather than the derived
meanings of words, on the theory that the former were the older.
Every other translator confronts the same difficulties in translating
a Book of Chilam Balam, and it seems obvious that more than one
independent opinion is desirable for an understanding of the contents of these remarkable compilations.

What emerges from the long and arduous effort is a significant
document. Interspersed among the prophecies are fragments of
history and mythology and references to religious ceremonials, as
well as frequent lamentations and exhortations to the Maya people to
hold fast to their ancient teachings. Much that is found in these
pages is confirmed by the writings of Landa and other Spanish historians; but there is also much that is new and vital, for this is the
"inside story" of the hidden life of the Maya under Spanish dominion,
the revelation of what they were thinking during the 250 years which
culminated in the great uprising of 1848. The book appears to be
a compilation of the writings of various Chilam Balam—the earlier
ones perhaps transcribed from the hieroglyphic books—which were
brought together around 1752, in a Katun 4 Ahau, for "4 Ahau is the
Katun for remembering past knowledge and recording it in annals."

PART I

The Book
of the Jaguar
Priest

page one

Thirteen Kan on the first of Pop. Katun 5 Ahau follows along its path,[1] the year being 1593, save that one year still remains to be checked off before the bearer of the future arrives.

Now in those days when Mayapan was captured in battle, they confronted the katun of affliction. During the migration of the remnant of descendants, the remnant of the descendants of Yaxum,[2] good fortune should have come to generation after generation of his sons; but instead there came all at once castigation,[3] oppression, vigilance in the night. That was a long time ago.

Three earthen walls were wholly demolished. Three symbols of the fatness of the Tree of Life failed. Could there come a time when the magic drawing of the days should cease? The sacred Long Count[4] shall be kept in order by magic enduring to the end! With rivers of tears we mourned our sacred writings amid the delicate flowers of sorrow in the days of the katun. Vale.[5]

We poured ourselves out in supplication. We entreated Ah Chaante the Wonderful, Kinich Chaan who dwells in the heavens, that he be kind. . . . Thirteen Kan passes. Then 1 Muluc comes on his day, with his prophecies in our behalf. Above the twisted earth

---

[1] Read as *chaoc u be katun.* It is partly effaced. Since *Ziic* may be a numeral classifier for counting on the fingers and toes, I have taken *yalkaba* as *yalkab a,* "the fingers of the hand." The meaning seems to be clearly that of checking off the count on the fingers.

[2] *Yaxum,* "the Ancestor." I derive it from *yax yum,* "first father."

[3] *tzek,* "skull or stony ground," I have taken to be meant for *tzec,* "castigation." The first part of the Chronicle seems to have been dictated.

[4] *kin tzul can chacil uaan,* "sacred day-count of great length," is probably the technical term for what we call the *Long Count.*

[5] *vale,* "next, later, it passes," is used to emphasize the completion of a sentence or paragraph.

3

we invoke Ah Vuc Chapat the Seven-headed Serpent,[6] asking him to carry his seven bundles as an extra burden during the next two *tuns;* also for the same period, the vestments.[7] For our sons still remember the calamities, the burning of men, the burning, the shattering, the destruction of those days.

Although after the days of shooting down the multitudes[8] we pleaded for mercy, they then kindled fires over the whole province. The heavens were sealed against us. When they had succeeded in reducing the population, the compassion of heaven set a price upon our lives. Should we not lament in our suffering, grieving for the loss of our maize and the destruction of our teachings concerning the universe of the earth and the universe of the heavens?

We are agitated by these sharp blows. We are moved to sorrow, sending up our pleas to Ah Bolon Yocte of the Nine Paths, and to Ah Bolon Kanan, of the Nine Precious Gifts. . . .

page two

Has this generation forgotten the emptying of the towns the entire length of the land? Then the sons of Ah Vuc, the Seven, availed themselves of the eleven penances.

During this period three katuns succeeded one another;[9] three great heaps of *cayman* meat; three great counts of the years and casting of lots concerning the days.[10] There was an excess of water,

---

[6] Pio Perez gives "A-*hac-chapat*, a fabulous serpent having seven heads." It is reasonable to infer that *Ah vuc chapat* is an earlier, more correct form of the name, as *vuc* means "seven." *Chapat* may also signify "centipede."

[7] The god of the katun is asked to defer his visit until time has mitigated the memory of recent suffering during the migration from Mayapan. Two tuns is just under two years.

[8] *Zon* was "to shoot with a blow-gun," before European firearms were introduced into Central America.

[9] Three katuns is an interval of nearly 60 years.

[10] *amob baxax:* Landa mentions "some small stones called *am* [amob is the plural form], of the kind which they used for the casting of lots." Tozzer 1941: 154.

too much dripping water. In this manner, three folds of katuns passed by, until the rigorous government of Katun 1 Ahau arrived.

Afterwards comes 3 Cauac, the day of activity at the wells throughout the land. The people will travel by good roads asking alms. They will travel in safety, even when going by night. They ask alms, sending out a clamor everywhere. In the *seven mouths* at that time, there was abundance of bread. They took heart because Ah Vuc, Lord Seven, is powerful, Ah Vuc Chapat, the Seven-headed Serpent.

Later, when the day of the katun has passed, they feed upon trees; they feed upon stones, mourning for that which took place at the Well of the Cavern. Dishonorable were the omens; dishonorable the lives of their rulers; yes, even their own lives in the days when they carried burdens; during the three tuns. . . . In this manner, furthermore, the Lord 13 Ahau arrives. . . . 11 Ahau, 9 Ahau. . . . These set them free from their burdens, fulfilling their days here on earth. Our leaders grieve for those who have departed from the kingdom. This is the day of 3 Cauac.

Next comes 4 Kan on his day, at the side of Katun 5 Ahau. In the days of this katun, there are three major afflictions. A multitude of intruders [11] make a loud clamor when they arrive. There are heaps of them. Then we pray that they may be lifted.

We complain in great sorrow, in loud voices . . . and death. Our grief is torment. We are pierced with a great longing to read the books of wood and the writings on stone, now in ruins. They contain the seven well-springs of life! They were burned before our eyes at the well. At noon-day we lament our perpetual burdens.

On 4 Kan when the year is interpreted, they plead for a judgment against the intruders; for a judgment against the white fangs and against the red fangs, and against the pestilence which they brought, which lasted five tuns Ahau. The people perform the eleven penances all the days of their prayers. They pray that the eyes of their children may read the writings (page 3) on the stone tablets.[12]

---

[11] *yaxcach*, here translated "intruder," is literally a "fly" or "pest."
[12] I have taken *maitun* to be a form of *mayactun*, for which Pio Perez gives "stone tables."

page three

In the days of the katun, the year being called 5 Muluc, white is our cotton, white our garments.[13] At this time there is . . .

How heavy are the burdens in our arms! How long the time! How rigorous the eleven penances! For eleven tuns, for eight tuns, we are crushed under our load.

When 9 Muluc fell on the first of Pop there came the tun which is known as 5 Ahau, as it is spoken in our language. Ah Vuc Yol Sip came to the festival as was his custom.[14] When he arrived we experienced a burning sensation, afterwards extreme cold. He caused our sons to tremble and the mothers of our sons to shake violently.

At the ceremonies in our presence, they offered gizzards of birds and virgin honey [15] to the deity of the day,[16] a god of the Itza, and there was a drawing of the days in silence to the very end.[17] There was also the burning of trees before our eyes. They scattered food; yes, they strewed maize about.

Wherever they reside, whether in the north or in the west, they study the aspect of the heavens. They say that it will rain when Ahaucan the Rattlesnake [18] is lifted high above the trees, above the

---

[13] White is the color associated with the Muluc year, according to Landa.

[14] The name may be interpreted as "Lord of the Seven Lineages of Sip." Seven Sip (or Zip) was the month-date of the hunter's festival according to Landa, who writes the name also as Dzip. In the latter form dzip means "to flay," and suggests that this deity may be the Aztec Xipe.

[15] The first honey taken from the hive, suyilcab or suhuyilcab.

[16] maxkin, "a demon" according to the Motul Dictionary.

[17] tzintzin does not appear in the dictionaries; but in the dialect of the Tizimin manuscript tz replaces th. Tzan, for example, is always written for than, "to speak." Thin or tzin is "to hold a drawing."

[18] This is clearly a reference to the culmination of the constellation containing the Pleiades (Taurus), which takes place close to the zenith in Maya latitudes. In a footnote Tozzer (1941:133) remarks: "This constellation has the same name as that of the rattle of the rattlesnake (tzab). The Pleiades is the most conspicuous star cluster of the constellation of the Dog [Aztec] forming the eye of the dog's head (Beyer 1908). In the Chumayel (134) we read, 'Itzamna,

rocks, above the houses, and above everything else, on account of
Ah Vuc Yol Sip, on account of his seven . . . his seven skins.[19]

When the cornstalks began to lean over at the usual time . . .
the katun, we were guilty in the eyes of our rulers. When a sufficient
number of prayers had been offered in the presence of the Maya
people, above the faces of the children, we started out early in the
morning upon the road. We traveled by day, so as to see the omens
in the sky.

When 10 Ix came on the first of Pop, at the time when the ruler
of the katun, Lord 5 Ahau, descended along the celestial road, we
smelled the fragrance of heaven. From the beginning, the ruler interprets his government to the people and declares it to the people,
and prepares the people for the march.

The people are well-grounded in the liturgy and in the ritual of
the chocolate cup and in the working of miracles, and in the ceremony of the mat and of the square-cornered bench of the god, today and in all future times when they shall make their libations
from the cup, that the people may be set free, delivered.

The prophecies declared it to the people on that day. Thus it
was ordained on the day when they were separated. Our wonder-
working religion is the foundation of everything. As trees grow in
the land, and stones . . . our prophecies will prove true, and the
heavens. . . .

page four

When we have been set free throughout the land, on the
day when *they* abandon the government, we will wash the choco-

---

Itzam-tzab, is his face during its reign.' Roys (1933, 134) suggests that, as
Itzamna is the god of the heavens, Itzam-tzab may be another name for the
constellation *tzab,* the Pleiades."

It is probable, therefore, that Ahaucan is a large stellar configuration containing the Pleiades. Perhaps the Hyades, also in Taurus, forms the snake's
head.

[19] *tzotz* signifies "a hairy skin."

late cups. We will cleanse everything in that day of goodwill in government.

As soon as they have departed we will no longer need to speak exceedingly softly when we cast our lots. And in that day there will be no more violent disputes. Our good fortune will unite us. We will be able to look at ourselves in the mirror without sadness. We will amuse ourselves once more when that day comes. Ah Vuc Yol Sip will take charge of the fire. In that day of deliverance from the covetous ones, from bewilderment and vexation, there will come salvation by reason of his authority and by reason of their departure.

No longer will our priest[20] have to conceal himself here and there in the village. For the first time, his hiding and his silent misery will be a thing of the past. We will face our father[21] squarely once more: Ah Zam[22] is his name, to whom is given authority for eternity. We will then unburden ourselves to him. He will look upon our eleven penances. These are what exalt the soul during great affliction.[23] In those times there will be some who clamor for "Just one shot! Why not?" But our good elder brothers will turn them back on the road. Our guide will ask intercession for them in that day when they put their trust in authority.

Being without strength the country would have been in grave danger in the past, had it not been for the thousands of the lineage of Ah Chac. Perhaps they will come to our aid in the future. In extreme wretchedness the remnant of the Itza nobility were followed by their aggressors when they left Mayapan. When the magic of the calendar is brought to an end, 10 Ix will be the day of the count.

Have you forgotten the downpour on the day when you carried the idol named Kan? Three symbols of the thickness of the Tree

---

[20] *ah kin,* literally "he who represents the sun," the common word for priest.
[21] *yum,* "father."
[22] *ah zam,* "he who works miracles"; pronounced *dzam.*
[23] The "eleven penances," *buluc chabtan,* is the term for drawing one's own blood in expiation of sin. In Tozzer 1941: 145 Landa declares: "And those who were devout had to draw their blood and to anoint the stone of the idol Chac Acantun with it. This service and sacrifice they considered as being agreeable to their god."

of Life! Three clusters of fruit from the tree of nourishment!

When our eyes were suddenly opened to the snatching of "alms"; when the common people began to suffer from the taking of "gifts" by the collectors; when the soldiers took property in the manner of warriors, it was as if a mountain had descended upon our shoulders. We lamented; there is no doubt about that. We entreated the gods to save Mayapan in some manner.

We offered them turkey feet, obtained both by capture and by purchase. We mourned the red cardinal birds and the red jeweled ornaments; likewise the handfuls of precious stones which lie in the midst of our fields.

This all happened, moreover, in the very katun in which it was most likely to meet with success, because it was also in a certain Katun 5 Ahau long, long ago, that the sky was new, having just been created. And it was so close to the earth that certain crafty fellows made a loud outcry, from amid the branches of the Tree of Life, entreating Lord 5 Ahau that he make an end to the drunken begging, an end to covetousness on the part of the rulers.

Then the priests performed seven enchantments with the cup, affirming the magic of the mat and interpreting it to the people. Since it was the month of Pop, the priests effected the exchange of years, and there was dancing among you as well as contests of courage. Then prayers were offered to remind the Seventeen of their responsibility. Afterward, everybody departed from the Well of the Cavern.

page five

Then it happened concerning the stammering Itza that they made supplications. . . . While the sons of light were offering many prayers in behalf of their kingdom, the sons of darkness [24] at the same time happened to be celebrating a festival among them-

---

[24] The two phrases are set side by side, in true Maya love of antithesis: *u mehen kin u mehen akab,* "the sons of the day, the sons of the night."

selves in honor of the earth . . . and leopards with burnished skins came one by one out of the forest.

Meanwhile the others were holding their solemnities, and it was on a day 4 Kan. After the festival the heavens were moved. The earth also was moved.[25] The priests were deeply disturbed. The lands throughout the province were greatly annoyed. Fierce warriors were among those who were dubious about the outcome, and they felt that further observances were required to celebrate the festival of the katun when 5 Muluc came, at the time of his taking office. Fruit was falling from the trees, and the elder brothers collected it in great quantities to save what they could.

Then when 5 Ahau arrived on his day within the year 5 Muluc, there was a crescent moon, omen of life. In another part of the province there was a flood of water. In great abundance it silently spread over all creation. The people begged to be told in what way they had offended against the law, whether in not speaking the words of truth, or in the silent rites, or in the magical incantations, or in the casting of lots. . . . From everywhere, by day and by night, they came one by one to see the solemn casting of lots. Over the entire country for many days, during that period. . . .

In one corner ended that which had begun in the day of the abomination at the Well of the Cavern. Because it thus came about that the Itza were lifted up by reason of their suffering, when the Seven said goodbye at the Well of the Cavern on the day when they departed from the land of trees and fruit and beans. . .

. . . Kinich. At the new moon, they prayed for the remnant of the days, the remnant . . . of the katun that was to follow.

The day of 6 Ix fell, and they totaled up the pebbles of the days, after they had divested themselves of breeches and other garments,[26] before the drawing of the days.

---

[25] While the Xiu worshiped heaven, the Itza prayed to the earth. The invocations of the former produced a tempest, while those of the latter produced an earthquake, it would seem from the text.

[26] i.e., they remove their clothing so that none of the small pebbles shall be lost in the folds, throwing the count of days into confusion.

At that time Ahaucan the Rattlesnake was lifted high on the back of the Leopard Chacbolai.[27] They sum up the days in order to determine how much recompense is due to the altar of Ah Pop and to the altar of Ah Zam when they come to the crossroads to devour the offering, stretching out their arms for it . . . mighty men in order not to extinguish. . . . Then the men of the Bat [tribe] are strong because of the coming of the sons of the deity. . . . Perhaps the lord will fasten securely that which is at loose ends . . . the deity of the day

page six

of the katun. They told about a vision of the earth and its four quarters, how great activity came from the north and a great stirring from the west.

On the name-day of the katun, the seven sons of Suhuy Sip[28] came down. Then there was the prophecy of Sip, the ancient Sip, who can play musical instruments on earth, and whose jingles resound through the heavens. When the count of the pebbles of the katun was taken, they estimated the [remaining] length of the katun cycle. When the pebbles had been completely separated and taken out one by one in this manner, then we saw before our eyes that which was heaped up in the sky, the multitude of clouds over the face of the Sun, over his face.

At that time there was only one count to be made. A single straight shot it should have been, if everybody had been honest and above-board. You who despise your mothers, you who despise your fathers,[29] are you fit to make the count of the katun cycle?

---

[27] The Leopard thus appears to be a constellation under Taurus.

[28] The "Seven Sons of Suhui Sip" may be a name for the Big Dipper, a conspicuous configuration of stars in the northern sky which "comes down" and dips below the horizon as seen from Yucatan.

[29] This reproach is undoubtedly addressed to the Itza who had the reputation of killing the old men of the tribe, lest they become wizards. Roys 1933: 178; Tozzer 1941: 20.

The heavens will increase the supply of provisions. They will increase them according to their promises. So when you are assembled together, dry your tears. Without breeches, without clothing, the idols our patrons though even without food demand nothing for themselves.

Seven Cauac arrives on his day in the seventh tun on the first of Pop, when the lord of the day, the god of the katun, created writing.

Afflictions came suddenly. Then came the bowed and chafed shoulders. Alas for the joy of living! They must strip bark from trees for food; and the claws of the lion's whelp draw blood, as they hide where we seek for food in the forest.

We go on the palms of our hands and the soles of our feet, because we greatly long for bread and we are in dire need of water. The teeth in the mouths of the lords chew, as the result of their custom of practicing the eleven penances and of scraping up the fire in their fists.

The generations of the Itza will comprise three folds of katuns on 8 Kan, the year-bearer which falls on 1 Pop in the eighth tun.

Five Ahau shall be the day of the apportionment of food at your wells. Mountains shall descend. They shall descend in your midst, kindling the fire of great brightness. Foreigners shall descend from the sea as of old. Why do they come? They come to harrass us!

The door leading to miracles shall be closed . . . the vigilance of the warriors of Tihoo. The rule of the Itza shall be completely established over us. We will accept their commands. They cherish the bursting open of the living rock.[30] They whistle when they look on at our ceremonies.[31] They whistle with impatience for the handing around of the medicinal herbs of the fields and mountains, and for the beneficial effects derived therefrom. In the fields they search for food.

---

[30] A euphemistic term for human sacrifice.
[31] *xob:* "to whistle with a finger in the mouth, as the Indians do" (Motul).

page seven

Eleven Cauac came on the first day of Pop in the eleventh tun. Our two priests of Pop and our two priests of Zam set the drinking vessels firmly beside the idols. The people recompense the idol of the Bacab, Ah Cantzicnal, who is seated upon the stone of the eleventh tun of the katun.[32] Then Ah Cantzicnal makes his presence known to us. And Ah Can . . . and Ah Sac Tzin are manifested to us.

On the day of the katun, when Cantzicnal took us under his protection, the people performed the figures of the dance known as Ix Toloch.[33] At the time of the magic ceremonies of the aforementioned katun, when the eleven penances had come to an end, the other rituals were then presented and the other heavens of the Moon were honored by appropriate dances to the gods on high, on whatever days should prove to be fortunate, according to the teaching.

Moreover, Ah Tem Pop and Ah Tem Zam interpreted the future road of the katun, after removing their breeches and other clothing in the presence of heaven and the lords. They read the auguries by the paths of Chacbolai the Leopard and Bolai Can the Fierce Serpent, and Chacbolai Ul.[34]

It was at this time that the Itza betook themselves almost into the heart of the forest and along its borders, where it was customary for the soul of the great stone to wander on the day of the katun in misery and torment by reason of its afflictions. They are restless, the

---

[32] Here Cantzicnal appears to be lord of the *Cauac* year. Landa, on the other hand, declares: "This year in which the dominical letter was *Muluc,* and in which the Bacab Can Sicnal ruled, they regarded as a good year; for they said that he was the best and greatest of the Bacab gods; and so they placed him first in their prayers." Tozzer 1941: 145.

[33] The Motul contains the form *ix tolil.* The name survives in the modern *Xtol,* characterized as "the most important dance of the modern Mayas." Tozzer 1941: 94, footnote No. 409.

[34] These are clearly stellar configurations. Chacbolai Ul may mean "Leopard Lodge."

sons of the generations of the day, and of the generations of the night. At that time there was the swarming of wasps in the heart of the forest and along the borders. Then . . . like the bees, they gathered the fruits of the land into large receptacles.[35]

In the tenth tun [36] when the day 12 Kan arrived on the first of Pop, there was the folding up of the days, and the speeches of the festival and the interpretation of the prophecies . . . and the fulfillment of the true sayings to the sons of the day and the sons of the night, which in due time shall take place on earth, and shall take place in the heavens.

During the twelfth tun the heavens will be aflame and the earth will burn with fire. We will reach the end of desire. Take care! Whatever happens . . .

The summer will be so dry that you will entreat Hunab Ku to have compassion upon you, lest the commonwealth be destroyed. For seven years there will be drought. The living rock will burst asunder.[37] The sacred pebbles will be consumed by fire. Finally the Hand will begin to use gentleness in order to save the fields and the mountain valleys.

Then they haggle at the Well of the Cavern over the offering of cooked food. Then the priest finally asks for a covering of green bark. Thirteen times he strips the flowers and leaves from branches. Then he binds the branches together . . . the face of the priest when he is on the point of entering the well

page eight

of the Cavern. Once more we listen to their orations in the Cavern, when the priests of Pop and Zam, Ah Tem Pop and Ah

---

[35] *xux* is interpreted as "wasp" by both Pio Perez and the Motul dictionary. The word translated "bees" is *yikilcab* which is taken to be a variant of the *ikelcab*, "abeja," of Pio Perez. *Ikil* or *yikil* is "like the wind," or "restless."

[36] This is obviously a typographical error for *lahca pistun*, "twelfth tun," as it is correctly stated a few lines farther on.

[37] Another reference to human sacrifice, in time of great distress.

Tem Zam, are about to destroy themselves on account of their grievous injuries, having come to the end of desire and to the end of being subjected to violence.

Then they walk twice around the cave and around the well,
stopping at the altars. One at a time they rub their hands over the
smooth stone and read the words: "Justice exists. Heaven exists."

Thereupon the great priest Chilam replies: "Perhaps so; perhaps not.[38]

"True, for the present we must carry the highly ornamental [39]
sons of the Itza on our backs, maintaining them in our midst, like a
great stone in our misfortune. But there will come a time when the
white flowers [40] will again be unsheathed in this land, from the Island of Cuzamil to Mayapan. It will come to pass on account of the
well, on account of the Cavern in this land of magic.

"In the day of the overthrow of the Red Eagle, in the day of
retribution, when it shall come to pass later over this beautiful land
of billowing mountains, then quickly shall come the day of vexation, the vexation of the Itza.

"How, then, can we remember the prophecies, if there are no
fathers of the days or of the festivals of the katun? [41] How can the
generations of the sons of the Itza tell us the days of the prophecies
and the days of the tun? How can we celebrate the rites of Lord 5
Ahau in the twelfth tun, when he comes in benign holiness, in the
katun of power and of the strength of the wooden idols, and the
magic of the cup, and the magic of the plate, and the magic of
the count of days, in Katun 5 Ahau, in the twelfth tun? [42]

---

[38] *hix binac hix mac:* Pio Perez gives *hix binaci ix maaci,* with the meaning
given above.

[39] *yalomal* is taken to be from *yala + olmal,* "excessively ornamented"; but *yala-
mal* would mean "an excessive number of times."

[40] There may be a play on words here: *sac* (or *zac*) means "white," and *zac*
(pronounced *dzac*) is "magic" or "medicine."

[41] Who will keep the count of days and regulate the calendar if the priests
whose function it is destroy themselves in the well?

[42] The word translated "magic" is *can ezlic,* which is assumed to be a variant
of *cancan ez,* "to remedy, counteract," according to the Motul Dictionary.

"When the thirteenth tun arrives on his day and 13 Muluc falls on the first of Pop, on the day 1 Oc [43] there will be majesty, when Pop shall descend, when Zam shall descend in Tun 13.[44] At the ceremonies there will be overwhelming grandeur, the impressive majesty of the heavens. As always there will be the cup, there will be the plate which they will heap up with great quantities of food, from the abundant rains. They will break up the mountains of food into portions and distribute them. The heap of food left over will be enormous.

"On the katun's day, on 5 Ahau, a great mound of cayman meat will appear, because of the cup into which the lords draw their blood with the flint knife of the katun, when it shall come to pass, in the temples of Xultun and Ichcansiho,[45] and of Saclactun amidst the meadows in the heart of the island. When the festival of the katun is appointed throughout the province of the Itza and it comes to pass in the midst of the open country, it may be that the prophecies will deceive the sons of the day and the sons of the night. Perhaps they will come to pass. Perhaps they will not come to pass. The prophecies may deceive you, if you have contempt for them, if you have contempt for the Ancestors."

page nine

In the fourteenth tun on the first of Pop, in the fourteenth tun on the Katun's day, the Itza recounted their grievances among themselves in great excitement . . . their burning needs, a tale of great distress, on the day in which they read their fortunes in the fangs of the fire.

---

[43] 1 Oc is the day following 13 Muluc, the year-bearer.

[44] The text has "Katun 13," but it seems to be a typographical error since the *13th tun* of Katun 5 Ahau is current, the twelfth tun having just been completed.

[45] The word for "temple" is *chac na,* "great house." Here is one of the numerous references to the drawing of their own blood by the lords, as an offering to the idols.

After they had assembled, they rejoiced to see the sky covered with clouds. On that day everyone saw it. Then the face of the sun was veiled, the face of the moon was covered. In the fourteenth tun the vegetation was fast disappearing, owing to so much cropping. Too many mouths in our houses; too many mouths for the number of calabashes.

The strength of many great warriors ebbs away. There is no one left on whom to lean. There is no one left on whom to lean, and the people are on the point of dying. They produce a tale of dire misfortune, when they discuss their troubles, and take counsel with regard to their afflictions.

There is no one left with sufficient understanding to set in order the days of the katun. And so there will be no great abundance of water.

The generations of the Itza! Once they came from the north, and once, later, from the west, the enemy in our midst. In great distress we were scattered among the forests and in the mountains.[46] This all happened in the fourteenth tun. The sorrows of those days! The sufferings of that katun! Ants descend upon us, with consequent great damage to the beehives.

We were provoked at the Well of the Cavern. We mourn the scattering abroad of the books of hieroglyphic writing.[47] It was in the fourteenth tun that it all happened. For months there was discord among the caciques, and all true men suffered deeply in the fourteenth tun.

Then the fifteenth tun arrives on its day, and 2 Cauac falls on the first of Pop. The katun paces on in our presence. When all the prophecies of the Lord 5 Ahau were made, there descended fatness. There descended purses of cacao-money. Ropes were manifested, and canes for arrows appeared, in the fifteenth tun.

O Sun! With thine eagle's eye look down upon our pleading before thy throne! O rolling Sun, our Deliverer and the Ripener of

---

[46] The phrase is *u bobil uitz*, "the *bob*-trees of the mountains." According to the Motul Dictionary, these are trees having very large leaves.
[47] The phrase *kulem zib* = "sacred writing" = "hieroglyph."

our fruit! All our days we are crushed as by a rock, we are crushed. . . .

When we pray thus from our roots, Kinich the Sun-face, Kinich Chaante the marvelous Kinich, will manifest himself in speech. The eleven penances will be performed. After that, our grief will be transformed into gladness.

Over the foreign lands, over the billowing mountains, there will be sudden death. Because *they* have not taken their gifts wisely, their kingdom will be overthrown. It deserves to be demolished! Our women [48] will conjure a vomit of blood. It will be entirely on *them.* In the fruit-bearing katun of 5 Ahau, the katun . . . on the first moon of the katun, the first moon of the year. . . .

page ten

The Itza are accustomed to make bundles of sticks of the individual years and bind them together, and they know nothing about our days and our katuns. They know only the passing of the days, and the passing of the nights. But their minds are inquisitive concerning our katun.

From the Milpa of the Dragon,[49] Cantzicnal comes down to fulfill his promises to the people. When the day of 2 Cauac arrives over this great land, then comes the descent of the katun headforemost,[50] the katun of Ix Toloch,[51] the playful katun to soften the

---

[48] *ix cah: ix* is the feminine prefix and *cah is* "people."

[49] The phrase is *u col canyel.* It suggests a part of the sky thickly sown with stars, such as the Milky Way.

[50] As explained in the Motul, *pacax* may signify "head-first" or "the fiesta of the sowing, as maize, beans, melons etc." The "head-first descent" recalls the pictures in the Dresden Codex where a beast or deity is depicted in this position, doubtless symbolizing the "precipitation" of the rain which usually appears during katun drawings.

[51] The name *Ix Toloch* first appeared on page seven in connection with a sacred dance. From the prefix *ix,* it appears to be the name of a goddess.

hearts of anger. The priest declares the auguries to be of good fortune, from the remote places of the spirit.

In the sixteenth tun, 3 Kan shall come on his day on 1 Pop, in the rain-bearing katun and the lords of the land shall be present also. They shall bind up the faces of the lords at that time, and no one shall speak for the jesting katun at the festival of 3 Kan.

They will despoil the trees of their black and red and white coloring matter.

The priests [52] of the Itza take fruit from the receptacle. They take out grains of corn. They are suddenly interrupted by a rain-squall, by a tempest of wind. Then the face of the god is revealed to Ah Pop and Ah Zam. And as it appears overhead, the people run among the trees, among the rocks! Take care that you recompense the idol for his protection!

In confusion, the people turn to authority. They go to the seat of power, to Lord 3 Ahau, for the interpretation of the path. When the other lords arrive, they place reliance on their words and upon their priests. They lean upon the warriors among their own number.

The people have come to depend upon the cup and the plate. [53] They lean upon their rulers who came long ago from the north and from the west. [54] Furthermore, in the sixteenth tun, they go about the island searching for the lords of the katuns, particularly for the current ruler, Lord 5 Ahau, until afterwards, even until the present time.

In the seventeenth tun when 4 Muluc arrives on his day in the fortunate katun, the warriors heap up food for themselves. They

---

[52] The word *balmil* is taken to be a contracted form of *balamil*, for which the Motul gives "a master or a priest."

[53] The word which appears to read *chuch* is here understood as a mistake for *luch*, "cup," in order to preserve the symmetry of the ritualistic phrase, *u luch y. u lac* (or *laac*), "the cup and the plate."

[54] This is one of several references to the two "descents" of the Itza conquerors from the north and later from the west. It is rare, however, to find a kindly feeling, expressed toward them by the authors of the Tizimin manuscript.

dine in secret. On that day at the end of a Balam or Jaguar year,[55] a gentle rain presages that we will be greatly afflicted by ghosts.

A drought will sweep the province bringing the pestilence in its wake in the days of bitter hunger. There will be no rain, and even the springs will dry up in this land of the south. There will be much blood-letting by way of appeasement. They will clamor for jars and basins [56] for the eleven penances. The Eleven Chuens [57] wear an aspect of agony. . . . The gods shall mourn, the people shall lament for a score of tuns. . . .[58]

page eleven

Death will consume the fathers of the three-fold katun. In bewilderment they will dwell underneath the trees; for such is the purport of the prophecy of the day, the words of memory for the seventeenth tun.

It is customary for the priests, the Chilam, Ah Kin Napuctun and Ah Kin Hun Uitzil Chac, to read from the teachings of the six eternal books at Uxmal. This is the revelation of the hieroglyphic writings [59] of the prophecies. And Ah Kin Chel Yaxnak is he who

---

[55] This statement seems to indicate that the year 4 Kan, immediately preceding a year 5 Muluc, was dedicated to the Jaguar-god. The following table gives the arrangement of tuns and year-bearers in the Katun 5 Ahau which began in 1593:

tun	year-bearer	tun	year-bearer
11th	11 Cauac	15th	2 Cauac
12th	12 Kan	16th	3 Kan
13th	13 Muluc	17th	4 Muluc
14th	1 Ix	18th	5 Ix etc.

[56] Jars and basins are required for catching the blood as it flows from the veins of the warriors.
[57] It is written *buluc te ti chuen*.
[58] A score of tuns comprises a katun of about 20 years.
[59] The word *anahte* is not found in the vocabularies of Pio Perez or of the Motul Dictionary. It is probably from the Spanish *anal*, "annal." The Book of

looks into them to see by what road guilt will be brought home to us. This is the expectation according to the Jaguar priest, the Chilam Balam, coming from Hunab Ku the One God, and from the Thirteen gods: [60]

"They will preserve a resting-place for us to stretch out in during the Balam or Jaguar year, and for almost a whole month later." These are the words of the book: "Perhaps; perhaps not."

Day and night, Ah Chapat the Seven-headed Serpent lies overhead. If we do not smear ourselves with soot in mourning for our lives, we shall lament for food because of this grievous fault, according to the words of the katun, according to that which is set forth in the hieroglyphic books of the katun.

The books tell whether we should go against Mayapan from the north or from the south; and when Ah Vuc Chapat shall reveal himself to us; and when little by little the vision of Ah Vuc Yol Sip himself shall be manifested to us.

When Lord 5 Ix, the bearer of the days, arrives in the eighteenth tun near the end of the katun, and the day 5 Ahau comes carrying his burden, then the war-captives with collars about their necks and in great distress, are led to the stone of life.[61] The drums set up a loud clamor. Words are spoken telling the important purpose of the ceremony, the reason being that the food of the people of Ix Toloch has been entirely consumed.[62]

When the beat of the drums is changed, the lords settle themselves expectantly. The seven war-captives are stretched out on their

---

Chilam Balam of Chumayel also uses the form *anahte,* but early Spanish writers give *analte* or *analteh.* See Tozzer 1941: 28, footnote 155.

[60] The *Thirteen gods* were probably lords of the numbers one to thirteen. Some modern Maya still look upon the day-numbers as distinct deities and address them in prayer. Lincoln 1942: 106-7.

[61] This is the most vivid description of human sacrifice that I have found in Maya literature. The act is usually euphemistically characterized as "the bursting open of the living rock."

[62] Ix Toloch, perhaps a Toltec goddess, appears here for the third and last time, the Xiu tribe being called "the people of Ix Toloch." It was first mentioned in connection with a dance, and then as the title of a katun.

backs, naked. This is the word of the eighteenth tun, after the return to the province: [63] "The Itza shall feel retribution."

The great idols are men of vigilance and they delight in the words of prophecy, even in the very midst of the rains. The people feel forsaken when the lords stir up discord and the auguries fail. When good rulers come, will not the people again place reliance on the cup and the vestments,[64] even in times of the most rigorous discipline? Those who whistle in derision shall paint the wooden idols . . . on 11 Ahau, when Balam and Pop [65] shall make a recompense to the wooden idols. The idols would wither away in close confinement because of the rainy weather.

For three days we looked on at the ceremonies celebrating the return to the Well of the Cavern, while our gallant sons entertained us with sports.[66]

"O Thou who standest at our side and fulfillest the rites of the sowing by sending the rains, how many prophecies from on high have come true since the days of the return of the Itza, since the second descent! On account of the bitterness. . . ."

page twelve

In another part of the cave where they interpret the movements of the heavens and the movements of the earth, quietly went the wooden idols Ix Chac and Ix Chuah [67] into the well of the Cavern, into the midst of the waves, because they have the power of bestowing wonderful nocturnal visions. Such are the instructions given by the katun of sufficiency.

---

[63] It appears that the Xiu and their Itza overlords have attacked and recaptured Mayapan, and are celebrating the victory in a way repugnant to the Xiu priests.
[64] Symbols of divine authority.
[65] The impersonators of the deities Balam the Jaguar and Pop, a calendar god.
[66] *u chenil ti yactunil*, "the Well of the Cavern," thus appears to be located in the District of Mayapan, recently recaptured.
[67] These are goddesses. The masculine forms, Chac and Ek Chuah, are well-known, the former as a god of the cardinal points and of rain, the latter as the patron of cacao-growers and travelers.

Six Cauac arrives on his day in the nineteenth tun, and they pray with outstretched arms because of the days of drought and of the pestilence, and the excessive anger of the Seven against us. Ah Chacmitan clears away the rubbish from the path of the katun.

Thus it came to pass that at the mouth of the sea the lords made sport with much good-humored chaffing. Then for five days they all confessed their sins to Kukulcan.[68] From the katun's undulations they counted out the pebbles to the very end. They counted the pebbles completely, and accepted the gifts when they appeared, summoned by their outstretched hands. In the festival of the nineteenth tun, they counted the completed katun.[69]

From the clouds they collect among themselves the auguries as to the earth, and there is almost rain in our presence.[70] The gods accept the gift of maize kernels. They accept the games and revelry of our sons. Thus our sons break the solemn silence of the drawing of the days; but they do not speak in our presence the words which should be spoken on that day, in the year of 6 Cauac, if we are to secure for ourselves much strength from the gods who stand at the four corners of the earth with their faces twice as high as the Tree of Life.[71]

Yaxum our forefather [72] cast aside the divisions of the katun pertaining to the moon. He was the first to make an arch. He was the first to carry an idol on his back. He was the first to concoct power-

---

[68] This celebration may have taken place at the Temple of Paalmul on the eastern coast of Yucatan, where the ruins of a circular structure such as were built by the followers of Kukulcan may still be seen. Tozzer 1941: 25; footnote 134.

[69] From this statement it appears that the Maya considered the nineteenth tun the final one, and the twentieth as the zero tun of the following katun.

[70] Rain was expected to fall during the drawing of the days.

[71] These are the Bacabs, gods of the four types of year and of the rain and harvest.

[72] Yaxum the Ancestor appeared on Page 1 of the Manuscript. He is here credited with reforming the calendar and other innovations. Ah Pilte is probably a descriptive title for him.

ful drugs.[73] And Ah Pilte, He-who-opens-the-eyes, appeared and accepted his offerings.

Would that he might return from the west,[74] uniting with us in commiseration over our present unhappy plight! This is the fulfillment of the prophecies of Katun 5 Ahau: the pottery jars shall be shattered into dust, when Tun 19 arrives! At that time there will be imprisonment among the lords, when the prophecies have come true. There will be vigils in the overburdened katun. So be it.

Good and virtuous shall be 7 Kan, and a day of great rejoicing. The people assemble to hear Ah Pop and Ah Zam [75] interpret the path of the katun, after they have concocted the cup of honey and water, on account of our afflictions during this katun.

Famine shall be turned aside. This shall be the witness of the Eight [76] who ask for offerings, when the days of the katun are drawing to a close. Thus they loudly declare the path by which it shall come in the heavens, as they divide the honey among themselves.

Then the aspect of the sustaining heavens changes, with the apparition of the Sun in the eastern sky, the Ruler of the Kingdom. The people draw together to contemplate his majesty. Then when the bundle of the katun shall be completely filled, they will tie it up. . . . The people must rely upon Zam. The people must rely upon Pop. . . . They must speak the words of the attested katun on 7 Kan, the day of.[77] . . .

---

[73] On Page 7 appeared mention of "the medicinal herbs of the fields and mountains and the beneficial effects derived therefrom."

[74] This phrase may also be translated "*to* the west." The allusion is reminiscent of the story of the departure of Quetzalcoatl or Kukulcan, and it is possible that Yaxum later became identified with the Mexican hero. Tozzer 1941: 22 et seq. contains an account of the Quetzalcoatl-Kukulcan legend.

[75] Ah Pop and Ah Zam, also written Ah Kin Pop and Ah Kin Zam, are the priests of the calendar deities who have charge of the drawing of the pebbles that mark the passage of the days, as well as the prophecies connected with them.

[76] *The Eight* may be the four Bacabs and the four Musencabs, who are mentioned oftener than the Chacs in the Tizimin chronicle.

[77] The last word looks like *pah*, "vinegar or suspicion," but as the influences of the Kan year were benevolent, it is omitted as a misreading.

However, there is the life of the katun to be considered, and it incites us to blood-letting and to our responsibilities, and it calls upon Kauil, when the day 7 Kan arrives in the avaricious katun.

page thirteen

Thirteen Oc should be the day for measuring the katun,[78] and 4 Cauac should be the day for taking a turn in the folds of the katun. These are the days which Pop and Zam declare.

The people assemble. The cup follows the mat, and the miracle-working [79] follows the cup. Then come the lords, carrying Lord 5 Ahau in a pack, looking backward, after he has accepted the offerings.[80]

The cup has gone. The mat has gone. The prophet has gone with his oration. If they arrive at the Pueblo of the Sleeping Earth, at the Tree of Life, at the divisions of the pierced earth, they will witness the completion of the katun bundle.

And if we mourn for Mayapan, perhaps we should not express our grief at the Well of the Cavern. One by one, death by the pestilence will come to the people, as it came to the first people from the ever-flowing source of life, on the day of the completion of the katuns, the one final fold of the katun.

Eight Muluc came on the first day of Pop and we lodged the square-cornered stone in its place, we who are called Ah Kauil Chel, Ah Napuctun, and Ah Xupan Nauat, priests and great and true men; and Hun Uitzil Chac, the Tutul Xiu of Uxmal.[81]

From the land of Mayapan they came to see the taking of the

---

[78] *chekoc*, "measure," is actually "to measure by feet, or by paces." The day-name *oc* signifies "the foot of an animal."

[79] *zam.*

[80] This description calls to mind pictures in the Dresden Codex of a priest carrying an idol in a pack on his back, particularly on pages 25-28 where New Year's ceremonies are probably depicted.

[81] These names appeared also on page 11 of the Tizimin Chronicle, but the title of "Tutul Xiu" was omitted there.

plate of Lord 3 Ahau,[82] in the hope that they might thus perhaps observe the engraving of the words upon the stone and see the drenching rain, when in all honesty and integrity I counted the pebbles of the days from the pouch of the katun, as wholeheartedly as when I first counted the katun here in Bakhalal.[83] I revealed in writing afterward my own correct knowledge. Of course anyone who spilled a pebble must have been a most unreliable man.

My property and hacienda are in the land called the District of Salamanca, in the section over against Chactemal, in the land division of Vaimil, where I established my grant in writing, it may be on the 18th day of Zac, on 11 Chuen, on February 15 in the year 1544.[84]

This is my memory of the ancient things as they descended from Hunab Ku the One God, and from the Thirteen gods, and from the One Thousand gods, as found in the words of the priests and prophets of Chilam Balam and recorded by Ah Xupan and Ah Napuctun, priests, and Ah Nahau Pech and Ah Kauil Chel, as we interpret the prophecies.

I make confession of these beliefs in order to clarify my words, but there is no one who understands my words or my teaching. When He-who-burns-the-trees [85] shall come, however, to spy out the land of Chilam Balam, his appearance. . . .

page fourteen

Here in our houses, however, such injuries will be done that the priests will look at the faces of the people to see if they really desire to listen to their speeches. For the people grieve deeply for their homes and their property. Consequently they interrupt with lamentations over the loss of all their possessions, whenever the

---

[82] Lord 3 Ahau is now installed as the ruler of the new katun.
[83] The modern Bacalar, on the southeast coast of Yucatan.
[84] For a discussion of this double date see Thompson 1935: 55, 56 and 74.
[85] The god of lightning, perhaps.

priests attempt to speak with confidence about the future. Then they make such a clamor that when the priests of our company who are trying to restore faith in the prophecies go about the country teaching out of their own knowledge, the people close their ears. They do not cooperate, although they should trust in the important teachings of our forefathers, according to their words.

When there are enemies in the land and the prophet Chilam begins to teach out of his own knowledge concerning the cup of the first katun and the cup of the dishonorable katun, and the footsteps of the Seven Subjugated ones, and about the baseness, not of our fathers but of the descendants of Yaxum, then nobody pays any attention to him. On that day they must choose representatives from among their own number when the priests arrive, lest there be no one to listen to them after they have come.

In the twelfth katun, as it is called, the Jaguar should be the head. So many ill-advised turtle-doves that pass for men! Men to be loathed! They trespass. They shoot arrows into men's hearts!

It is better to spill from overflowing vessels. It is better to eat food.[86] Perhaps there will be speeches. Perhaps they will even be heeded. Perhaps lying mischievous words will no longer deceive the thoughtful among us, and the former government of the land will be imitated by our younger brothers. Here in the Peten, bones will be scattered all about, the burden of the land.

When your teen-age daughters give birth to children in the coming days, you yourselves will understand why I, your elder brother, grieve.

Do you buy the katun-bundle, when it comes, without first casting lots? When you sincerely feel that you are cleansed, I will yield my place to anyone whom you may select.

Do not cast your lots in houses of straw! Cleanse away anger from the root and branches of the tree. O Xiu! [87] Do not cast your

---

[86] Can these be Maya proverbs: "It is better to spill from overflowing vessels" than from one only half full."It is better to eat food" than to waste it.

[87] This is the first time the authors have called themselves *Xiu*. They were previously called "the people of Ix Toloch." The Xiu were probably Toltec. Roys, R.L. 1933: 192-193.

lots in houses of straw! Thus death will come to your people by reason of it.[88] Here on this earth, we will keep the festival at Uchmal,
in the midst of the Maya land. When Mayapan was named, the
heavens were filled with omens of good luck, as they have appeared
in other skies and in other katuns.

Now you wander about in restless searching from one place to
another, having no fixed settlements. Sunset may find you arriving
at an unfortunate situation. In time of pestilence, let them hide
themselves in the forest, who have become indifferent to Pop and
to the words of Hun Sip, and to the heavens of Hun Sip, and to the
katun of Sip and the three divisions of life, and the three-fold flowery katun.

When 13 Pop, the day of life, arrives, we will see the treasures
of Chilam on the powerful shoulders, and the casting of lots . . .
the passing of divining by lots, now when good things are considered to be the result of evil desire. Vale.

page fifteen

When that day comes, then with great vigilance we will
enjoy the fruits of our heritage; but vigilance here below will gradually relax, the more forceful becomes the heavenly anger directed
against the Christians.

Justice must come when our plots of land will be enlarged,
when suspicion has dried up and the country has been put in order.
There will still be great grief until the fulfillment of the katun of
dishonor. Nobody will keep his promise when the foundation itself
happens to be blameworthy. And so, great trees which formerly
towered to the sky over the whole country are no more. This is the
prophecy of the dishonorable katun: "There will be no good purpose
served by the Christian bishop when he arrives. He will seek to
destroy this generation. Likewise, he will restrict your beliefs. He

---

[88] For Landa's account of the burning of the straw-thatched houses in a winter's
hurricane and consequent loss of life, see Tozzer 1941: 40-41.

will destroy you. He will eradicate your true knowledge. In the end he demands that we shall accept the Christian teaching, as it is called."

When there are beatings, when finally the rulers shall make an end of good things among you, then shall arise vigilance against lascivious guests who call upon your wives by name.

Little by little you will clamor for me to unfold to you our own stirring teachings as to how these harsh persecutions from dishonorable men may be brought to an end. Now when we would speak of our literature, they entice our youth away.

Little by little you will begin to clamor for the holy things also. May the gods guard your feet from the left-hand path! If any among you would acquire learning, let him heed. The Christians in our midst will expose our most profound teachings. Take warning of this!

Fully four katuns have passed since we ate the herbs of hunger, when the nobles acted as hosts to Sr. Antonio Martinez.[89] . . . Xaul is his name, as one who aspires to heaven. Little by little we are being degraded.

Little by little, you will observe the women of the nobility openly taking lovers, although they have been taught very serious matters right along, even about death,[90] and are strictly forbidden to do so. For seven years they have accepted money for that which is an exchange, and they have become aware of the ruin which comes from seeking gifts.

When the original *thirteen baktuns* were created, a war was waged which caused the country to cease to exist. Little by little, however, our enemies came to hear the prophecies of Ahau; but finally even the hope of hearing Ahau is brought to an end, because of the words of opposition.

When the need arises for the high authority at the head of the mat to safeguard our children, then we feel deeply the tragedy of being captives in war; also when we are ordered to obey.

---

[89] See the story of Martinez in the Chumayel; Roys, R.L. 1933: 123.
[90] The penalty of death, perhaps.

Among the great things which those who speak the exact truth have taught us is the covering of our bodies with soot in deep humility and in true knowledge.[91]

Presently, at the arrival here below of a cross of iron, I will suddenly come into your presence. I will be a companion to you in prison. Go you to the war-captain. . . . I will protect your trembling backs.

The Nine shall arise in sorrow, alas. . . . And when over the dark sea I shall be lifted up in a chalice of fire, to that generation there will come the day of withered fruit. There will be rain. The face of the sun shall be extinguished because of the great tempest.

Then finally the ornaments shall descend in heaps. There will be good gifts for one and all, as well as lands, from the Great Spirit, wherever they shall settle down.

page sixteen

Presently Baktun 13 shall come sailing, figuratively speaking,[92] bringing the ornaments of which I have spoken from your ancestors. Then the god will come to visit his little ones. Perhaps "After Death" will be the subject of his discourse.

What good can it do to wail childishly in loud voices on account of these men who are spreading everywhere? Where is your faith? Daily at noon I press my hands on the head of the well. After sprinkling the sacred objects of our religion and the holy products of the sea, I look upward at the divine face of the heavens. Standing on the stone pavement at the mouth of the well, I look for the guide-posts on the face of the sky, to see whither they navigate.[93] No man speaks

[91] Several illustrations in the Dresden Codex depict men or deities with their bodies blackened.

[92] The completion of a great cycle of thirteen baktuns would indeed be an occasion of the highest expectation. It involves a count of approximately 5000 years from the normal date, 13.0.0.0.0 4 Ahau 8 Cumhu. See Commentary, the chapter on the Calendar.

[93] This is an example of divination by clouds, the time of day being noon.

to me without a grievance. My part is to interpret to you. Your part later, as well as my own, is to be born again.

Although they overturn slowly, nevertheless I shall yet prove my name, that my name is Martinez.[94]

Even if they publish seven sacred books[95] our priests will read them. The priests Ah Xupan, Ah Kin Chel and Napuctun will make themselves known in three scrolls. Gradually the Priests of the Jaguar, the Chilam Balam, will compose seven holy books for our altars, in which we will explain the manner of offering invocations, so that finally the katun will arrive as in ancient times with no diminution in the power of the prophecies.[96]

As for those who make themselves known to our conquerors in an excess of submissiveness, O my people, forgetting the existence of the other half of their countrymen, then let my people speak of beatings and of reprisals. I tell you the situation shall be reversed!

At this time I speak to you of Justice,[97] for the purpose of vexing the Christians. Nine souls shall be baptized by the dishonorable men, and shall be asked questions by them which not even the nobles in the pueblo would be able to answer. When they shall appear in this land of trees, in this land of rocks, and shall settle down in the towns, there will be no one to understand these things. Then sorrow and misfortune will follow.

When Katun 9 Ahau shall arrive later on, then they must all profess my teachings, when that day comes . . . without forsaking them, in the final days of misfortune, in the final days of the tying up

---

[94] Antonio Martinez was mentioned on Page 15. He does not appear in the writings of the Spanish historians according to R.L. Roys. See Roys 1933: 120-124.

[95] Here the word for books is the Spanish *libro*, instead of *huun* or *vooh*, indicating that the "they" refers to the friars. The word translated "priests" in the next sentence is the usual *ah kinob*.

[96] This paragraph explains why the Books of Chilam Balam were written: the younger generation was not permitted to learn the hieroglyphic writing and were trained by the monks in Spanish script only.

[97] The Latin form *Justitia* is used.

of the bundle of the thirteen katuns on 4 Ahau,[98] then the end of the world shall come and the katun of our fathers will ascend on high.

Are you not accustomed to raise your voices in song when you fan the katun upon its arrival, when you sound the flutes for your sins as the ancient day approaches?

These valleys of the earth shall come to an end. For those katuns there shall be no priests, and no one who believes in his government without having doubts. They are broken, the omens, because of the katun of dishonor. This is due to the fact that the days foretell events through visions, whether in the daytime or in the night-time. Pay heed to the truth which I present to you in the katun of dishonor. Shall my intercession, my pleading, be in vain?

I speak to you! I, Chilam Balam, the priest of the Jaguar! I recount to you the words of the true gods, when they shall come. . . . Then it will come to pass that afflictions will consume our sons. . . .

page seventeen

Am I not a priest and a prophet? There will be abundant rains to record during Katun 9 Ahau. Vale. The heavens will shield themselves with darkness, as in the first division of world history.

Nahau Pech, his statement

In former times there was understanding of the Moon, in the time of our fathers. With compassion the government redeemed us. Vale. That was four katuns ago.

I will ask intercession of the Holy Father,[99] if he will hear me, when you forget the omens and neglect them. When the Itza came to our country as guests of our fathers, they all together sowed discord among you. This saying came from the mouth of Nahau Pech,

---

[98] The date would be 13.0.0.0.0 4 Ahau 3 Kankin, falling in 1752, if a Katun 5 Ahau began in 1594.
[99] *kul yum.*

the priest of the lunar calendar,[100] in Katun 4 Ahau, on the final day of the katun. Vale.

the prophecy of Yabun Chan

In former times, the priests of this country were allowed to speak freely. Yes. Our fathers expected divine manifestations. And the priests were the ones who cut the honey from the hives in olden times. You will grant that they understood the good omens of abundance when they sought for them in the fire.

Your souls shall accept the truth and hold it in high esteem. . . . You Itza are altogether provoking, when you forget the Lord Ahau and sow discord among the holy ones. It will come to pass that you shall adore the divine truth, and the government of our ancestors will stand always in readiness forever.

the prophecies of the Jaguar priest
sung by him at Cabal Chen in Mani [101]

Thirteen Ahau is the day of the opening of the sealed katun. Then the Itza shall. . . . There shall be the customary observances in the presence of the fathers of the people. The sign of Hunab Ku the One God is in the heavens. His word shall disclose a gallows to the people, in order that the Ancestors may establish order upon the earth.

Do the humming-birds take unfair advantage of one another? Do the humming-birds envy one another? When the gods of the ancients return, they will give us a sign.

Priests are the fathers of mankind. One cries the invocation to the gods. To another falls the task of playing upon a musical instrument. Let the earth awaken!

One goes forth as ambassador. Another awakens Itzamna Kauil

---

[100] *ah kin tu kini uil.*

[101] "The Chumayel text reads Cauichen, but the Tizimin version calls it Cabalchen, which is still the name of the cenote at Mani. It is in a cave and approached by a path, but there is also an opening like a well in the roof of the cave directly above the pool." R.L. Roys 1933: 167, footnote 4.

in the west. The lions' whelp come, the Itza fathers. The people come. The enchanters work their magic with the precious stones.

The temple receives its guests, the bearded ones from the lands of the Sun. They are bringers of a sign from our Father God: blessings in abundance! This is the word of the god as he enters the temple.

The people came to hear the prophecies on the day of universal life. . . . The Lord and Father of the whole earth, Hunab Ku, inflicts upon you the penalty of stripping the bark from trees for food. . . . Finally . . . the prophecy of the Holy Father.

It is sufficient that the enchanter scan the heavens for a sign. Let the conjurers make a double recompense. Shall the seers deceive the people? . . . the discordant sea. . . . Your recompense shall appear. In the last days, learn about the Tree of Life. . . . Remember your blessings. Lean upon the protection of the Tree. Yes, this sign is your assurance that

page eighteen

they come from heaven.

These sacramental objects of yours, O Itza, these holy things of yours, derive from Kukulcan. [102] Find your holiness in truth and penitence. Find holiness with the people of god . . . in the words of Hunab Ku, the One Supreme God. He comes to you from heaven in the drops of rain.

It is good, what I say unto you assembled here, O Itza. Let the earth awaken when They tread upon it, and attend, in another katun later on.

Sufficient unto themselves are my words, for I am Chilam Ba-

---

[102] The spelling here is *ku u kul canale*, "God the holy one of heaven." By this play on the name *Kukulcan*, "Feathered Serpent," the supreme deity of the Itza, the prophet tried to draw the Itza and the Xiu closer to one another in their worship by identifying Kukulcan with Hunab Ku. "Whom . . . ye ignorantly worship, Him declare I unto you."

lam, the Jaguar Priest. I repeat my words of divine truth: I say that the divisions of the earth shall all be one! This is the ninth year of Katun 1 Ahau.

the interpretation by the priests

The great prophetic words of the priests and the wisdom of the prophets.[103] Hear ye their commandments! So let it be done! The prophet of the Jaguar, Chilam Balam, shall be Ah Xupan Nauat during Katun 13 Ahau. Ah Xupan is his name. In the eighth year of Katun 13 Ahau, the priests proclaim to their listeners their judgments concerning the arrival of the foreign visitors.

Although you have respect for the Ancestors, although you begin to have faith in the truth, you must follow in your fathers' footsteps. Moreover, the highly valued katun must be earned, and we advise you to put your affairs in order.

This is the ancient interpretation: the priests called Ah Bobat, the Searchers, will make the customary count of our fathers. They will set Pop in its place.[104] They will fill the katun's pouch to overflowing. Our sons and warriors, meanwhile, must have faith in us.

Three years to the day we were accustomed to spend in polishing our words to awaken the gods above, we prophets.[105] Now I am greatly heartened to hear that you are learning the ways of peace, now at the moment of the earth's awakening.

The Thirteen gods hear the words of the devils, seven of them.[106] For there are seven devils called Satai, and they are from the foundation of the heavens. Formerly they were the bearers of

---

[103] The Spanish *profeta* is used instead of the Maya *chilam*.

[104] This obviously refers to the annual count of days and checking of the calendar, Pop being the first month of the year.

[105] Can this mean that three years were devoted to engraving the stela or katun-marker?

[106] The word translated "devils" is *cisin*. *Satai* suggests *Satan*, and there is a strong Biblical flavor about the whole statement. On the other hand, the Maya root *sat* or *zat* means "to destroy or ruin"; and *dzata* is "to cause discord," according to the Motul. Hence the *satai* may be genuine old Maya in origin. The foreign Itza may have introduced devil worship.

messages. At the time the heavens were established, there were seven inhabitants who created discord. That was because foreigners came in large numbers in ancient times. But the government of the devils came to an end a very long time ago, after we began counting within the folds of the days.[107]

Pay attention, all of you! Your sins have become heavy burdens. It is almost time for the Lord 1 Ahau to come down from above: 1 Ahau in the heavens, 1 Ahau in the earth, according to the ancient prophecies.

His communications are the means by which he governs everyone, and there will be the additional burden, the excess weight, of the descendants of the Itza from times past. Sorrowful shall be our vigils! The soul shall dwell in goodness. All the vile qualities within us are washed away by sorrow. These are within every one of us.

Xupan Nauat, as he is called, is he who will explain the order of the world. Ah Kin Chel, Nahau Pech, Napuctun, the war-captain Balam, and the prophet Chilam Balam—these are the priests who know the future, and the order of the world and of the katuns. [Written] in the first tun of Katun 13 Ahau at Mayapan.

page nineteen

These are the words spoken by the Thirteen gods through their prophet, Ah Kin Chilam, the Priest of the Jaguar, who carries in his pouch the lottery of life. A little more, a little less— and what are your chances? He who impersonates the god casts lots to determine the final outcome of the country's affairs such as: when the needs of the land shall be supplied; when there shall be many ceremonials to gaze upon; the times of abundance all through the mountains; the time when malevolent men in the land shall be apprehended; the time of confused agitation; the times for unrolling the scrolls of the many genealogical trees of our lineage; the times for standing firm; the times for attaching three seals to the Tree of

---

[107] i.e., after the magic ritual of the calendar was established.

Life; the times for completing the three bundles and distributing the excess; the time when whispering between the teeth shall be brought to an end; the time for delving into the drawing of the days; and the times for scattering underneath the trees and under the branches.[108]

Hunger will descend on Chacmitan. They shall interpret the road of the katun.

They came sweeping down from the west; they came from the north.[109] Many of the sons of God lost their lives. There was great dismay under the trees, beneath the branches.

Finally there came the great, the excessive sorrow of the sons of our wretchedness, when the foreigners descended from the sea. That was a long time ago. The war-captain for defense was buried without having committed an offense by the malevolent men, in the beginning of the count of Pop.

Then there was great desire on the part of the Thirteen for their offerings, in return for having produced the sweetness of the honey, the bountifulness of the land, so that all who looked upon it might well wonder.

The state of Chactenel must be abandoned. The forest trees shall be destroyed by fire, even the great roots at their feet. Then they shall come and scatter great quantities of grain, the staff of life, by the handful. They shall destroy the flowers by the handful.

So sudden will be the violence of that day, when it appears in the heavens, revealing the fleeing multitude! They shall grieve for Chactenel in its affliction.

Then the state of Sactenel shall be depopulated. On a day 13 Ahau 9 Chen, the thirteen treasures of the Itza shall be shattered and swept away. Strong trees will be uprooted. A fire will be kindled in the very midst of the pueblo, when the prophecies shall be fulfilled amongst us.

The priests search out the road in the pages of the book of the

---

108 As the result of drought and famine, or invasion by an enemy.
109 A reference to the two "descents" and the permanent occupation of the country by the Itza.

idols where the words are painted in many colors, telling the path which must be followed.

As the priests were unable to tie up the bundles of the years, they placed them in pottery jars and carried them in their arms when they fled into the darkness. And in the morning when they worshiped the rising sun they beat upon the jars with their hands, pretending that they were the drums of the inhabitants of the state of Chactenel.

When the time approached for the katun to arrive, they were determined that the count should not become confused . . . and to put it in order, each one independently of the others.

So when the time came to inquire into the pouch of the thirteenth katun and into the treasure of the country, they sought out a village in the heart of the forest, on an island, where the precious objects descended. When it came time to roll up the mat of the katun, we were wise by reason of our suffering. In adoration we lifted up our voices to the stars.

With abuse and ridicule heaped upon our heads, the migration will arrive at Chacmitan; and at Chacmitan, we will take warning to lead better lives. At that time, the surface of the state of Chacmitan will extend a great distance.

At the time of the great pestilence, they will worship as lord of the sky the Jaguar war-god.[110] We will pledge the day of establishing the katun, when it comes, by lifting up our voices at noon, on the day of the lord of the baktun.[111] . . .

The migration will begin like the last one from Suiva, as they lament for rain. . . . The state of Sactenel will be depopulated . . . the tenth of the moon.

---

[110] The phrase is *sinic balamil*. The Motul Dictionary gives for *sinbalam*, "to struggle; to make war."
[111] The phrase appears to be *u bak ahau*.

page twenty

During the migration from Holtun Suiva and the one from the Five Provinces also, it chanced that there should be no idols of carved wood. In those days, the Lord of the Canul governed the five divisions of the country to our utter misery, to our degradation and to our sorrow. There was Ah Canul in the midst of the country of the Canul, and the number of those who were severely punished by his government at Saclactun was legion.

The pottery jars which were used for the storage of food were kept closed, and the food was sold for high prices, after it had been carried down from the mountains. Seven multitudes of bearers were engaged in this operation.

Thus was fulfilled the prophecy of the katun that there should be seven years of drought in all. Seven times, the year of the waxing katun was changed in the usual manner. For seven years there was pestilence. But that which was to affirm the completion of the katun's treasure, they guarded there for seven years as if it were the very life of the Earth. For Saclactun is situated in the heart of the Island of Cuzamil and of them all.

At the expiration of the period of the prophecy, there came the Sun of our life, and whichever one of the four Musencabs [112] it was who measured the earth by his paces. And there was the utmost astonishment when the Lords of the Days, 13 Ahau and 1 Ahau, came to the festival, in spite of the fact that the enemy in our midst harrassed us day and night.

When they came down and ranged to and fro over the earth, the Thirteen gods and the Nine gods, they put in order that which they had created, and that which Itzam-cabain, Itzam the Earth-monster, had put in order.

The knife of the Sun protects his people. When the heavens

---

[112] For a discussion of the four Musencabs, who appear to have been associated with the cardinal points, see R.L. Roys 1933: 64.

cease to be, we shall all die and four-footed creatures will destroy the land.

Even when the Thirteen gods once had their beginning in ancient times, when there was rigorous discipline upon the earth and the Earth-monster tore up great trees by the roots, still the prophecies of the katun-folds were fulfilled, even when he once threatened to shake the earth.

The prophecies of the katun shall be fulfilled! And the Nine gods, when they cut the throat of Itzam-cabain and created the island out of his body, had no desire to destroy the works of his hands, or his books. Nevertheless, we do not invoke him by name or burn incense to him, when the lords bind up the face of the tun at the present time.

On 11 Ahau when Ah Musencab arises, they bind the faces of the Thirteen gods and they do not even know the names of the deities.[113] "The holy elder brothers," these are the names which they invoke. Nor do they observe their faces either, when they direct their feet upon the earth. Nor do they know when they themselves are being greatly deceived.

But when the Thirteen gods are rightly called by name and the Nine gods, then corn descends, salt descends, precious stones descend, trees descend. Then come the carvers in wood and stone, and then come the treasures of the Thirteen gods, even with a great crash of drums. And their faces are seen, even when they are covered up.

When Canhel the Serpent destroyed the cornfields and ground them to powder, then they created the new growth from the old,[114] lest the divine vigor waste away, lest our gains crumble away. May the gods grant the fulfillment of our prayers!

When the Bolon Tzacab, the first Nine Wisemen in the thirteenth level of the heavens, heap up everything in abundance in-

---

[113] This must refer to the Itza priests who have assumed the functions of the Maya priesthood, without sufficient knowledge of the rituals.

[114] The phrase is *ix kukil ix yaxum,* which might be rendered "both descendants and ancestors."

cluding quantities of jewels, and when the path leads straight to the heart for the sake of the Thirteen gods, there shall be no more pain or suffering. Then their hearts shall be provided with food. So be it.

When they crumble away in death, being without

page twenty-one

the help of the Ancestors, and they suffer affliction, being without teeth, and living their lives without heart, then they will conceal their uncertainties in the midst of their withered fruit as in the midst of the sea.

Once there was truth, which we drew from the Serpent in ancient times, from the clear unclouded heavens to the evil-knotted earth beneath. But when the enemy warriors came, the folds of death became the swaddling clothes of our babies. Similarly, the folds of the katun were made on the day 3 Oc, and on the day 1 Cimi the prophecy of the katun was afterwards fulfilled.

Now it should be said of the four gods, the four Bacabs, that they stretched out the earth.[115] And when they had finished stretching out the earth, they planted the red *Imix*-tree.

They receive a handful of offerings as a token of their having stretched out the earth. These Bacabs shake the tree. Perhaps the moon germinates the plants.

And they planted the white Imix-tree in the north. Perhaps they will grant us a sign, a symbol of the stretching out of the earth.

Although they place a black Imix-tree at the west of our land

---

[115] Following the principle that the simpler and more fundamental meanings of words are the most probable in a document such as the Book of Chilam Balam of Tizimin, I have translated *hayal cab* as if it came from *hay, ah,* "to stretch," and *cab,* "earth." The Motul Dictionary, however, also gives *haycabil* or *haycabal,* "the destruction of the world," and it is thus that Roys has interpreted the phrase (Roys 1933: 100). Pio Perez, on the other hand, gives *haycab, tah,* "to destroy," not "to destroy the world." It seems to me that my interpretation above is more consistent with the concept of planting trees.

as a sign of their having stretched out the earth, the black face of this black Imix-tree in our midst will frighten the multitude.

The yellow Imix-tree stands to the south of the land as a sign of the stretching out of the earth. It stands there, yellow, to tell the news.

Finally there is the green Imix-tree in the middle of the country, to commemorate the stretching out of the earth. The people are instructed concerning the origin and existence of the katun. So be it.

Eleven Ahau was the day of the descent of the words of the Bolon Tzacab, the Nine Wisemen, and the prayers which were folded within the bundle of Katun 9, the bundle which descended on the day 4 Kan. Vale.

When the bundle was completed, when it descended, the time arrived in the heart of the heavens for the second birth of the Nine. Searching for resting-places, the Nine descended in a company and were not consumed.

Sweet was the ancient fruit, and succulent on the tongue; sweet to soften the hard heart, to mollify the angry passions! Chac Vayab the Bat,[116] he it is who sucks honey from the flowers.

During five days Ix Haunab, Mother Despair, Ix Huznab, Mother Terror, and Ix Kuknab, Mother of Lies,[117] eat from the red-painted bowl, from the white-painted bowl, from the black-painted bowl, and from the yellow-painted bowl.

After a while they cease from smelling the yol-flowers and from eating them by the handful. Then they perform a rite against steril-

---

[116] vayab may derive from vaay which the Motul interprets as "the familiar of a sorcerer." The word vayben signifies "a sorcerer." For the Chumayel version of this passage see Roys 1933: 104.

[117] One of the meanings of nab which forms the common base of the three names, is "mother." Ix is the feminine prefix corresponding with the masculine ah. Speaking of the tabus of women, Landa says: "Nor did they allow them to go to the temples for the sacrifices, except on a certain festival, at which they admitted certain old women for its celebration. For their child-births they had recourse to the sorceresses, who made them believe their lies, and put under their beds an idol of a goddess called Ix Chel who they said was the goddess of making children." Tozzer 1941: 128-129.

ity, including the penance of blood-letting by cutting, and they sip from the hollow hearts of the *yol*-flowers and from the bellies of the *yol*-flowers.

Let the flowers spring forth from the bowl!

The Maya people learn about the gateway to the house of flowers. The priests smell the flowers. The lords smell the flowers. The warriors smell them. This is the treasure of the Lord of Flowers which he brought when he descended. Is not life the burden of the flowery katun, and of the precious stones?

The penances dear to the heart of Ku Mitnal, God of the Underworld, did not arrive, either, when the Nine Wisemen, the Bolon Tzacab, descended for the penance of the flowers.

Now the wizards vie with one another in taking the shapes of the blue heron and of the humming-bird. Then flowers descend from the source and from the folds of the Hand, nine flowers. When the hearts of the flowers appear, the priests place four branches of flowers on the burning altar of the Sun.

Then as in ancient times the Thirteen gods appeared. But the sin of the mat [118] did not recognize their descent, when their words came down. Excepting the flower of the mat and the flower of the bench, envy shall be enthroned. Envy shall reap. Envy shall be in their hearts.

page twenty-two

Those are words of great mischief when the Lords of the Days complain about the sacred food, when they desire to eat their food according to the time-honored custom. They look at the foot of a bird and speak distastefully of their fare to the god Sip, and

---

[118] The *mat* is used as a symbol of the highest authority as the *throne* is employed in other cultures. The rulers mentioned here were doubtless the Itza overlords. Sanchez de Aguilar remarked that the Maya had been vassals of the Mexicans for 600 years prior to the arrival of the Spanish. Tozzer 1941: 21; footnote 123.

he makes a note of their words in his mind. They bind up their faces as they sit.

His people understand. The people of Pop plead with their Lord lest, having forgotten the fathers and having forgotten the mothers, he should fail to recognize the sons of the fathers and should not recognize the houses of the wizards.

No longer are there stones which speak a little.[119] He does not sit down to rest with his burden, the gifts of the Nine gods. The seven devils descend, bringing a condition of ruin, even utter darkness. But when they slit our throats and string us up by the neck, they are not reckoning with Hunac Sip and the prophecy of Ah Bobat the Searchers. So be it.

The priests of Sip are here, of the mighty Lord Sip. The warriors of Sip are here. All these evils shall cease when *they* are overwhelmed, when they are all overthrown by the Guardians, when they are all overthrown by the Anointed Ones.

The number of men here in our land shall be increased tenfold, and when they arrive, they will fulfill the words of the warriors of the katun. May the drunkards be torn up by the roots! May Ix Tab [120] carry them dangling from her hands, even before we have tied up the face of the katun.

They shall be punished in our midst, wounded in many places by our lances and by the flowers of death of the priests and the wisemen and the lords and the warriors. The prophecies will be made manifest in the current katun, in the ninth tun, when it shall come to pass that the government shall be cut off by the lords and nobles and the priest Ah Kin Chilcoba and the Sweepers.[121]

I do not speak the words of the Thirteen gods when they despatched three different groups of men upon the earth in order that they might fold the katun three times. Vale. At the time of the overturning of great mountains, we are as withered fruit.

---

[119] This may be a poetic allusion to the stelae with their engraved inscriptions.
[120] Goddess of suicides and of hangings.
[121] The Sweepers, *ah miscit,* are mentioned several times in the Chumayel. Roys 1933: 65, 74 etc.

At the height of our afflictions, the stammering Itza called our sons to their aid, in order that together they might surpass the perfection of the powerful Christian warriors. Vale.

Eight Ahau came on his day and we swept the market-place, and the world looked on in wonder when the words of the Thirteen gods descended, on 8 Ahau, at Chichen. The faces of the Thirteen gods smoked, and those upon whom the responsibility of government rested turned pale, when there came the words of the Thirteen gods on 8 Ahau at Chichen.[122]

In response to the fervent prayer of the Lord of Uxmal, Chacxibchac came carrying animals on his back. Then when Kukulcan, He-who-causes-the-flowers-to-open, descended they petitioned him to remove the Itza far away, saying that when the Itza arrived without warning and settled on our soil, they overran us. They picked the ears of corn, and their feet trespassed against us. Lord 8 Ahau was our guest then, also.

Like the strong and enduring Tree of Life they increased twofold. One twist in the road; one shot from a musket. Vale.

Anciently on 8 Ahau we were the guests of our blood-relatives, the people of Itzmal, because Sip was there as the guest of the lords. When they opened the sealed katun in earlier times during the 17th katun, they pleaded for the satisfaction of our needs by the holy heavenly Itzam-caan,[123] and for his apparition as Lord of Heaven, and for the opening of heaven to our kindred, the people of Itzmal, by the god their guest, as in ancient times the sons of holy Itzmal declared it.

---

[122] The Katun 8 Ahau after the Conquest ran from 1693 to 1713 if a Katun 5 Ahau began in 1594, as stated on page 1 of the manuscript.

[123] Itzam-caan is in antithesis to Itzam-cabain, which I have called the Earth-monster and which Roys translates as the "Earth-crocodile." *Cab* is "earth" and *ain* may mean "cayman." Roys 1933: 101.

page twenty-three

When the lord of the katun appeared in the ancient kingdom of Itzmal, the people of Itzmal completed the count, absorbing the teaching, even in the midst of afflictions.

We had as our guest Yaxbolai. We had as our guests Chacbolai and Chacxibchac, three very unlucky spirits. Their gift, when it descended in our midst proved to contain great suffering for our relatives here in Itzmal at the hands of that evil-doer, the King of the Canul.

He ensnared our honorable sons into revealing the secret teachings to him. After he had learned from them the whereabouts of Kukulcan, he cut the throats of all of them and theirs. When the bodies of our noblemen lay stretched out upon the base ground, the heavens opened, and our leaders laid the frightful deed upon our oppressors.

Then began the experiment of Itzam-caan to effect the reformation of the King of the Canul from his wicked ways. When the Lord of Heaven was manifested to the people of Chichen where Ah Canul had no power, they listened with careful attention.

When Lord Thirteen appeared he made their burdens lighter with his solution, for the sake of their forefathers who once fought for them with all their might.There were many idols of wood, and their duplication caused quarreling and bloodshed.

The pestilence enters the houses, stealing in secretly. There are pleadings muttered in the throat. They tear their clothing. They yearn with a great longing.

This is the burden of the katun in the days of the Christians, in the days of the lascivious men, when such terrible suffering came in the folds of Katun 8 Ahau from the Thirteen. Vale.

Then it came to pass that our governors, the lords of the Itza, pleaded with lamentations asking, "With whom will perfection rest among dishonorable men?"

These nine lords, when they build a wall to defend worthy men and provide canes for arrows, will prevail against the enemy by means of the magic of the book.

At Ichcansiho they opened the sealed katun at the end of the tribulation of Katun 11 Ahau.[124] Shining were the faces of the Lords of the Heavens who were on the point of entering the concealed heavens, the sweet-smelling heavens. They are agitated by the drums. They are deeply moved by the drawing of blood.

On a day 9 Oc the first strutting turkey-cocks arrived.[125] On that day there were whippings at Chakanputun. The people subsisted on trees; they subsisted on stones.

When the invasion came during Katun 11 Ahau, even the Heavens pitied themselves. They blamed it on the Moon when our warriors cut their own throats. The women singers must chant invocations to Yaxal Chuen, the First-born Chuen, for the protection of the people. Great numbers assembled and they all sang together to the gods.

There was he who advises about new moons;[126] and he who advises about attaining man's estate; and he who advises about buying and selling; and he who advises about the prime of life; and he who advises on the problem of marriageable daughters.

Your expectation is from the gods and from your elder brothers. Lest your visitor, the god of the white face, make you change your manner of dressing and turn you into effeminate fellows, you must cut off the white, bearded strangers from Ichcansiho. Whip them from the land!

And the priests of the living God, the true God, shall write in the sacred book of the universe concerning the earth when He descended and His effulgence grew brighter and brighter.

Gradually in this land there shall be no more sculptured Temples of the Jaguar for you, when these men extend their sway among

---

[124] 1535-1555. A new sequence of katuns starts at this point.

[125] Clearly a descriptive term for the dress and demeanor of the Spaniards.

[126] *ah kainom pal:* kainom may be construed from *kai*, "to sing;" but I have derived it from *kaay*, "to admonish or advise." The Tizimin manuscript and the Motul frequently disagree in the matter of doubling a vowel; *i* and *y* are interchangeable. *Pal* is "new moon."

the heavens, when they reach the Source, the origin of the three-fold majesty of the heavens, when . . . This is the burden of Katun 11 Ahau.

page twenty-four

Nine Ahau.[127] Seven times the opening of the sealed katun of 9 Ahau has taken place.[128] On this day at sunset, the men of responsibility met to consider the question of guidance, not only the instruction of the chiefs and priests, but that of the war-captains also, as well as the lords of Pop and Zam, all with one heart and mind.

Then in company with Lord 9 Ahau descended the words of that well-known Sip, the ancient Sip, the warrior of the nobility and of days 9 and of the nine Zam, in the kingdom of Ah Vuc Chapat the Seven-headed Serpent, whose shield is the sun.

When this mighty warrior arrived, descending the road of the Stars of the Abundant Life and of the living Katun, on the day-sign of Sacvacnal, the faces of the lords were suffused with living tears, with tears like rain.

When the battle for our lives was joined, our warriors looked very ferocious as if hungering for warfare, for a universal conflict. They went into battle with high courage, first acknowledging the authority of the day 9 with a few words.

It is the katun of the forcible withdrawal of the Hand,[129] yes, from the granting of the prayers of warriors. The lords were vanquished, and there was much praying for their lives and shedding of tears at the end, as they lay stretched out on the mats trying to staunch the flowing blood, or lying flat on their backs in heaps. These are the words of the katun.[130] So be it.

---

127 1555-1575 approximately.

128 A given katun, such as 9 Ahau, occurs seven times in about 1800 years.

129 The phrase is *u col kab katun.*

130 A record of the events of each katun was jotted down in the Book of the Katun, for future reference. See Commentary, chapter 1.

The opening of the sealed katun of 7 Ahau [131] took place at Mayapan. Katun 7 Ahau belongs to Ek Chuuah. The faces of the lords of Pop and Zam were stern,[132] and the faces of the enchanters were grave when the lords began to perfect the blossoming of the nine *yol*-flowers, and when they reproduced the *yol*-flowers, the flowers of life, the flowers of rain and of tears.

The true men work miracles to protect the people. The priests, *ah kin,* work wonders. The Searchers, *ah bobat,* work wonders. Nobody will be left out. They thoroughly cleanse the lords, their faces and their hearts. Will you, the foremost division of earth-dwellers, be taken captive lying flat on your backs, while your feet are still able to carry the whole of you?

Should meditation during the day, and meditation during the night, be considered the sin of the day, and the sin of the night?

Great is the tenderness of the hearts of Ah Bobat, true men, when alas your arms are laden with burdens like stones and, without houses, without parents, you look upon yourselves and your feet are confused.

The men of Katun 7 Ahau speak a great madness of words. They run to and fro in frenzy. In Ichcansiho *they* will soon begin to take possession. They will bring to pass the final days and the end of all protection of the people, all. The nine magic rituals of life, the nine magic incantations for rain in abundance and for new growth in abundance were given us by the authors of our life.

Whether by taking medicine or by eleven vomitings, our daughters may become both good and beautiful, and whether they are beautiful or not, there will be no defenders to guard them in the days to come, in the seven days of collecting tribute. Men with trumpets are making the rounds of the country. Only seven days remain to our government. Then come the men to dig to the very bottom to fill their baskets. . . . They lay waste the property of our people, making destitute the houses of our rulers. The holy symbols on the altars will allure them. They will covet the precious masks.

---

[131] 1575-1594.

[132] *amayte,* literally "squared."

page twenty-five

These men will laugh in the faces of our countrymen and of the people of the province, and of our rulers and lords. Having at heart the welfare of Pop and Zam and of the government, true men will deny, when they are asked, that they have any property. These avaricious rulers are the governing lords of Katun 7 Ahau.

The opening of the sealed katun of Sozil the Bat, Katun 5 Ahau: [133] the faces of the lords will be clear and shining.

One irregular file of boys out of step will confuse their watching kindred. So it is at times with the things which concern the security of the people. In such a manner do true men meditate that no person shall love the lords of the earth.[134]

A wave of disgust sweeps through the house of the gods, because you forget Life, you forget your own ancient teachings. Within your very doors, the avaricious lords are your punishment in the living katun.

The Thirteen! Suiva, City of Eternal Life! [135] The story of the road from Suiva to the kingdom of affliction. They strip the skin from the rattlesnake. They stretch the skin of the jaguar.

For three days the circles of a double rainbow adorned the blue sky of Ichcansiho.

The mouths of our white oppressors declare the things pertaining to the *year* [136] to be only wind. They even go so far as to say that there will not be a throne in the heavens, shining like the

---

[133] 1594-1614. This is the Katun 5 Ahau of the first twelve pages of the manuscript.

[134] The Spaniards.

[135] I derive *suiva* or *suyva* from *suy-vah*, "eternal life." Roys remarks in the Chumayel (page 192): "The name Zuyua is inseparably connected with the Toltec penetration of Yucatan, which left a number of Nahuatl words in the Maya language. The Xius believed that they had come from a place called West Zuyua, and Brinton has identified Zuyua with the Mexican Zuiven, 'the name of the uppermost heaven.'"

[136] In other words, they ridicule the Maya calendar.

sun, to be adored in its majesty. But the dying lords of the land of Pop and Zam accept the eleven penances on faith, as they cut their throats on the altar of Pop and on the altar of Zam.

The jaguar, the mountain-lion, the innumerable *sacbob* and *chacbob* all love the native lords. In sorrow they turn away to Chacvenco and Sacvenco,[137] who are insolent and disobedient to their parents, who belittle their fathers and mothers.

The ancient people strove to attain perfection. In olden times they recognized the miracles performed by the heavenly Hunab Ku, the One God. Formerly, Ichcansiho knew how to protect all the people.

The security of our land, the security of the province shall return! Our faces shall be set free! Our hands shall be set free! Our feet shall be set free!

If the earth is shattered, if there is pestilence, if destruction comes to the rulers of Katun 3 Ahau,[138] they will forget the sight of the stripping bare of the altars of Pop and Zam. Then their necks were stretched, during the three days of government, the three days of Zam, mourning again for their eternal homes, lamenting the invasion, mourning for the casting of lots before starting on a journey. We will find Zam and Pop in the heavens.

There are some who deny their ancestors, who deny their ancient houses when the covetous sons, the covetous sons arrive. Then descends the opening of the sealed katun of 1 Ahau.[139] Ropes descended. Clay descended. When the descent of the hills came, as was customary, they were resentful.

The lust of the belly, the lust of carnal sin, the lust for noble family, the sin of arrogance, all these are vices which come quickly, the evil desires of our rulers in Katun 1 Ahau. So be it. The sculptor of the gods.[140] . . .

---

[137] These are minor nature deities, classified by the Motul Dictionary as "refined villains."

[138] 1614-1634.

[139] 1634-1654.

[140] *amaite kauil ku.* I take *kauil* as equivalent to *kabil* or *kavil*, "one who works with the hands."

page twenty-six

The surface of the earth will be moved. How can the people be protected, thus disturbed in the midst of the earth, in the sculptured land of Ichcansiho, when all around us there are beggars soliciting alms? They will appropriate the idols and the vestments of Pop and Zam from the lords. The burden of our land will be: how much will it take to satisfy these avaricious rulers?

The sons of the Sun are sorrowful, and wisely so, for they lament the intruders,[141] and they feel poignantly the ridicule of the casting of lots. They doubt that protection of the people will result from scoffing at the Bacabs.

There are some who smooth the way, who placate and seek to calm the angry words of Katun 1 Ahau by the authority of the altar of Pop and the altar of Zam, when the words of Chacvenco and the many Sacvencos themselves dart forth. God grant that there may come a Deliverer from our afflictions, who will answer our prayers in Katun 1 Ahau!

According to the omens above the earth and the prophecies, the disturbers of our land shall eventually turn back, after the years of avarice have passed and our sons have used concealment after concealment. The hearts of the lords are sorrowful when they hear the piercing words which are the burden of Katun 1 Ahau.[142]

In Saclactun is held the opening of the sealed katun of 12 Ahau,[143] the katun of Yaxal Chuen, First-born Chuen. The lords watch for the coming of Hunac the Knower, Hunac the Artist, Hunac the Enchanter.

He will teach the priests the complete magic of Zam and Pop. And the Jaguar will measure out the six magic formulas of government: these involve good chiefdoms, a good aristocracy, good men, and good sons, throughout the earth.

---

[141] *yaxcach* is literally "a fly."
[142] 1634-1653.
[143] 1653-1673.

He will bring food and water on his back, regardless of borrowed Pop and borrowed Zam. When *they* arrive each day in the midst of the land, they will find themselves in an uninhabited desert.

When good men are oppressed and their towns destroyed, there will be no more mountain-lions in the land, no more foxes, no more ferrets in the ravines. There will be no niggardly king. There will be no deliverer to save *his* kingdom. There will be no licking of [the feet of] rulers.

No longer will the theft of our idols continue. This is the burden of Katun 12 Ahau: "There will be the majesty. There will be the nobility. There will be the religion." But if they do not merit life, the pestilence will come to end the deception.

When an end finally comes to the troublesome days of the troublesome katun, He-who-crushes-the-rocks will bring to pass six good years followed by six bad years, in order that once more there may be an intercessor in our midst. The wicked knife of the warrior will wound grievously and destroy. We look forward to the good things of holy 10 Ahau, when happiness will finally come to the land.

There will be no more foxes, no more towns, no more ferrets in the ravines. There will be no more noble descendants adorning the lion's den. It will be better if the world comes to an end. It will be better if our land comes to an end, in the 13th fold of Katun 12 Ahau. Vale.

Ten will interpret the opening of the sealed katun of 10 Ahau.[144] One looks at the face of Citbolon or at the face of the sky of Citbolon,[145] one at the sun, one at the forests, one at the trees, to determine what kind of remedy the heavens will provide, to be written down [in the Book of the Katun] for future years: "The business of life will be difficult, and retaining the breath of life full of sorrow."

---

[144] 1673-1693.

[145] *Cit Bolon Tun* is mentioned by both Cogolludo and Landa as a god of medicine. Tozzer 1941: 155.

page twenty-seven

The lords bind up their faces in pain because true men swelter in toil, and hunger is their burden, and because of their bad conscience about protecting the people.

They are agitated by the drums. The Bat is awakened by the drums. The four Bacabs ride to earth on the back of a green rainbow. One by one the stars fall.

The lords hold their breath in the throat and make true their promise about setting Pop in order. It has become perverted by this time, a stain on the good name of our people. When the bearer of Katun 10 Ahau arrives, there will be great sorrow among the lords on account of the year-bearer.[146]

Eight Ahau is the katun of settling down [in a new place] as of old Mayapan was depopulated. In the south, at the opening of the sealed katun of 8 Ahau,[147] we were in the presence of ten statues, representations of the forms of the Lords of the Abundant Life. At sunset, towards the end, Citbolon himself reviewed the blood-letting for bread, the blood-sacrifice for rain.

The warrior will employ his prowess on nobody. When they are taught about the abundant life, they will have compassion on the fields. They will have compassion on the mountains. They shall be followed for the benefit of all concerned, so that there shall be no more sorrow in the fields, no need for distress in the mountains, because the whole province and the entire earth were stretched out by the Bacabs.

When Kinich Kakmo [148] shall descend in majesty, then those of other lands shall descend also, when they can be set free straight-

---

[146] The calendar has fallen into confusion, but not irreparably so; for the lords are pledged to set the New Year's day in its correct time in the tzolkin.

[147] 1693-1713.

[148] Kinich Kakmo is mentioned several times in the Chumayel, usually in connection with the city of Izamal, where he was worshiped. Roys 1933: 66, 82, 141 etc.

way from the insolent and lawless men, and from those who look with scorn upon our ancestors and upon our noble lineage. This is the offense of the lords of Chichen, the lords who came from the sea.

The Bacab who lives in the northern land; when our rulers shall presently fulfill all their obligations, perhaps there will descend arrows, perhaps there will descend shields to shelter the homeless ones.

Our sons sprinkle with their tears the majesties of the altar of Zam and the altars of the Pops. They take delight in the words concerning the path of truth, recollecting the furious speeches at the solemnities on account of the cupidity of the lords.

Ah Kinich Kakmo having revealed himself as cause during Katun 8 Ahau will be recompensed on the threshold when he comes, cleaving the heavens, darkening the earth.

Then as in ancient times parting the sky, Sip will arrive. Now let true men be revealed to the people. They will break the necks of the lords of creation, because they secretly scoff at the altar of Zam and at the altar of the Pops.

However, when the country is on the point of being turned upside down, the humiliation of the overturning is a great evil in itself, the denial of perfection. They lament the invasion. They mourn for the casting of lots in order to learn the path for arriving at the divine goal. This is the prophecy of 8 Ahau.

He by whom Mayapan was anciently depopulated set limits to the katun prophecies, in a manner of speaking. There will come a stopping-place for the prophecies when the government has been restored once more, according to the words of Ah Kin Chilam the Prophet, when he writes about the aspect of the katun during 8 Ahau.

page twenty-eight

Seven times there has been the opening of the sealed katun of 6 Ahau, the katun of Kinich Kakmo, at Uxmal. In the appointed union, the faces of the lords express their appreciation of his words, when he enters. Suffice it that they concede the enchantment of the authority of Pop and the authority of Zam in operation.

Suffice it that they learn the true nature of the stars. And if they should misunderstand, they ask that they may be corrected promptly. The men ask for a judgment in silence. The people in our midst shall grieve for food until the passing of the katun of 6 Ahau. At Chacmitan also there will be much subsisting on trees, much subsisting on stones. Hunger will be their burden.

They die, he who is of Pop and he who is of Zam. If true men cut their own throats, to the people will be left only what resembles the approach to a blank wall, a being left on the outside. Since no one ever arrives who travels by an evil road, the people weigh their words, whatever they may be, lest there be almost no end to lies.

When trees grow in the land, when rocks grow in the land, when it happens for the third time that they dwell in peace and serenity of life in Chacmitan, then there will come a recompense for the ancient hunger.

Three times for government they will have the authority of Zam, three times the authority of Pop. In the fourth tun they shall see an increase in the prosperity of the state and in the prosperity of the lords. Finally a day will come when there will be no more uprooting in the land, when it has been overthrown once again. There will be no more festival days to honor the authority of Pop and the authority of the Zams.

And why should healing not come to the country? This is the prophecy of the katun when it comes. This is the aspect from ancient times of Katun 6 Ahau.[149] Vale.

Seven times the opening of the sealed katun of 4 Ahau [150] has taken place; seven times, the rigors of the people of Chichen whose feet were bruised with much walking. The omens of the great ones are of toil and wretchedness, and the gnawing of bark for food to preserve the holy people lest they close their eyes in death.

The gods give us the bread of heaven in their mercy. Let there be obedience to their laws. Is not the desire to obey, is not obedience

---

[149] 1713-1732. [150] 1732-1752.

itself the duty of the lords? Their throats will be silent when the life of abundance comes to an end, and with it esteem for one blood-relationship. And there will no longer be obedience through veneration for one western tongue in the land of Pop and Zam. The pestilence shall be their burden.

When discord comes among the rulers may the gods forbid that true men among the people shall perish! The vomit of blood shall be the burden of the katun. The day shall come when you will withhold the bread of life from these white-skinned effeminate fellows, from their very teeth.

Our descendants shall pierce them with the lance. Our Ancestors shall pierce them with their hands tied together. The chanter of news [151] shall pierce them. The horse shall strike them down with despair. The horse shall pierce them in secrecy. It is decreed.

At Chichen one-half the katun shall be good; one-half shall be without good. There will be the majesty of the throne of him who speaks the magic language of the stars of heaven submerged in blue water, Yax Ah Cocaimut is his name. And no one is gallant enough to hear the news calmly when everyone is involved in the omens of Katun 4 Ahau.[152] Vale. Likewise the pestilence will enter our houses.

There is also reason for suspecting that even now the year-bearer will continue to be an important and grave problem of Ah Kin Chilam when he teaches about the bearer of the katun.[153]

page twenty-nine

The day of 4 Ahau arrives at Chichen Itza. Four Ahau is the katun for remembering knowledge and compressing it within *annals*.[154] There was the time, [for example], when the friars[155] came

---

[151] *ah kayom mut.*   [152] 1732-1752.

[153] This is the second reference to confusion in the year-count.

[154] There can be little doubt that *anahteil* was derived from the Spanish *anales*.

[155] The word translated "friar" is *yum* or *yumil*, also written *yunil*. It is the common word for "father." The Chumayel has *lumil*, "lands," in its version of this passage. Roys 1933: 146, 147.

among us at Nitunzala and Chactemal and Tah Vaimil and Holtun Itza, and the high-handed manner in which we tore up the writings of the friars, the *Reportorio* for the remission of sins.[156]

In order that our people may recognize deception when it comes, we have written down the auguries of the days of the katuns one by one, telling by what signs the burden of each katun may be recognized, and the manner in which the count of the bearer of future events is safe guarded when he comes; also the road by which the wisemen shall arrive on the day when they come, that it may become the road of the believers themselves. In the katun of trouble the warriors quietly blacken their faces.

Eleven Ahau [157] was the first and original katun of the count, and it was also the name of the first katun after the arrival of the white men in Ichcansiho in time for the establishment of a katun. Alas for us when the great ones, the bearded ones, the sons of the Sun, the white men came along the trail! On that day we became the victims of their evil desires.

The bearded ones, the ones who shoot—this is the signal of the white god—were arriving. Six sons of heaven, some aged and infirm, came shouting to announce the news, spreading it over the country. They were present in every clump of trees, behind every heap of rocks, the friars, all exactly alike in appearance, negotiating for our souls and haranguing us about the "true god."

When you tried with all your hearts to emulate them [158] they obstructed your efforts to protect the people. At our ceremonies we prayed to the gods above, asking intercession for our brothers, when they arrived.

You meditated on the words of God, never deceiving us with regard to the road of the future still to be made firm, the road of bondage. The Father of Heaven and Earth will hear your prayers,

---

[156] In the Chumayel manuscript the Spanish word is misspelled "repuldoryo."
[157] This is a new sequence of katuns beginning with 11 Ahau, 1535-1555.
[158] It is a historical fact that the Xiu received the Spaniards in a friendly and peaceable manner.

when you come to cast lots in the presence of the people in the matter of the *tuns*.

On 9 Ahau we put the katun in order when we counted the days in four different ways to establish the katun.[159]

Little by little we began to grow weary of the maiming of the people by the Christians, when I should have liked to protect the people and guard the country. They gradually began to plant a church in the middle of Tiho. This did not do much harm to the katun treasure.

Gradually, they began the hangings again for the second time, and they kindled the fire on the stone. The offenses of the white people are all alike, even against those who surrender themselves or their relatives, everywhere they go. Brothers plead for justice in their throats. Gradually we discover that the Christians are great liars. Little by little we realize that they are great cheats.

Little by little, whether they take seven sacraments or not, their prayers are heard by their powerful God.[160] You cast your lots. The people come. You set in order the enchantments.

Katun 7 Ahau [161] is the third katun since the count was first begun at Ichcansiho. When the sealed katun was opened, immediately the eyes of the lords opened wide when they saw, to the accompaniment of the throbbing drums, that we were requited by the cleaving asunder of the heavens, and the descent of the flowers of life, the flowers of rain.

This is the burden of the katun: "Little by little they will begin to esteem our learning and our knowledge of the unrolling of the face of the universe for the protection of the fathers of the people from ruin and the descendants of our ancestors."

"The face of the squared stone from the mountains shall again be made beautiful." These are the prophetic words of Balam the Fox, Balam the interpreter of miracles. No lie shall he make when he counts the katun.

---

[159] 1555-1575.

[160] *dios*, not *ku*.

[161] 1575-1594.

page thirty

. Now the priests begin the customary drawing of the katun days. Now they begin to name one at a time in their hands the great heap of small stones, passing them from hand to hand. Then there came into your dwelling, there came the men who want you to become Christians, into the midst of the ceremony. Vale.

Katun 5 Ahau [162] was counted at Ichcansiho in the fourth period at the opening of the sealed katun, during the government of the katun of misfortune. Gradually the hanging of the great men among us began to take place, the extinction of noble lineages. Gradually began our sorrow for our daughters, our sorrow for our sons, for the foolish behavior of our daughters and the foolish behavior of our sons, made purposely so.

The omens of the gods must go, the omens of Kavil must go, and those of the Sky-serpent, of Canhel the Sky-serpent, alas!

Little by little began the offering of prayers to the Devil. Little by little came the days of spying and lying, when we began to go hungry and our feet were bruised with much walking for the protection of the people.

When they lifted up the necks and held in their hands the heads of nobles of high lineage, when they held up the neck of Chac Ahaucan of the lineage, when they began on the two priests of Zam and the two priests of Pop, and on Balam the Fox, Balam the interpreter of wonders, the Dog, then our hearts were broken when we heard the news.

The wretched men inquired minutely again and again as to how to be able to recognize the days of the moon-count, and the katun-bearer, and the prophecies of the gods above. Vale.

Three Ahau.[163] It was the fifth time the katun had been counted

---

[162] 1594-1614.
[163] 1614-1634.

at Ichcansiho. At the opening of the sealed katun, Ek Cocaymut [164] showed himself in the presence of the lords. There was watchfulness on their faces. There was courage on their faces. There was intelligence on their faces.

When you descend to covetousness and avarice and the invocation of the Devil, then you reach the lowest abyss of falsifying the words of Hunab Ku above. The swindlers ridicule the year-count of the Jaguar. The white men invent a system of spying on our great ceremonials, on the cherished rituals of the Jaguar Balam.

The stonings, the grievous hangings, all the cutting down and the wearisome bearing of heavy burdens have exhausted and bruised and pierced us. And when the katun-bearer arrived seven years ago, we made enchantments for protecting the people. And the mourning for the three-fold learning, and the great yearning for a return to the occult teachings kindled a fire which finally burst forth in Ichcansiho. The fact that the flaying of the mountain-lion in the open plaza has been forbidden brings us to stony ground. We have burned great quantities of copal on account of the hangings.

When the katun-bearer finally arrived and the burden of our afflictions was unfolded, we saw the look on the faces of the two priests of Zam and the two priests of Pop, when they read the prophecy of the katun which does not lie, the words of the God in the holy heaven. And you, my brothers, mourned for the casting of lots and lamented the coming of the intruders, when you learned the divisions of the road which we are to follow in the genealogical tree, when we receive the gifts of Ah Vuc Yol Sip.

Katun 1 Ahau [165] was the sixth katun and it arrived in the pueblo of Emal. At the opening of the sealed katun there descended both recompense in the form of *yol*-flowers and at the same time, alas, three prophecies, three precepts, three hindrances to medita-

---

[164] The parallel passage in the Chumayel reads: "The fifth katun. 1620. Katun 3 Ahau was the fifth katun. The katun was established at Ichcansiho. Ek-Cocah-mut was its face to the rulers, to the wise men. Antichrist was its face to the rulers." Roys 1933: 153.

[165] 1634-1653.

tion, three hindrances to seeking the wisdom of the Sculptor of the Squared Stone, before the faces of the lords, when he polishes his words concerning the other affairs, the other teachings.

page thirty-one

There will be deep distress in spite of our yearning to protect the people, and they will be disturbed by divisions. There will be agitation in the midst of the land when "Justitia" descends upon the teaching of our sacred religion, and upon the words of the true God, and our obligation to protect the people from the abyss.

A thousand scaly warts descended when we were bitten by the serpent seven years ago. When we were bitten by the serpent seven years ago, a thousand scaly warts appeared, after *they* came.

Shame descended on our fields when the spectacle of battle arose, the spectacle of war when it descended. We suffered from the absence of the venerable ones, the representatives of our people.

O Lord of Council, Lord of Strength, grant that the abundant treasures of the sandy beaches and the treasures within the ocean may not come to an end, when *they* descend! Be with us!

When those who pour out libations come face to face with dangerous warriors, they cut their claws and hang them up in a row. When the wolf descends with the burden of taxation, when the Christians arrive, when ropes descend from heaven,[166] when great avarice comes, and the pestilence, and the vomit of blood, and a famine at Chacmitan, this is the burden of Katun 1 Ahau standing on the threshold.

Mourning for our leaders, mourning for the casting of lots to determine the road by which the katun approaches and where its resting-place shall be. One by one the mysterious flowers fell when we reached the end of the concealment of the katun bundle, in the prayer for completion and the longing for the gift of perfection, when the avaricious hagglers intruded upon the katun ceremonies.

---

[166] A reference to the hangings.

Twelve Ahau [167] was the seventh katun since the new count was begun and it arrived at Saclactun. At the opening of the sealed katun of Yaxal Chuen, the first-born Chuen, the faces of the lords were in mourning for the teachings of the day and the teachings of the night.[168] This is the burden they shoulder: to dig to the bottom of the food-baskets.

When the power descended with great force sprinkling the faces of fierce warriors, they trembled and shuddered with fear. Immediately their hearts were grieved at the condition of affairs here on earth in the katun of perplexity, in the majesty of the katun, the lordship of the katun, the words of the katun, the food of the katun, the holiness of the katun, the march of the katun, the occupation and purpose of the katun, the great sons of the katun, the great daughters of the katun, the children of the katun, the warriors of the katun, the young men of the katun.

When *they* came, demanding entrance into our houses and assuming the power of government, on one day there was one cell for Zam and Pop, in the current katun. Oh the wretchedness of a country when trees and rocks rise up and join in the battle!

One-half the remainder of the katun will be lucky, one-half will be unlucky—six years of misfortune and six years of good fortune. When all the mourning of the eternal katun 12 Ahau has been placed on high, when the seven lineages are exalted after the custom of the country, when the sacred prophecies regarding the conditions of domestic affairs in our land have come to pass, then you will again receive your replies by the casting of lots. There will be a laying down of burdens. There will be a shout of joy.

There will come a thousand scaly warts, however. This is the burden of the katun: "There will be three breaks in the lineage, three hindrances to speech, to the speeches of the fathers in the houses of grief during the katun and to the pride of the fathers, the

---

[167] 1653-1673.

[168] The reference is probably to their profound interest in astronomy, as well as to the reading of auguries by the stars.

pride of the house of the one God, Hunab Ku, when they plead with him, lamenting the Tree of Abundance of the people of Pop.

page thirty-two

The spirit of Katun 12 Ahau was certainly expressed in the numerous rainbows. Rainbows arched over the island. Rainbows stood in the midst of the land and circled from border to border over the center of the island.

When the present government came into existence in the interests of the people, there happened to be many Maya who ridiculed their kindred. The conditions of local affairs throughout the country will rapidly reach a very low ebb. It will be a katun for shooting arrows, a katun for discharging muskets in battle. There will also be the shooting of our mischievous sons and daughters. In the course of time, when the prophecy of the katun ends in exhaustion, when the remedy comes and the gods descend, what kind of sculpture shall be unveiled?

With regard to the internal affairs of the country, the omens appear black indeed, because of the entanglement of the katun. Little by little, the government of the people will be divided, when the rulers keep asking them for money.

There will always be those who labor. There will always be wisemen. Yes, they spring up in this land of trees, in this land of rocks. The lords will take counsel together. They will cut the claws of those whom they will hang up in a row, when they scratch the bowed backs of the wolf and the foxes. They will burn fiercely on the altars. Then there will be no more foxes, no more wolves.

Then there shall be the great Life, the Life of the Katun, the spirit of the katun, and a benevolent government. There will be rejoicing in the people's welfare. From the mouth of the sea they will obtain *och*-fish. Then the Katun, the flower of the Tree of Life, shall be established. After that, drought and blood-vomit will bring happiness to an end. Finally, when they are asked to reduce the amount of food that they eat, there will be much sorrowing, but rejoicing will return with the day of the katun.

Ten Ahau [169] is the eighth katun and it is counted at Saclactun. At the opening of the sealed katun of 10 Ahau, in the presence of guests from the pueblo of Chable, they will violently break the thongs which fasten the ladders of wood over the heads of the lords of the land. Three lives, three lives, are consumed by fire. [170] The sacred pebbles are shattered on the living rock. Malevolence shall be consumed. Secrecy shall be consumed. In the mouth of the sea are the words of God in heaven. The perfect One will guard our backs. The perfect One will guard our presence. Vale.

Eight Ahau [171] will be the ninth katun and they will count it at Itzmal. When the sealed katun was opened in the presence of our guests, once more the Shield descended, and arrows descended above Chakanputun where the Garden of Sculptured Stones stands within its walls, the fulfillment of the desire of Kinich Kakmo, at the opening of the sealed katun. Vale.

Six Ahau [172] will be the tenth katun, when they count it at Uxmal. *They* negotiate among themselves. Their faces are impudent. They speak insolently to the lords. There will be lying speeches of madness, as in former times when the attack of evil tongues descended. They will cut our throats. This is the burden of 6 Ahau when the katun comes. Vale.

Four Ahau [173] is the eleventh katun and they count it at Chichen Itza. At the opening of the sealed katun they shall redeem the descendants. They shall redeem the ancestors.

---

[169] 1673-1693.
[170] A reference to human sacrifice, in times of extremity.
[171] 1693-1713.
[172] 1713-1732.
[173] 1732-1752.

page thirty-three

They shall redeem the standard of the temple, Ah Kantenal. They shall redeem the vomit of blood for the fourth time. They shall redeem Kukulcan, carried on the backs of the Itza [priests] in four ceremonies.

Two Ahau[174] is the twelfth katun and it is counted in the district of Mayapan. At the opening of the sealed katun, one-half will hasten to depart; one-half will awaken in Katun 12 Ahau. Vale.

Thirteen Ahau[175] is the thirteenth katun and they shall count it in Cabal. In the assemblage of people they shall open the sealed katun. At dusk they will smell the fragrance of the flowers. Day shall be turned upside down. Their faces shall be disturbed. The genealogical tree shall descend. Stones shall descend and Heaven and Earth shall be universally consumed by fire.

They shall make a divination concerning the living and the dead: "The dead shall live! Dying from old age, they shall immediately ascend into heaven. They shall ascend quickly by good roads. Evil roads descend, spreading out on the earth."

At the end, in the final days of the katun, we will hear the words of the father of heaven and earth regarding the government of Katun 13 Ahau during his days, at the completion of the katun. Vale.

■■■■■■■■

Now, however, Ahau is subservient to the year-bearer of the south, 3 Cauac on the first of Pop, the year being 1552.[176] The god Four is submerged on that very day, 4 Ahau.

Each score of years has its bearers. When each has collected his debt, then there come four years without names. For this reason there are five years of idleness and amusement. When the katun ar-

---

[174] 1752-1772.

[175] 1772-1791.

[176] An obvious mistake for 1752. It is corrected on page 35.

rives in the future—Kaan—nevertheless, they will call upon it by name. And they will speak of the five deceptive days at the end of each year, although they are without names and thus fall, each year, at the very end of the year.

It is similar with the katun: for five years they amuse themselves by collecting the fragments of the katun. When the time comes to read the auguries of the katun, they explain to the people how it first originated, and they count the years since the birth of the various pueblos.

There is one Jesus Christ, the very most correct count above all counts. Yes, and when they are all in order, He protects their backs from the pressure of the ancient Maya teachings in the land.

And when they count, they are deceived as to the year-bearers of the teaching, like an old wound breaking out afresh, when they teach the three counts of the deceptive katun. At this time the guests of the hewn stone will be recognized in the years of grief. At this time, the pestilence will come upon us. We will speak with emotion of our afflictions. But if no crop is sowed there will be enormous wastefulness from now on for a period. It should be understood that whoever, in the presence of the elders, counts the days which are found in the *uinal,* will find *one score* of days.

There are twelve enchantments, of course, to meet all sorts of needs. Our kindred know the days of "food by the handful." In the cornfields they help themselves to handfuls of corn. They pick beans by the handful and eat them by the handful. They eat the *jicama* root by the handful, and all that they sow is nonsense, however much they may be able to count the days of the uinal at a certain time, in our presence.

If they have failed to keep the commandments of God,[177] but increasingly without noise, without agitation, *without writing it down,* our kindred on the road of love desire with all their hearts to change back, in order to satisfy their yearning [for the ancient practices] at the times of the great festivals, may they then be preserved from all evil! They will be offered the heaps of good things

[177] The Maya *ku,* not the Christian *Dios.*

by the gods in the appointment of each katun, when they have confidence in the prophecies of the four score years, in the sixteenth

page thirty-four

and nameless katun. As each of us pauses, those of us
who have not forgotten, *they* are suspicious of our being together.

A time will come when the katun-folds will have passed away,
when they will be found no longer, because the count of tuns is reunited. And after that there will come years in which there are tuns,
either four or three in number.

Eight Ahau, 6 Ahau, 4 Ahau, 2 Ahau: four score and one years
to the first tun of Katun 13 Ahau. Thirteen Ahau, 8 Ahau,[178] 6 Ahau,
4 Ahau: there arrived at Chacnabiton the Tutul Xiu Mekat. One
year less than five score.

In 8 Ahau a long time ago, Chichen Itza made itself powerful.
A long time ago they wrote down the history of the province in a
chronicle. So be it.

Four Ahau, 2 Ahau. In 13 Ahau, they counted Pop in its order.
Eleven Ahau, 9 Ahau, 7 Ahau, 5 Ahau, 3 Ahau, 1 Ahau: for ten
score years they had governed Chichen Itza. Then they abandoned
it and settled in Chakanputun where there were houses built by the
consecrated men of the Itza.

Six Ahau, in the land of Chakanputun. Four Ahau. 2 Ahau, 13
Ahau, 11 Ahau, 9 Ahau, 7 Ahau, 5 Ahau, 3 Ahau, 1 Ahau, 12 Ahau,
10 Ahau. In 8 Ahau, they abandoned Chakanputun. For thirteen
score of years they had governed Chakanputun. They went away
because the men of the Itza returned to construct their flimsy houses
for the second time. When they lost the road to Chakanputun during the two katuns of evil fortune, the Itza had wandered under the
trees and beneath the branches, under the stars of misfortune.[179]

---

[178] Thirteen Ahau should be followed immediately by 11 Ahau. This appears
to be merely a recapitulation of the previous statement.

[179] I have read *ek*, "stars," in place of *ak*, "reeds."

Six Ahau, 4 Ahau. After two score years we returned to build houses, for the second time since we lost the way to Chakanputun.

Two Ahau, 13 Ahau, 11 Ahau, 9 Ahau, 7 Ahau, 5 Ahau, 3 Ahau, 1 Ahau, 12 Ahau, 10 Ahau: they appointed as Elder Brother Ah Suitok, the Tutul Xiu of Uxmal. Ten score years passed after they settled in the land of Uxmal.

Eleven Ahau, 9 Ahau, 7 Ahau, 5 Ahau, 3 Ahau, 1 Ahau, 12 Ahau, 10 Ahau, 8 Ahau: The Xiu, true men, abandoned Chichen Itza to the threatening words of Hunac Ceel.

Ah Sinteyut Chan, Tzumtecum, Taxcal, Pantemit, Xuchuvet, Itzcoat, Kakalcat [180]—these are the names of the seven men of evil repute, known for their lives of destruction. And Ulil was the ruler of Itzmal.

Thirteen folds of katuns passed after they had abandoned the city to Hunac Ceel, because of the flayings they had heard about.

Six Ahau, 4 Ahau: two score of years. Two Ahau, in the beautiful citadel of Ichpaa, in Mayapan, because of the men of the Itza, the rulers of the country, on account of the sinful words of Hunac Ceel.

Two Ahau, 13 Ahau, 11 Ahau, 9 Ahau, 7 Ahau,

page thirty-five

5 Ahau, 3 Ahau, 1 Ahau, 12 Ahau, 10 Ahau, 8 Ahau. They succeeded in demolishing the stone buildings of Ichpaa, the walled city of Mayapan, by means of a break in the surrounding walls as the result of the joint government of the state of Mayapan.

Six Ahau, 2 Ahau, 13 Ahau. It was then that the first foreigners made hideous the landscape of the land of Yucatan, four-score and thirteen years ago.

Eleven Ahau, 9 Ahau, 7 Ahau, 5 Ahau, 3 Ahau, 1 Ahau, 12 Ahau, 10 Ahau, 8 Ahau, 6 Ahau, 4 Ahau, 2 Ahau, 13 Ahau, 11 Ahau. In 8 Ahau, the pueblo of Mayapan was abandoned on account of the

---

[180] For information regarding the seven cruel Mexicans see Roys 1933: 178.

mountains of foreigners. Ten score and four score years had passed.

Six Ahau, 4 Ahau: the pestilence arrived on the thresholds of Ichpaa. Four Ahau, the smallpox[181] came.

Thirteen Ahau: at that time they killed Ah Pulha when there were still six years to run before the count of Katun 13 Ahau would be completed.

In former times, it may be, there was a count of years governing from the east. Four Kan, with all his magic rituals, sat at the head of the mat of Kan.

On 15 and 3 Sip, on the day 9 Imix, Ah Pulha died. It was then the year 1536, its government.

In 11 Ahau the foreigners came, the men of God.[182] From the east they came. When they arrived they took possession of the country. In 9 Ahau the Christians began for the second time to convert us, and this continued throughout the katun. Then Toral, the first bishop, arrived, and the year when he came to govern was 1544.

During Katun 7 Ahau Bishop Landa died.

Five Ahau was the year in which the Fathers came from Spain to Mani, and the year in which they came was 1550.

By the time these years had passed—1552 to 1559—they were everywhere.

Then came the Hospital.[183]

1560 this was the year Dr. Quixada arrived, the first man of integrity to come to this country.

1562 the year in which the hangings took place.

1563 the year of the arrival of the Marshal.

1569 the year of the smallpox.

1610 the year in which people were hanged on trees in the forest.

1611 the year in which we wrote letters about the hangings, asking for justice. It is right that the King should ponder these things.

■■■■■■■■■

Cauac fell on the first of Pop and the earth was renewed once more.

---

[181] *noh kakil,* "the great fire."

[182] *kul uincob.*

[183] Written *Kispital.*

the days of the years of the jurisdiction of 4 Ahau,
beginning with 3 Cauac, in Katun 4 Ahau

1752	3 Cauac	1753	4 Kan	1754	5 Muluc
1755	6 Ix	1756	7 Cauac	1757	8 Kan
1758	9 Muluc	1759	10 Ix	1760	11 Ahau [184]
1761	12 Kan	1762	13 Muluc	1763	1 Ix
1764	2 Cauac	1765	3 Kan	1766	4 Muluc
1767	7 Ix [185]	1768	6 Cauac	1769	7 Kan
1770	8 Muluc	1771	9 Ix		

These years comprise the burden of Katun 4 Ahau. . . . There still remain four years without names at the very end of the katun.

page thirty-six

After that, there will be established 2 Ahau, the "united for a cause" katun.

1772	10 Cauac	1773	11 Kan
1774	12 Muluc	1775	13 Ix

Now 2 Ahau, when it follows immediately upon 1 Cauac, awakens twice the day of 1 Pop. These sayings are there in the bundle and their functions are declared in the pouch of the year at Saciapan. The sealed katun of 2 Ahau is opened in the square of Saclactun.

In former days when Mayapan negotiated the katun, there descended soothing things from heaven. There descended gifts. Now there will descend the sorrow of pestilence and great heaps of rocks and skulls. Yes, the government, yes, the auguries of Katun 2 Ahau with his burden of eleven penances bound upon his back.

The coils of Hun Yapotik [186] restrict the bread of life; they com-

---

[184] It should read "11 Cauac."
[185] It should read "5 Ix."
[186] The name of this serpent-deity does not appear in the indices of Tozzer 1941 or Roys 1933.

press the bread of life one-half. The burden for the year is "Good conditions for life." But there will be tears. And the rule of the lords for one-half the time will be a condition of great wretchedness. But in the wonder-working of Zam and Pop good will accrue to the community from the lords of the land, when there comes an appraisal of conditions in the land.

In recompensing the white men, the beardless men, throughout their days the people will become united, likewise. So speaks the priest Chilam. The day will come when our elder brothers will themselves smooth away obstacles, likewise.

You shall again retain your food in your stomachs. You shall wear your accustomed clothing. The worms. . . . Shall we root up the small palms to make hats for them? You shall talk to me and I will talk to you. Perchance the Lord of the Katun. . . . All this wrangling over the buying and selling of merchandise!

And in the season of the opening of flowers, when we yearn for the flowers and lie down on the flowers, no one of us is allowed to rest, while we weep for 11 Ahau. Vale. The purpose of our uniting for a cause will unfold during Katun 11 Ahau. Vale.

The count of Katun 2 Ahau, when it follows immediately after 1 Cauac, is:

1776	1 Cauac	1777	2 Kan	1778	3 Muluc
1779	4 Ix	1780	5 Cauac	1781	6 Kan
1782	7 Muluc	1783	8 Ix	1784	9 Cauac
1785	10 Kan	1786	11 Muluc	1787	12 Ix
1788	13 Cauac	1789	1 Kan	1790	2 Muluc
1791	3 Ix	1792	4 Cauac	1793	5 Kan
1794	6 Muluc	1795	7 Ix		

These complete the term of office of [Katun] 2 Ahau, except that at the end of the katun there come four years without name, before the arrival of 13 Ahau:

1796	8 Cauac	1797	9 Kan
1798	10 Muluc	1799	11 Ix

When Katun 13 Ahau is current, following upon 12 Cauac, the katun of 13 Ahau will be established at Kinchilcoba, not at Mayapan.

These are the words which must be spoken:

"The prophecies are a solemn trust from ancient times. They are the first news of events, and a valuable warning. There are omens of a famine at Chacmitan, a restriction on bread, a stringency on the bread of life. For five years there will be severe necessity, but there will be the bread of diligence. There will be tears also." Ten Ahau, 8 Ahau. . . .

page thirty-seven

1758	1 Kan—from the east	1779	9 Muluc
1759	2 Muluc	1780	10 Ix
1760	3 Ix	1781	11 Cauac
1761	4 Cauac	1782	12 Kan
1762	5 Kan	1783	13 Muluc
1763	6 Muluc	1784	1 Ix—from the west
1764	7 Ix	1785	2 Cauac
1765	8 Cauac	1786	3 Kan
1766	9 Kan	1787	4 Muluc
1767	10 Muluc	1788	5 Ix
1768	11 Ix	1789	6 Cauac
1769	12 Cauac	1790	7 Kan
1770	13 Kan	1791	8 Muluc
1771	1 Muluc—from the north	1792	9 Ix
1772	2 Ix	1793	10 Cauac
1773	3 Cauac	1794	11 Kan
1774	4 Kan	1795	12 Muluc
1775	5 Muluc	1796	13 Ix
1776	6 Ix	1797	1 Cauac—from the south
1777	7 Cauac	1798	2 Kan
1778	8 Kan	1799	3 Muluc

1800	4 Ix	1805	9 Cauac
1801 [187]	5 Cauac	1806	10 Kan
1802	6 Kan	1807	11 Muluc
1803	7 Muluc	1808	12 Ix
1804	8 Ix	1809	13 Cauac

This is the Calendar, the summation of the years or Calendar Round.[188] This array of years is continuous to its expected completion, and when the count begins with 1 Kan it ends with 13 Cauac. Then it repeats over and over forever, protected by the enchantments of the Zam above, ever since the first katun. There are four groups of years. This is the truth.

page thirty-eight

the names of the days which
continually wander through the Uinal

1 Kan	16 July	Pop [189]
2 Chicchan	5 August	Uo
3 Cimi	25 August	Zotz
4 Manik	11 September	Zip
5 Lamat	2 October	Tzec
6 Muluc	22 October	Xul
7 Oc	13 November	Yaxkin [190]

---

[187] These years are written 18001, 18002 etc. in the text.

[188] It seems likely that *bubukil* is actually the Maya word corresponding to our "Calendar Round," the period of 18,980 days or 52 vague years during which every possible combination of tzolkin and month-days may be found. Although *bubukil* itself is not in the vocabularies of Pio Perez or the Motul, *bukxoc* appears with the meaning "to sum up." *Xoc,* "to count," may be understood in the present connection. Bubuk is the reduplicated form.

[189] Opposite *Pop* is written "One score. The first burden," referring to Column 1 which contains the first 20 days of a year beginning with 1 Kan on the first of Pop. I have adopted the conventional spelling for Zip, Zac, Zotz, Cumhu and Eznab.

[190] Written *Zeyaxkin,* "Little Yaxkin."

8 Chuen	3 December	Mol
9 Eb	23 December	Chen
10 Ben	12 January	Yax
11 Ix	1 February	Zac
12 Men	21 February	Mac
13 Cib	13 March	Ceh
1 Caban	2 April	Kankin
2 Eznab	22 April	Muan
3 Cauac	12 May	Kayab [191]
4 Ahau	1 June	Pax
5 Imix	21 June	Cumhu
6 Ik	00 days of misfortune 5	
7 Akbal		

One score of days there is in the Moon's treasure, the *uinal*. These are their names. Now recall the Burners. There are four of them in the uinal.

First, there is 4 Chicchan. On 10 Chicchan he carries the fire, and on 11 Chicchan he extinguishes the fire.[192] He is the uinal-bearer from the east.

Then there is 4 Oc. On 10 Oc he carries the fire, and on 11 Oc he quenches the fire. He is the uinal-bearer from the north.

Then there is 4 Men. On 10 Men he carries the fire and on 11 Men he extinguishes the fire. He is the uinal-bearer from the west.

Finally, there is 4 Ahau. On 10 Ahau he carries the fire, and on 11 Ahau he quenches the fire. He is the uinal-bearer from the south.

Now these Burners, when they set out on the uinal-road in the very beginning, started the count with [1] Kan so as to arrive at 2 Chicchan in the second place of the count. Searching for that which is forgotten, we come to the above 4 Chicchan.

Thus they seek to bring to light the origin of the four Burners in the uinals, [to determine] whether it begins in Pop or in Uo. In

---

[191] *Kayab* and *Pax* should be interchanged.
[192] From 10 Chicchan to 11 Chicchan is an interval of 40 days; and similarly for 10 Oc to 11 Oc and so on.

either case, whatever you will have to eat each year will depend on your continuing the count unbroken.

page thirty-nine

Prudence is very much needed if there is to be protection from the things which inspire fear, in order that we should obtain merit by making a good appearance, so that there will be good corn in the ear, and abundance of food in the cornfields everywhere until the days of new growth or we reach the time of sowing.

You say there is far too much whipping because you gather grain and other foods as you wish, according to the moon, whether the moon culminates [193] in the signs of Taurus, Cancer, Virgo, Libra or Capricorn. All these signs rise occasionally for the sowing, and they are propitious for forming whatever it is you plant in the milpas.

The cornfields shall become as they once were when we kept the ancient day-by-day count. I will secretly uproot [our enemies]. There shall again be a yield in our cornfields!

The harvest of the corn-crop shall be apportioned as follows [194] [among the various years]:

Sunday	Sun	great abundance
Monday	Moon	one-half a crop
Tuesday	Mars	hunger
Wednesday	Mercury	one-half
Friday	Venus	great abundance
Saturday	Saturn	hunger
Sunday	Sun	great abundance
Monday	Moon	one-half
Wednesday	Mercury	one-half
Thursday	Jupiter	great abundance

---

[193] *tian,* "hits the mark."

[194] The table predicts the yield for 28 years beginning with the various days of the week, found by combining the seven days with the four years of the Julian leap-year cycle.

Friday	Venus	great abundance
Saturday	Saturn	hunger
Monday	Moon	one-half
Tuesday	Mars	hunger
Wednesday	Mercury	one-half
Thursday	Jupiter	great abundance
Saturday	Saturn	hunger
Sunday	Sun	great abundance
Monday	Moon	one-half
Tuesday	Mars	hunger
Thursday	Jupiter	great abundance
Friday	Venus	great abundance
Saturday	Saturn	hunger
Sunday	Sun	great abundance
Tuesday	Mars	hunger
Wednesday	Mercury	one-half
Thursday	Jupiter	great abundance
Friday	Venus	great abundance

One score and eight years are given in the above table. So be it that the count may express what is under the heavens. The count unrolls again and again the course of the unfriendly years. There is just the one count. And once it is exhausted it repeats these years of misfortune from the bottom to the top of the table continuously. When one arrives at the end, one year is missing. Concede it and start again with Sunday in its measure.

■■■■■■■■

1628: This was a most remarkable year in the past. One night there was a terrific hurricane which mowed down all the trees and houses. In fact, everything which stood in its path fell before the wind.

1629: This year, likewise, was one of unusual destruction to the corn in the ear, because with such terrific force the ripened grain was thrown to the ground along its path. Because there was insufficient remedy [195]—that which wards off death, and cleanses, the ancient magic—there was dire distress all the way to Cupul.

Now on April 19, 1629, there came a shaking and destruction, and everything was thrown together in heaps, the bundles of food falling violently to the ground in ruin. On the very last day of Yaxkin the great manifestation of the earthquake finally relaxed its shaking.

page forty

Should January [first] fall on a Thursday, there will not be many lol-flowers on the trees for the honey-bees. There will be fierce suns. There will come floods, filling all the low places with their waters, bringing danger of disease. There will be separation among all the people. The corn will form.

Should January [first] fall on a Friday, there will be both good and evil. It will produce fierce suns and there will be much sickness. There will be misery, and afflictions will come from cruel and inhuman men during the katun, because there will be oppression. The corn will form and there will be little need.

Should January [first] fall on Saturday there will be drought, and they will pound the corn slowly. Nobody will pick the fruit because, although it looks sound, it is rotten within. The corn will form a little, a quarter. There will be very high temperatures. There will be a shearing by death. People will become very lean in these lands. Everyone will be dismayed and bitter. Things of high quality will become putrid. There will be fire over men, so that trees will scatter their fruits. All sowing, all sowing will cease. Death will range to and fro in the land.

Should January [first] fall on a Tuesday, there will be widespread animosity. There will be twisting and wandering throughout the year. Back-breaking labor will fall to their lot. There will be drought. They will chew the corn slowly and gnaw the kernels.

---

[195] I have read *zac,* "medicine, magic," in place of *sak,* "the itch."

But, meanwhile, the fatness of the nobility will not mock them and add to their misery, because a pestilence will affect even the highest of the wicked aristocracy. Without a remedy, there will be little corn.

Should January [first] fall on Wednesday, there will be a year of good fortune. The spring sun will be kind and occupations and service will be constructive. There will be fruits of all kinds. There will be benevolence. Good learning is kindred to justice, because without justice there would be widespread migrations throughout the land, and travelers find many roads that lead to death. Death comes to all, digging deeply, to children as well as to those in the prime of life. There will be few hungry days and men will die [only] because guilt falls upon them. One-half the corn will form.

Should January [first] fall on Sunday, there will be drought and a division in the kingdom of God. One-half the days will be without strength; one-half will be watched over from above, as well as on earth. They will weep over their memories. Drums will beat in all the land. There will be misfortune and destruction. There will be . . . The first sowing will turn out badly. There will be war, because men without compassion will cause distress. But there will be retribution when the great prophecy is fulfilled. There will be despair over that which is destroyed in the corn-baskets, everywhere.

Should January [first] fall on Monday, there will be the gift of misery. And there shall befall a very great flood of water. It will be the very spirit of chance, if the country is saved. There will be much sickness. Broad will be our burdens. Then the five gods of Ah Chalamat will restore order by carrying the waters into the sea. The corn will form but not too well; only one-half.

page forty-two

bottom of page

On the 6th of June in the year 1629, there was a swarm of locusts above the houses. The people then stopped up all the openings in the houses as in ancient times, for several days, to preserve their own lives. The cornfields were destroyed and all the food everywhere among the pueblos. The locusts came to Chikin and to Cupul. They oppressed Mani. The locusts scooped up the food by the mouthful, ravenously.

Then the people formed a circle around the daughter of Don Franco Cocom and seized her, placing a rope around her neck, on account of the destruction of the crops and the dire need of Hunab Ku for food.

O wretched people! Why are you so agitated by hunger, all of you, just because of your afflictions by reason of the locusts!

At Chanucan, some distance from here, there came to be food, and all the people did not die, but lived to bless their benefactress for the food, because she took upon herself the guilt of the locusts which were destroying all that the people had sowed.

page forty-three

bottom of page

During the year 1622, likewise, there was famine in Chacmitan; in fact, all over the Peten. All suffered, and they hastened to make the bad news known.

And when they purchased corn, they twisted the fibers of the husks into ropes and went into the highlands in order to trap the mountain-lion, so that there would be no more hunger among the people as in former times, and they caught the wild waterfowl. Finally, they guarded the people from falling as they gathered food from trees. Many sank down. Some died. Even the lords, in their hunger, went into the forest.

page forty-four

bottom of page

Seven Roads. One penance. Three vigils against offenses. On the 7th of May in the year 1627, locusts destroyed the corn in the ear and ate the beans and the cooked corn and the large beans. Everywhere they went, the locusts destroyed even the medicinal plants, even the stored food.

Finally, the plague of locusts in our land was brought to an end by magic, and deliverance from the wicked locusts came quickly when there was a sudden downpour of rain. This, in truth, helped to bring about the destruction of the locusts.

page forty-one

January   31 days

1	10 Oc	lucky	The fire is kindled.
2	11 Chuen	lucky	
3	12 Eb	lucky	
4	13 Ben	lucky	
5	1 Ix	unlucky	In which death comes to men.
6	2 Men	unlucky	
7	3 Cib	lucky	
8	4 Caban	lucky	
9	5 Eznab	lucky	
10	6 Cauac	lucky	
11	7 Ahau	lucky	
12	8 Imix	unlucky	In which *Yax* enters.
13	9 Ik	unlucky	The feather of flint; [196] there will be sickness.

[196] The sacrificial knife used for opening one's veins.

14	10 Akbal	unlucky	
15	11 Kan	lucky	The end of the rainy season.
16	12 Chicchan	unlucky	
17	13 Cimi	lucky	The Great Spirit.[197]
18	1 Manik	lucky	The guilt of our sons unites us.
19	2 Lamat	unlucky	
20	3 Muluc	unlucky	
21	4 Oc		The Burner announces his name.[198]
22	5 Chuen	unlucky	
23	6 Eb	lucky	Searching the forest for deer.
24	7 Ben	unlucky	
25	8 Ix	unlucky	
26	9 Men	unlucky	
27	10 Cib	unlucky	
28	11 Caban	lucky	
29	12 Eznab		
30	13 Cauac	lucky	
31	1 Ahau	unlucky	Rain appears in Chacmitan.

page forty-two

February   28 days

1	2 Imix	unlucky	In which *Zac* enters.
2	3 Ik	unlucky	
3	4 Akbal	unlucky	
4	5 Kan	unlucky	
5	6 Chicchan	unlucky	
6	7 Cimi	lucky	In which there is much rain.
7	8 Manik	lucky	
8	9 Lamat	unlucky	
9	10 Muluc	unlucky	

[197] Or "great vigor."
[198] *Ah toc* signifies either "the Burner," or "the Deliverer."

10	11	Oc	lucky	The Burner quenches the fire.
11	12	Chuen		The culpability of our priests. Vigils.
12	13	Eb	unlucky	
13	1	Ben	unlucky	Sickness; heat.
14	2	Ix	unlucky	
15	3	Men		The Burner carries the fire.
16	4	Cib	unlucky	Vigils.
17	5	Caban		Blame falls on the seers.
18	6	Eznab	unlucky	
19	7	Cauac	unlucky	
20	8	Ahau	unlucky	Then comes our enemy, Satan.
21	9	Imix	unlucky	*Ceh* enters.
22	10	Ik	unlucky	
23	11	Akbal		The sin of our religion.
24	12	Kan		The sin of eating men. St. Mark.
25	13	Chicchan	unlucky	
26	1	Cimi	unlucky	
27	2	Manik	unlucky	
28	3	Lamat	unlucky	

page forty-three

March   31 days

1	4	Muluc	lucky	The day of great purification.
2	5	Oc	unlucky	
3	6	Chuen	unlucky	They unite in disorder.
4	7	Eb	unlucky	
5	8	Ben	unlucky	
6	9	Ix	unlucky	
7	10	Men		The Burner kindles the fire of great purification.
8	11	Cib	unlucky	
9	12	Caban	unlucky	The great sunset is here.

10	13 Eznab		A handful of food [left]; the first rain comes.
11	1 Cauac	unlucky	
12	2 Ahau	unlucky	
13	3 Imix	unlucky	Here *Mac* enters.
14	4 Ik	unlucky	
15	5 Akbal	unlucky	
16	6 Kan	lucky	On which the rain begins.
17	7 Chicchan	lucky	
18	8 Cimi	lucky	
19	9 Manik	unlucky	
20	10 Lamat	unlucky	
21	11 Muluc	lucky	
22	12 Oc	unlucky	
23	13 Chuen	unlucky	
24	1 Eb	unlucky	
25	2 Ben	unlucky	
26	3 Ix	unlucky	
27	4 Men	lucky	The Burner announces his name.
28	5 Cib	lucky	
29	6 Caban	lucky	
30	7 Eznab	lucky	A handful of food on this day.
31	8 Cauac	lucky	

page forty-four

April   30 days

1	9 Ahau	lucky	God the Creator, Himself.
2	10 Imix	unlucky	*Kankin* enters.
3	11 Ik		New growth appears in profusion from days of rain.
4	12 Akbal	lucky	
5	13 Kan		The kernels of corn which God asks for.

6	1 Chicchan	lucky	
7	2 Cimi	lucky	
8	3 Manik	lucky	
9	4 Lamat	lucky	
10	5 Muluc	unlucky	
11	6 Oc	unlucky	
12	7 Chuen	unlucky	
13	8 Eb	lucky	
14	9 Ben	lucky	
15	10 Ix	lucky	
16	11 Men	lucky	The Burner quenches the fire.
17	12 Cib	lucky	
18	13 Caban	lucky	
19	1 Eznab	unlucky	
20	2 Cauac	unlucky	
21	3 Ahau		The Burner carries the fire.
22	4 Imix	unlucky	*Muan* enters. A handful of food.
23	5 Ik	unlucky	
24	6 Akbal	unlucky	
25	7 Kan	unlucky	The first day of Pop.
26	8 Chicchan	unlucky	
27	9 Cimi	lucky	
28	10 Manik	unlucky	
29	11 Lamat	unlucky	
30	12 Muluc		

page forty-five

May   31 days

1	13 Oc	lucky	A day of rain.
2	1 Chuen	unlucky	
3	2 Eb	unlucky	The Holy Cross. Only a handful of food.
4	3 Ben	unlucky	Searching through the forest.

5	4 Ix		Recalling the sins of our rulers.
6	5 Men	unlucky	
7	6 Cib	unlucky	Perchance going into the forest [for food].
8	7 Caban	unlucky	Luring the deer with good things.
9	8 Eznab	unlucky	When men sing.
10	9 Cauac	lucky	For the lords of the land.
11	10 Ahau		The Burner fans the flames.
12	11 Imix	unlucky	For the caciquedom. *Pax* enters.
13	12 Ik	unlucky	A spirit in the hearts of men.
14	13 Akbal	unlucky	In which there is a vigil.
15	1 Kan	unlucky	A calm upon the spirit. The moon is completed.
16	2 Chicchan	unlucky	
17	3 Cimi	unlucky	
18	4 Manik	lucky	
19	5 Lamat	lucky	
20	6 Muluc	lucky	The count of strong suns.
21	7 Oc	unlucky	
22	8 Chuen	unlucky	
23	9 Eb	unlucky	
24	10 Ben		
25	11 Ix	unlucky	
26	12 Men	unlucky	
27	13 Cib	lucky	
28	1 Caban	lucky	
29	2 Eznab	lucky	For people to visit on this day.
30	3 Cauac	lucky	
31	4 Ahau	unlucky	The Burner announces his name.

page forty-six

June   30 days

1	5 Imix	unlucky	On which *Kayab* enters.
2	6 Ik	unlucky	
3	7 Akbal	unlucky	
4	8 Kan	unlucky	
5	9 Chicchan	lucky	
6	10 Cimi	lucky	
7	11 Manik	unlucky	
8	12 Lamat	unlucky	
9	13 Muluc	lucky	
10	1 Oc	lucky	The day of a very great event.
11	2 Chuen	unlucky	
12	3 Eb	unlucky	
13	4 Ben	unlucky	
14	5 Ix	unlucky	
15	6 Men	unlucky	
16	7 Cib	unlucky	
17	8 Caban	unlucky	
18	9 Eznab	lucky	
19	10 Cauac	lucky	
20	11 Ahau		The Burner covers the fire.
21	12 Imix	lucky	In which *Cumhu* enters.
22	13 Ik	unlucky	
23	1 Akbal	unlucky	
24	2 Kan	unlucky	St. John.
25	3 Chicchan		The Burner carries the fire.
26	4 Cimi	lucky	The Holy Spirit.
27	5 Manik	lucky	
28	6 Lamat	unlucky	
29	7 Muluc	unlucky	
30	8 Oc	lucky	

page forty-seven

July   31 days

1	9 Chuen	unlucky	
2	10 Eb	unlucky	
3	11 Ben	unlucky	
4	12 Ix		The festival of the Jaguar Year.
5	13 Men	lucky	Rewards are multiplied. Vigil.
6	1 Cib	unlucky	
7	2 Caban	unlucky	
8	3 Eznab	lucky	Now is the time to call for a measure of the stores of food.
9	4 Cauac	unlucky	
10	5 Ahau	unlucky	
11	6 Imix	lucky	
12	7 Ik	unlucky	
13	8 Akbal	unlucky	
14	9 Kan	lucky	For giving presents.
15	10 Chicchan	lucky	The Burner fans the flames.
16	11 Cimi	lucky	Now enters *Pop*.
17	12 Manik	lucky	For the crops.
18	13 Lamat	unlucky	
19	1 Muluc	lucky	Calm skies for the crops.
20	2 Oc	lucky	
21	3 Chuen	lucky	
22	4 Eb	lucky	For one's desires.
23	5 Ben		The spirit recalls the sharp pain of the flint knife.
24	6 Ix	unlucky	
25	7 Men	lucky	
26	8 Cib	lucky	
27	9 Caban	lucky	
28	10 Eznab	lucky	
29	11 Cauac	unlucky	

30	12 Ahau	lucky	On which wise men are born.
31	13 Imix	lucky	

page forty-eight

August   *31 days*

1	1 Ik	lucky	For the nobility.
2	2 Akbal	unlucky	
3	3 Kan	unlucky	
4	4 Chicchan	unlucky	The Burner announces his name.
5	5 Cimi	unlucky	In which *Uo* enters.
6	6 Manik	unlucky	The Transfiguration.
7	7 Lamat	unlucky	
8	8 Muluc		For keeping vigils.
9	9 Oc	unlucky	
10	10 Chuen		Sudden death while in full vigor. St. Lawrence. There will be a tempest.
11	11 Eb	unlucky	
12	12 Ben	unlucky	
13	13 Ix	unlucky	
14	1 Men		All kinds of sudden death.
15	2 Cib	unlucky	The Assumption.
16	3 Caban	unlucky	
17	4 Eznab	unlucky	
18	5 Cauac	unlucky	A storm.
19	6 Ahau		Cutting appears at Chacmitan.
20	7 Imix	unlucky	
21	8 Ik	unlucky	
22	9 Akbal	unlucky	
23	10 Kan	unlucky	
24	11 Chicchan		The Burner covers the fire. St. Bartholomew.
25	12 Cimi	unlucky	In which *Zip* enters.

26	13 Manik	unlucky	
27	1 Lamat		The fire causes the Jaguar pain.
28	2 Muluc	unlucky	
29	3 Oc		The Burner sets the fire free.[199]
30	4 Chuen	unlucky	
31	5 Eb	unlucky	

page forty-nine

September   *30 days*

1	6 Ben	unlucky	
2	7 Ix	unlucky	
3	8 Men	unlucky	
4	9 Cib	lucky	
5	10 Caban		The strength of our rulers.
6	11 Eznab	lucky	
7	12 Cauac	lucky	
8	13 Ahau	lucky	The Nativity. There will be wind.
9	1 Imix	lucky	
10	2 Ik	lucky	
11	3 Akbal	lucky	Now there is much rain.
12	4 Kan	lucky	Now there is much rain.
13	5 Chicchan	lucky	
14	6 Cimi	lucky	In the power of the God of life.
15	7 Manik	lucky	
16	8 Lamat		The One Lord [200] eats corn by the mouthful.
17	9 Muluc	unlucky	
18	10 Oc		The Burner kindles the fire.
19	11 Chuen	lucky	

[199] The text has *u cha;* but if the "h" is barred, the translation should read: "The Burner carries the fire."
[200] *Hun Ahau,* not *Hunab Ku.*

20	12	Eb	lucky	
21	13	Ben	lucky	
22	1	Ix	unlucky	On which rulers are born.
23	2	Men	unlucky	
24	3	Cib	lucky	For the honey harvest.
25	4	Caban	lucky	
26	5	Eznab	lucky	
27	6	Cauac	lucky	The first day of Pop.
28	7	Ahau	lucky	
29	8	Imix	unlucky	St. Michael.
30	9	Ik		The feathered flint knife. There is sickness.

page fifty

October   31 days

1	10	Akbal	unlucky	
2	11	Kan	lucky	Floods of water.
3	12	Chicchan	unlucky	
4	13	Cimi		Great vigor. *Tzec* enters.
5	1	Manik		The guilt of our children falls upon us. There is sickness.
6	2	Lamat	unlucky	
7	3	Muluc	unlucky	
8	4	Oc	unlucky	The Burner announces his name.
9	5	Chuen	unlucky	
10	6	Eb	lucky	For going hunting in the forest.
11	7	Ben	unlucky	
12	8	Ix	unlucky	
13	9	Men	unlucky	
14	10	Cib	lucky	
15	11	Caban	lucky	
16	12	Eznab		There will be very terrible death.
17	13	Cauac	lucky	

18	1 Ahau	unlucky	Cutting will appear at Chacmitan.
19	2 Imix	unlucky	
20	3 Ik	unlucky	
21	4 Akbal	lucky	
22	5 Kan	unlucky	
23	6 Chicchan	unlucky	
24	7 Cimi	lucky	Great vigor. *Xul* enters.
25	8 Manik		
26	9 Lamat	unlucky	
27	10 Muluc	unlucky	
28	11 Oc		
29	12 Chuen		
30	13 Eb	unlucky	
31	1 Ben	unlucky	

page fifty-one

November   30 days

1	2 Ix	unlucky	All Saints day.
2	3 Men		The Burner carries the fire. Synod.
3	4 Cib		Guilt falls upon the seers. Vigils.
4	5 Caban	unlucky	
5	6 Eznab	unlucky	
6	7 Cauac	unlucky	
7	8 Ahau	unlucky	
8	9 Imix	unlucky	
9	10 Ik	unlucky	
10	11 Akbal		Guilt falls upon the descendants.
11	12 Kan		For the death of rulers.
12	13 Chicchan	unlucky	St. James
13	1 Cimi	unlucky	*Yaxkin* enters.
14	2 Manik	unlucky	
15	3 Lamat		
16	4 Muluc	lucky	There will be a great stirring.

17	5 Oc	unlucky	
18	6 Chuen		Memories of ancient times are confused.
19	7 Eb	unlucky	
20	8 Ben	unlucky	
21	9 Ix	unlucky	
22	10 Men		The Burner kindles the fire.
23	11 Cib	unlucky	
24	12 Caban	unlucky	
25	13 Eznab		Great handfuls of food arrive from the harvest.
26	1 Cauac	unlucky	There will be cold weather.
27	2 Ahau	unlucky	There will be cold weather.
28	3 Imix	unlucky	
29	4 Ik	unlucky	
30	5 Akbal	unlucky	St. Andrew.

page fifty-two

December   *31 days*

1	6 Kan	lucky	Rain begins.
2	7 Chicchan	lucky	
3	8 Cimi		*Mol* enters.
4	9 Manik	unlucky	
5	10 Lamat	unlucky	
6	11 Muluc	lucky	
7	12 Oc	unlucky	
8	13 Chuen	unlucky	Conception.
9	1 Eb	unlucky	
10	2 Ben	unlucky	
11	3 Ix	unlucky	
12	4 Men	lucky	The Burner calls his name.
13	5 Cib	lucky	
14	6 Caban	lucky	

15	7 Eznab	lucky	Great handfuls of bread.
16	8 Cauac	lucky	
17	9 Ahau		God the Creator Himself.
18	10 Imix	unlucky	
19	11 Ik		The Great Festival.
20	12 Akbal	lucky	
21	13 Kan		The corn of the Kingdom of God.
22	1 Chicchan	lucky	
23	2 Cimi	lucky	*Chen* enters.
24	3 Manik	lucky	
25	4 Lamat	lucky	The Nativity of Jesus.
26	5 Muluc	unlucky	
27	6 Oc	unlucky	
28	7 Chuen	unlucky	
29	8 Eb	unlucky	
30	9 Ben	lucky	
31	10 Ix		

[*End of Translation*]

PART II
Commentary

CHAPTER
ONE

Character and Contents

THE MAYA BELIEVED THAT HISTORY TENDS TO REPEAT ITSELF
in regular cycles. They drew their prophecies of future events from
the abundant records of the past; and when they chronicled historical
data on monuments of stone or in books of bark paper, it was with
full recognition of their importance in determining the "shape of
things to come."

The interval upon the completion of which History might be expected to retrace the same general course consisted of thirteen katuns
or approximately 256 years, the cycle in which the *tzolkin* days,
though not the Calendar Round dates, fall in the same position in
the 7200-day katun. From the statistics of centuries each katun—
named curiously enough for the day on which it ended—had ac-
quired an individuality and character all its own. Eight Ahau, for
example, was the "katun of settling down in a new place," and the
great mass-migrations of the Maya appear to have taken place during these 20-year periods. Ten Ahau was termed "the holy katun."
Four Ahau was the "katun for remembering knowledge and writing
it down in the Books of Chilam Balam." Two Ahau was the "united
for a cause" katun.

Thus during the progress of each katun, the principal events
such as invasions, wars, hurricanes, droughts, floods, earthquakes,
epidemics and so on, were recorded year by year in the *Book of the
Katun.* When the final day of the period arrived and the pebbles of
the days were tallied with solemn ceremonies, the Book of the Katun was read and the record closed. It was then folded fanwise in

97

the manner of Maya books, tied securely within board covers and placed in the temple archives. It might not be opened again until, after the expiration of 256 years, another katun of the same name should arrive once more. Since the close of one katun corresponded with the opening of another, the lord of the new katun was then welcomed with the opening of the books of records which had been made some multiple of 256 years earlier. The prophecies obtained from these sources appear to have been read year by year or tun by tun; but the Books of the Katun were searched whenever special direction was needed in times of crisis.

This cyclic repetition of events was not to go on endlessly, however, for we are told in the Book of Chilam Balam of Tizimin that the time would come when the katun prophecies would cease to be effective:

Page 27: "He by whom Mayapan was anciently depopulated set limits to the katun-prophecies in a manner of speaking. There will come a stopping-place for the prophecies when the government has been restored once more, according to the words of Ah Kin Chilam the Prophet, when he writes about the aspect of the katun during 8 Ahau."

As each *year* also possessed a character of its own, there was considerable variation within a given 20-year period. This pattern is brought out in clear detail in the first twelve pages of the Tizimin manuscript, where the events of certain Katuns 5 Ahau in the past are recorded and are related year by year to a current Katun 5 Ahau which began in 1594, as we are told on page 1. From this important fact of the incidence of a Katun 5 Ahau in 1594, the approximate positions of all other katuns can be established in the Christian calendar.

The following quotations illustrate how the character of Katun 5 Ahau changes from year to year, or from tun to tun:

Page 8 (of the Tizimin manuscript): "How can we celebrate the rites of Lord 5 Ahau in the twelfth tun, when he comes in benign holiness in the katun of power and of the strength of the wooden idols, and the magic of the cup, and the magic of the plate, and the magic of the count of days, in Katun 5 Ahau in the twelfth tun?"

On page 9 we read of the *"fruit-bearing* katun of 5 Ahau" in the fifteenth tun, and the following passage from page 10 is illuminating:

"From the Milpa of the Dragon [the Milky Way, perhaps] Cantzicnal comes down to fulfill his promises to the people. When the day of 2 Cauac arrives over this great land, then comes the descent of the katun headforemost, the Katun of Ix Toloch, the *playful* katun to soften the hearts of anger. The priest declares the auguries to be of good fortune, from the remote places of the Spirit. In the sixteenth tun, 3 Kan shall come on his day on 1 Pop, in the *rain-bearing* katun and the lords of the land shall be present also. They shall bind up the faces of the lords at that time, and no one shall speak for the *jesting* katun at the festival of 3 Kan."

The correspondence between katuns of the same name, separated by 256 years or some multiple thereof, is illustrated by an interesting passage in which the author, writing at a time when the Spaniards were leveling a grueling tribute, bemoaned the despoliation of the land by Itza conquerors in a certain previous Katun 5 Ahau:

Page 4: "When our eyes were suddenly opened to the snatching of 'alms'; when the common people began to suffer from the taking of 'gifts' by the collectors; when the soldiers took property in the manner of warriors, it was as if a mountain had descended upon our shoulders. We lamented; there is no doubt about that. We entreated the gods to save Mayapan in some manner. We offered them turkey-feet, obtained both by capture and by purchase. We mourned the red cardinal birds and the red-jeweled ornaments; likewise the handfuls of precious stones which lie in the midst of our fields.

"This all happened, moreover, *in the very katun in which it was most likely to meet with success,* because it was also in a certain Katun 5 Ahau long, long ago, that the sky was new, having just been created. And it was so close to the earth that certain crafty fellows made a loud outcry from amid the branches of the Tree of Life, entreating Lord 5 Ahau that he make an end to the drunken begging, an end to covetousness on the part of the rulers." This lament was signally appropriate in the century following the Spanish Conquest.

Before penetrating further into the Maya mysteries, it would be well to establish as far as possible such fundamental facts as the names of the authors of the book and their tribal affiliation, as well as the time or times when this remarkable document was written or compiled.

The protagonists in the tragedy enacted in the pages of the Tizimin manuscript appear to have belonged to the tribe of *Xiu*. On page 14 there is an impassioned plea: "O Xiu! Do not cast your lots in houses of straw!" In another place reference is made to "our blood-relatives at Itzmal." Itzmal, or Izamal as it is sometimes written, was the province of Ah Kin Chel, who married the only daughter of Ah Xupan, a great and famous priest at the head of the house of Xiu.[201]

The tribe is also variously referred to as "the people of Ix Toloch" and "the people of Pop." Ix Toloch is a most interesting name and it is not found in the index of Tozzer's well annotated edition of Landa's *Relacion*. The prefix *ix* suggests that it is the name of a goddess, whereas the *tol* implies a possible Toltec origin. Roys[202] gives *ix tolil* as the name of a dance and in another passage states reasons for believing that the *Xiu* family were of Toltec derivation.[203]

The Tizimin manuscript speaks briefly of an early migration from *Suiva*, written *Zuyua* in the Chumayel Book of Chilam Balam. According to Roys:[204] "The name Zuyua is inseparably connected with the Toltec penetration of Yucatan. . . . The Xius believed that they had come from a place called West Zuyua, and Brinton has identified *Zuyua* with the Mexican *Zuiven*, 'the name of the uppermost heaven, the abode of the Creator, Hometecutli, the father of Quetzalcoatl, and the place of his first birth as a divinity.'"

---

[201] Tozzer 1941: 40
[202] R.L. Roys 1933: 153.
[203] R.L. Roys 1933: 193.
[204] Ibid. 192.

The derivation of the name Suiva appears to be from *sui* and *vah*, signifying "everlasting life," a name appropriate to the thirteenth and highest heaven.

The name Ix Toloch is found only in three places in the Book of Chilam Balam of Tizimin, in the phrases: *the people of Ix Toloch, the Katun of Ix Toloch,* and in the name of a dance which was performed in Cauac years in honor of the Bacab Cantzicnal. In the latter meaning the name has come down to modern times as the dance *Xtol,* "the most important of the modern Maya dances," according to Tozzer.[205] The great *cenote* of Chichen Itza which supplies the pueblo with water (not the Cenote of Sacrifice) was named *Xtoloc Cenote.*[206] All these survivals indicate that the name Ix Toloch was of historical significance and they do not contradict the suggestion that it may have belonged to an important Toltec goddess.

The second descriptive name of the tribe, "the people of Pop," indicates that the tribe considered itself the originator and custodian of the Maya Calendar, as Pop was the God of the Calendar. He is usually associated with Zam.

Only a few personages connected with the Book of Chilam Balam of Tizimin are mentioned by name, but these names are repeated in the following passages:

Page 11: "It is customary for the priests, the Chilam, Ah Kin Napuctun and Ah Kin Hun Uitzil Chac, to read from the teachings of the six eternal books at Uxmal. This is the revelation of the hieroglyphic writings of the prophecies. And Ah Kin Chelyaxnak is he who looks into them to see by what road guilt will fall upon us. This is the expectation according to the Jaguar priest, the Chilam Balam, coming from Hunab Ku the One God, and from the Thirteen gods."

Page 13: "Eight Muluc came on the first day of Pop and we lodged the square-cornered stone in its place, we who are called Ah Kauil Chel, Ah Napuctun, and Ah Xupan Nauat, priests and great and true men; and Hun Uitzil Chac, the Tutul Xiu of Uxmal."

Page 13: "This is my memory of the ancient things as they de-

---

[205] Tozzer 1941: 94, footnote 409.
[206] Ibid. 109.

scended from Hunab Ku the One God, and from the Thirteen gods, and from the One Thousand gods, as found in the words of the priests and prophets of Chilam Balam, recorded by Ah Xupan and Ah Napuctun, priests, and Ah Nahau Pech and Ah Kauil Chel, as we interpret the prophecies."

Page 16: "The priests Ah Xupan, Ah Kin Chel and Napuctun will make themselves known in three scrolls. Gradually the Priests of the Jaguar, the Chilam Balam, will compose seven holy books for our altars, in which we will explain the manner of offering invocations, so that finally the katun will arrive as in ancient times, with no diminution in the power of the prophecies."

Page 18: "Xupan Nauat, as he is called, is he who will explain the order of the world. Ah Kin Chel, Nahau Pech, Napuctun, the war-captain Balam, and the prophet Chilam Balam—these are the priests who know the future, and the order of the world and of the katuns. [Written] in the first tun of [Katun] 13 Ahau at Mayapan." If a Katun 5 Ahau commenced in 1594, this entry must have been made in one of the following years: 1515, 1259 or 1003 . . . approximately.

On the other hand the statement of Nahau Pech on page 17 concludes with the words: "The saying came from the mouth of Nahau Pech, the priest of the lunar calendar in Katun 4 Ahau, on the final day of the katun." A katun-ending day 4 Ahau fell in 1496, 1240, 984 and so on. At least nineteen years must, therefore, have elapsed between these entries. The discrepancy can be explained by assuming that these statements were abstracted from different katun books, in charge of different priests. There seems to be little doubt that the period in which these priests lived antedated the coming of the Spanish invaders. The following passages from Landa's *Relacion*[207] throw considerable light on the identity of two of the men named in the Tizimin narrative:

"They say that among the twelve priests of Mayapan there was one who was very wise, who had but one daughter, whom he married to a young nobleman named Ah Chel, who had sons who bore

[207] Tozzer 1941: 40.

the name of their father according to the custom of the country.
. . . And the latter knew a great deal of the sciences of his father-in-law." Also footnote 194: "This 'very wise' priest was Ah Xupan
. . . founder of Mani and the ancestor of the Xius. The Chel dynasty
. . . starts from the marriage of the daughter of Ah Xupan to Ah Chel,
or, as he was called later, Ah Kin Chel."

Another statement on the same page may explain the exhortation quoted from page 14: "O Xiu! Do not cast your lots in houses of straw! Thus death will come to your people by reason of it."

Landa narrates the following story: "During a winter's night, about six o'clock in the evening, there arose a wind which kept increasing and soon changed into a hurricane of four winds. This hurricane overthrew all the large trees causing a great destruction of every kind of game; and it destroyed also all the tall houses which, since they were covered with straw and contained fire on account of the cold, were set on fire, and they burned up a large part of the people. If any escaped, they were crippled by the blows which they received from the (flying) wood. This hurricane lasted till the next day at noon, and it was found that those had escaped who dwelt in small houses."

The expression "cast your lots" should be taken quite literally in this connection; for the casting of lots was thought to cause an excitation of the elements resulting in wind and rain. Many instances of such a belief are found in the manuscript.

In this section of the *Relacion*, Landa presents a summary of events which may be of assistance in understanding the contents of the Tizimin narrative. When the katuns are computed roughly on the basis of a Katun 5 Ahau beginning in 1594, they form the following sequence:

Katun		*event listed by Landa—approximate year*	
8 Ahau	1437-1457	1441	Fall of Mayapan
6 Ahau	1457-1476	1464	Great hurricane and fire in Itzmal
4 Ahau	1476-1496	1480	Pestilence
2 Ahau	1496-1515	1496	Intertribal warfare
		1516	Great Plague

Landa continues ". . . so that according to this computation there are 125 years since its abandonment [Mayapan's [208]] during which the people of this land have passed through the calamities which have been related without counting many others, after the Spaniards began to enter it, caused by war and other chastisements which God sent; so that it is a marvel to find so many people as there are still here, though they are not very many."

The "calamities and chastisements" which Landa thus touches upon form the principal subject of the Book of Chilam Balam of Tizimin, together with the "many others" caused by the invasion, which he does not give in detail.

If the seven or eight priests explicitly mentioned in the Tizimin manuscript were the original authors of the hieroglyphic books from which excerpts were taken, the next step is to look for the identity of the man who read the ancient writings in the late 16th or early 17th century and dictated them to a scribe versed in the modern script of the Spanish friars.

The first twelve pages describe the events of a certain Katun 5 Ahau in the past with occasional excursions into a more remote past or predictions as to an indefinite future. The years are clearly indicated by year-bearer, and the tuns in which they fall are numbered. Tun 5 Ahau is named, probably because it has the same name as the katun. Finally the katun ends on the appointed day, 5 Ahau, the pebbles of the 7200 days are counted, and the Book of the Katun is folded together. Then the Lord of the new katun, 3 Ahau, is welcomed:

Page 13: "From the land of Mayapan they came to see the taking of the plate of Lord 3 Ahau, in the hope that they might thus perhaps observe the engraving of the words upon the stone, and see the drenching rain, when in all honesty and integrity I counted the pebbles of the days from the pouch of the katun, as whole-heartedly as when I first counted the katun here in Bakhalal. *I revealed in writing afterward my own correct knowledge.* Of course anyone who spilled a pebble must have been a most unreliable man."

---

[208] Assuming that Landa wrote in 1566.

The author then goes on to establish his own credibility as a respected citizen, saying: "My property and hacienda are in the land called the District of Salamanca in the section over against Chactemal, in the land division of Vaimil, where I established my grant in writing it may be on the 18th day of Zac on 11 Chuen, on February 15 in the year 1544."

Assuming that the year 1544 is approximately correct and that the unknown author was over 21 years of age when he received title to his property from the Crown, he must have been in the nineties when he counted the katun-pebbles of 5 Ahau in 1614, some 70 years afterward. The statement that he "revealed his knowledge in writing" may well mean that he read the hieroglyphic books of the katun and the contents were duly recorded in the new script. He concludes:

"I make confession of these beliefs in order to clarify my words, but there is no one [left] who understands my words or my teaching. When He-who-burns-the-trees shall come, however, to spy out the land of Chilam Balam, his appearance . . ." The rest is obliterated.

On the hypothesis that a very old man was reading from an ancient book, often interpolating remarks of his own drawn from memory, frequently lamenting the current unhappy state of the country and exhorting his hearers to keep to the old way of life, the Book of Chilam Balam of Tizimin becomes more understandable. The first twelve and a half pages constitute what may be called "The Book of Katun 5 Ahau." This cannot be the Katun 5 Ahau which began in 1594, because it starts with the fall of Mayapan. On the other hand, the abandonment of Mayapan described on page 1 cannot be the event listed by Landa as occurring in 1441, because that particular fall of Mayapan took place in a Katun 8 Ahau.

Other Katuns 5 Ahau commenced in 826, 1082 and 1338 approximately, but it is impossible to fix the period on the internal evidence alone. In the first section of the manuscript, through page 28, there is the intermingling of two streams, the story of a bygone era when the arrogant invading Itza were the hated enemy, and a passionate plea to the living Maya of the early 17th century to keep the faith of their fathers under cruel Spanish domination in the promise that peace and happiness, prosperity and freedom would one day return again to the land they loved. The similarity of their situation under the two widely-separated conquerors is striking, and it is not strange to learn that they believed in the repetition of historical events.

On page 29 a new section begins:

"The day of 4 Ahau arrived at Chichen Itza. Four Ahau is the katun for remembering knowledge and compressing it within annals. There was the time, for example, when the friars came among us at Nitunzala and Chactemal and Vaimil and Holtun Itza, and the high-handed manner in which we tore up the writings of the friars, the *Reportorio* for the remission of sins."

The whole intent and purpose of the Books of Chilam Balam are set forth in the next paragraph: "In order that our people may recognize deception when it comes, we have written down the auguries of the days of the katuns one by one, telling by what signs the burden of each katun may be recognized, and the manner in which the count of the bearers of future events are safeguarded when they come; also the road by which the wisemen shall arrive on the day when they come, that it may become the road of the believers themselves."

This explanatory statement introduces a series of 13 katuns beginning with 11 Ahau:

"Eleven Ahau is the first and original katun of the count, and it was also the very first katun after the arrival of the white men in Ichcansiho in time for the establishment of a katun. Alas for us when the great ones, the bearded ones, the sons of the Sun, the white men, came along the trail."

The first katun-ending day 4 Ahau after the Conquest fell in 1752. According to the time-honored method of counting, therefore, the later portion of the manuscript would have been recorded between 1732 and 1752. On page 35, however, there appears a list of the twenty years said to comprise Katun 4 Ahau and *beginning* with 1752 in a year correctly stated to be 3 Cauac. One must therefore conclude that 200 years after Landa destroyed all the sacred hieroglyphic books he could lay hands on, the katun-period had come to be named for its beginning day.

A statement which would assist in dating a portion of the manuscript if a reference point could be established, is found on page 30: "Three Ahau [1614-1634]. It was the fifth time the katun had been counted at Ichcansiho. . . . The swindlers ridicule the year-count of the Jaguar. The white men invent a system of spying on the great sacraments, the cherished rituals of the Jaguar Balam. The stonings, the grievous hangings, all the cutting down and the wearisome bearing of heavy burdens have exhausted and bruised and pierced us. *And when the katun-bearer arrived seven years ago* we made enchantments for protecting the people. And the mourning for the three-fold learning, and a great yearning for a return to the occult teachings kindled a fire which finally burst out at Ichcansiho."

It is not clear from the context whether the record was made seven years after beginning of Katun 3 Ahau, i.e., in 1641, or seven years after the "katun of remembering" began. If the latter, the record was made in 1739 in the old way of reckoning katuns or in 1759 on the basis of a Katun 4 Ahau *beginning* in 1752.

Setting forth the laws of the katuns as well as the names of the towns in which each should be consummated, the sequence which began with 11 Ahau on page 29 has the ring of authenticity. But suddenly a new note is interpolated, a false teaching regarding the katun-count quite out of keeping with everything that has gone before. The true record closes with the following paragraph:

Page 33: "Thirteen Ahau is the thirteenth katun and they shall count it at Cabal. In the assemblage of people they shall open the sealed katun. At dusk they shall smell the fragrance of flowers. Day shall be turned upside down. Their faces shall be disturbed. The genealogical tree shall descend. Stones shall descend and Heaven and Earth shall be universally consumed by fire.

"They shall make a divination concerning the living and the dead: 'The dead shall live! Dying from old age, they shall immediately ascend into heaven. They shall ascend quickly by good roads.' Evil roads descend, spreading out on the earth. At the end, in the final days of the katun, we will hear the words of the fathers of

Heaven and Earth regarding the government of Katun 13 Ahau during his days, at the completion of the katun. Vale."

Then comes the new note introducing the third section of the manuscript. It should be pointed out, perhaps, that none of these divisions is indicated in the manuscript itself, which has apparently been copied in the same handwriting throughout from earlier versions. It is a pitiful attempt to explain the details of the Maya calendar, and it commences with the startling statement that a katun is composed of 24 years, the last four of which, by analogy with the final five days of the year, are *nameless*. A misprint occurs in the date, 1552 being given where 1752 is clearly intended. It is given correctly in the table of years a few pages farther on.

Page 33: "Now, however, Ahau is subservient to the year-bearer of the south, 3 Cauac on the first of Pop, the year being 1752 (corrected). The god Four is submerged on that very day, 4 Ahau. Each score of years has its bearers. When each has collected his debt, then there come four years without names. For this reason there are five (four?) years of idleness and amusement. When the katun arrives in the future—Kaan—nevertheless they will call upon it by name. And they will speak of the five deceptive days at the end of each year, although they are without names and thus fall, each year, at the very end of the year.

"It is similar with the katun: for five years they amuse themselves by collecting the fragments of the katun. When the time comes to read the auguries of the katun, they explain to the people how it first originated, and they count the years since the birth of the various pueblos."

This last statement is doubtless a reference to such sayings as: "Seven times there has been the opening of the sealed katun of 6 Ahau, the katun of Kinich Kakmo, at Uxmal." As 6 Ahau can occur as katun-ending day only once in 256 years, this statement imputes an age of over 1800 years to Uxmal; but if the words "6 Ahau" are taken to be in apposition to "katun," the age would be approximately 140 years.

The passage quoted from page 33 continues: "There is one Jesus Christ, the very most correct count above all counts. Yes, and when they are all in order, He protects their backs from the pressure of the ancient Maya teachings in the land."

The explanation ends on page 34: "A time will come when the katun-folds will have passed away, when they will be found no longer, because the count of tuns is reunited. And after that there will come years in which there are tuns, either four or three in number." This is a manifest absurdity.

I quote this passage in all its obscurity because it immediately precedes the final list of katuns with their principal events which so closely resembles that of the Book of Chilam Balam of Mani as to have been copied from it, unless both were abstracted from a third and older chronicle, no longer extant.

This record begins with a Katun 8 Ahau: "In 8 Ahau a long time ago Chichen Itza made itself powerful. A long time ago they wrote down the history of the province in a chronicle. So be it." Page 34.

A statement on page 35 is of interest: ". . . 13 Ahau. It was then that the first foreigners made hideous the landscape of Yucatan, *four score and thirteen years ago.*" If a Katun 5 Ahau began in 1594, a Katun 13 Ahau commenced in 1515. This entry must have been made, therefore, between 1608 and 1628. This period agrees very well with 1614, the year of the ceremonies of Katun 5 Ahau, as well as with the years of certain news items in the latter part of the Chronicle, 1622, 1627, 1628 and 1629.

The final statement in this sequence of events, however, declares: "Five Ahau was the katun in which the Fathers came from Spain to Mani, and the year in which they came was 1550." The year is confirmed by the next statement: "By the time these years had passed, 1552-1559, they were everywhere." As this chronology is entirely inconsistent with that of the earlier parts of the Tizimin manuscript, it is reasonable to infer that the concluding part of the book was not in the original manuscript. Exceptions to this statement may be the marginal notes telling of events in 1622 to 1629, which have been copied in wherever there was a little space.

After a short record which begins with the arrival of Dr. Quixada in 1560 and ends with 1611, "the year in which we wrote letters about the hangings, asking for justice. It is right that the King should be concerned with these things," the explanation of the false katun-count is resumed.

On page 35 there commences a list of 20 years beginning with 1752 3 Cauac, and bearing the explanatory note: "These years comprise the burden of Katun 4 Ahau. There still remain four years without name at the very end of the katun." This erroneous information is a continuation of the section which began on page 33 with the statement, "Now, however, Ahau is subservient to the year-bearer of the south, 3 Cauac on the first of Pop."

On page 36 we read: "After that, there will be established 2 Ahau, the 'united for a cause' katun." The author then lists four years 1772-1775 inclusive, which he says make up the "nameless" years of Katun 4 Ahau. They are followed immediately by a prophecy for Katun 2 Ahau, which is to be celebrated in the square of Saclactun. The intention of assigning 24 years to each katun is clearly set forth in the next passage, entitled "The count of Katun 2 Ahau when it follows upon 1 Cauac." It contains a table of 20 years and their year-bearers from 1776 1 Cauac to 1795 7 Ix, with the explanation: "This completes the term of office of 2 Ahau, *except that at the end of the katun there come the four years without name*, before the arrival of 13 Ahau." The latter are then named: 1796 8 Cauac through 1799 11 Ix. Only a brief prophecy is given for Katun 13 Ahau and no Christian years are listed. It was to be observed at Kinchilcoba, not at Mayapan.

On page 37 the author lists the 52 years of a Calendar Round beginning with 1758 1 Kan and ending with 1809 13 Cauac. This section provides us with a valuable new fact, the Maya name for the period which has been named the Calendar Round. It is *bubukil habob*, "the summation of the years." [209]

On page 38 the author presents the names of the 20 days "which continually wander through the *uinal*," commencing as in the previous list with 1 Kan. A second column contains the Christian month-dates of the first days of the uinals on the basis of the so-

[209] See footnote 188.

called "Landa typical year" which couples July 16 and 1 Pop. The third and last column gives the names of the *uinals* beginning with Pop, and with Kayab and Pax interchanged. Complying with Landa's statement that the last five days of the year are without names, the author writes 00 where July 11 is to be expected, but characterizes the period as *u heh kin,* "the days of misfortune." In the third column, where Uayeb is expected, he writes merely "5." It was universally recognized that the five supplementary days of the year were days for staying quietly indoors in order to avoid misfortune. In the description of the false katun of 24 years, therefore, the statement that the last four "nameless" years were to be devoted to idleness and amusement introduces a discordant note and throws considerable doubt on the authenticity of the whole section.

The explanation of the list of days and uinals begins: "One score of days there is in the Moon's treasure, the uinal. These are their names," referring to the previous table. The author then lists the so-called Burners and their days and makes a feeble and unsuccessful attempt to get at their significance. It is of interest to note that Ah toc, "burner," may also mean "deliverer."

Pages 39 and 40 contain a most interesting section in which prophecies are set forth for seven years beginning variously with the seven days of the Christian week. Supplementing these, there is a table containing the years of a 28-year cycle, obtained by combining the seven days of the week with the four-year leap year period of the Julian calendar. I quote from my article in the Southwestern Journal of Anthropology: [210]

"The 28-year cycle must have appealed strongly to the 17th century Maya scholars for several reasons: It was of the same order of magnitude as the katun. It came into being through the permutation of seven days and four Julian years, thus representing a mathematical way of thinking familiar and pleasant to the Maya mind. Moreover, the number 28 had a place in their reckoning, since the ritual or computing year may be thought of as composed of 28 13's or of 13 28's."

---

[210] Makemson 1948: 398.

The final twelve pages of the book contain a list of the 365 days of the year together with notes as to their bearing on the welfare of humanity. But crowded in margins and almost illegible are found several extremely interesting jottings of events which transpired in the years 1622, 1627, 1628 and 1629, though not in chronological order. They treat of earthquake, tempests and plagues of locusts and seem to have been jotted down soon after they occurred, wherever an inch of space could be found. They have no connection with the other material on the various pages; but they must represent a modern attempt to recapture the spirit of the ancient books of the katuns in which records of all important events affecting the welfare of the people as a whole were meticulously entered.

In closing this chapter, I should like to quote one of these records in full, because of the light it casts on the tenacity of the ancient customs, a century after the Spanish invasion. One must remember, however, that the Maya had been deprived of their great spiritual leaders, during the decades of persecution, with the exception of the few who had successfully espoused the cause of their conquerors on the surface, at least.

Page 42: "On the 6th of June in the year 1629, there came a swarm of locusts above the houses. The people then stopped up all the openings in the houses as in ancient times, for several days, to preserve their own lives. The cornfields were destroyed and all the food everywhere among the pueblos. The locusts came to Chikin and to Cupul. They oppressed Mani. The locusts scooped up the food by the mouthful, ravenously.

"Then the people formed a circle around the daughter of Don Franco Cocom and seized her, placing a rope around her neck, on account of the destruction of the crops and the dire need of Hunab Ku for food.

"O wretched people! Why are you so agitated by hunger, all of you, just because of your afflictions by reason of the locusts!

"At Chanucan, some distance from here, there came to be food, and all the people did not die but lived to bless their benefactress, because she took upon herself the guilt of the locusts which were destroying all that the people had sowed."

CHAPTER TWO

The Historical Aspect of the Book of Tizimin

AS A FACTUAL RECORD OF THE MUNDANE AFFAIRS OF A people, the Book of Chilam Balam of Tizimin leaves much to be desired. The primary emphasis is not placed upon the historical data, although these are not lacking. Considered as the *spiritual* history of a cultivated Maya tribe, however, the document becomes truly significant.

"People of Pop," "people of Ix Toloch," "descendants of Yaxum," these are some of the terms by which the tribe was described. The last name signifies merely "forefather," from *yax-yum*, "first father." In the opening sentence of the Book of Chilam Balam of Chumayel, as it has come down to posterity, there are given the names of the four ancestors of the four Maya tribes, hailing from the north, east, south and west respectively. Among them Yaxum is declared to have been the first man of the *Cauich* family; but I have not found the name Cauich in the Tizimin manuscript. The word *yaxum* is found in three passages in the Chumayel: on page 63 of the Roys translation it is taken to be the name of a man; on page 74 it is interpreted as the *quetzal* bird, and on page 99 *yaxum* appears as the name of a tree. In the Tizimin, however, *yaxum* seems to apply only to the deified progenitor of the tribe which is probably of Xiu lineage. The name Yaxum does not appear in the index of Tozzer's edition of Landa's *Relacion*.

On the first page of the Tizimin manuscript the Christian-Maya year is named explicitly as 1593 13 Kan, with the statement that in

113

the following year (1594 1 Muluc) a Katun 5 Ahau would commence. The next eleven pages enumerate the Maya years and tuns of this katun, and they serve as a loom on which the Jaguar Priest has woven a pattern of events from past history, not only from other Katuns 5 Ahau but from intervening periods as well. That it is actually *ancient* history is indicated by the fact that the invasion of Yucatan by the Europeans is not mentioned until page 15; but one can hardly escape the conclusion that a parallel is being vividly and intentionally drawn between the situation of the tribe under the domination of the cruel and arrogant Itza and its circumstances under Spanish rule.

If, as seems inescapable, these early pages were transcribed from hieroglyphic documents which had miraculously escaped burning in Landa's *auto da fe* fifty years earlier, part of the contents may have been condensed or suppressed by the interpreter as unimportant, whereas other paragraphs may have been elaborated from his own memory.

In the opening lines, Mayapan has fallen to an enigmatic enemy,[211] probably the barbarous Itza. Under their onslaught, the subjugated Xiu, descendants of Yaxum, find themselves homeless, wandering in the forest and confronting innumerable hardships. But their deepest grief concerns the destruction of the highly-prized books:

Page 1: "With rivers of tears we mourned our sacred writings amid the delicate flowers of sorrow in the days of the katun. . . . For our sons still remember the calamities, the burning of men, the burning, the shattering, the destruction of those days. . . . Should we not lament in our suffering, grieving for the loss of our maize and the destruction of our teachings concerning the universe of the earth and the universe of the heavens?"

That these calamitous events transpired in a *past* Katun 5 Ahau is supported by the statement on page 2: "During this period three katuns succeeded one another. . . . In this manner three folds

---

[211] The name *Itza* appears first on page 3 of the manuscript.

of katuns passed by, until the rigorous government of Katun 1 Ahau arrived."

Dishonorable and cruel rulers governed during the katuns 13 Ahau, 11 Ahau and 9 Ahau. Freedom was obtained only in the release of death. Another Katun 5 Ahau arrived in his season, bringing a swarm of new intruders, like flies. The loss of the books for predicting the future course of events was still vital, after the lapse of 260 years.

Page 2: "We are pierced with a great longing to read the books of wood and the writings on stone, now in ruins. *They contain the seven well-springs of life!* They were burned before our eyes at the well. At noon-day we lament our perpetual burdens. . . . They plead for a judgment against the intruders; for a judgment against the white fangs and against the red fangs, and against the pestilence which they brought and which lasted five *tuns Ahau.* . . . The people perform the eleven penances [of blood-letting] all the days of their prayers. *They pray that the eyes of their children may read the writings on the stone tablets.*"

The first two pages thus appear to cover two or three hundred years of bondage to a warlike people known to us only by the Maya epithet *itza,* "the astute, the skilled, the wise ones." They are sometimes termed "the holy, or consecrated men." They were skilled astronomers, for example, and also knew how to predict the weather from the appearance of the sky. Such "magical" knowledge may have given rise to their name "Wise ones."

Page 3: "Wherever they reside, whether in the north or in the west, they study the aspect of the heavens. They say that it will rain when Ahaucan the Rattlesnake is lifted high above the trees, above the rocks, above the houses, and above everything else."

The Itza were also looked upon as black magicians, "sons of darkness" in contrast to the "sons of light" as the people of Ix Toloch styled themselves. A curious episode is related on page 5. While the Xiu were celebrating the advent of the year-bearer 4 Kan, the Itza were invoking the Earth in certain observances of their own:

Page 5: "Then it happened concerning the stammering Itza

that they made supplications . . . while the sons of light were offering many prayers in behalf of their commonwealth, the sons of
darkness at the same time happened to be celebrating a festival
among themselves in honor of the earth . . . and leopards with
burnished skins came one by one out of the forest.

"Meanwhile the others were holding their solemnities and it
was on a day 4 Kan. After their festival the heavens were moved.
The earth also was moved [by the entreaties of the Itza]. The priests
[of the Xiu] were deeply disturbed. The lands throughout the provinces were greatly annoyed. Fierce warriors were among those who
were dubious about the outcome." There must have been a tempest
and an earthquake, to judge from the agitation produced and the
propitiatory rites which followed.

There has been inconclusive speculation as to the origin of the
Itza. Sanchez de Aguilar was told by natives that the Maya had been
vassals of the Mexicans for 600 years. That would place the invasion in the early tenth century. Very likely the Itza "skilled ones"
were these Mexicans, since the Itza yoke had evidently lain upon
the peace-loving Maya for several centuries. The Tizimin manuscript informs us that the chief deity of the Itza was Kukulcan;
also, that they did not understand the Maya calendar, but tied up
their years in bundles in what may be supposed to have been Mexican fashion.

Page 10: "The Itza are accustomed to make bundles of sticks
of the individual years and to bind them all together, and they
know nothing about our days and our katuns. But their minds are
inquisitive concerning our katun." They must have eventually
learned the secrets of the Maya calendar, however, for a little later
we are told that they participated in the calendar ritual and the
counting of the sacred pebbles of the days.

If the Itza did not understand the Maya ceremonial magic,
they nevertheless demonstrated their appreciation of the spectacles
of the great festivals with appropriate noises, and their priests appear to have insisted upon the ritual of human sacrifice in times of
famine and distress:

Page 6: "The rule of the Itza shall be completely established over us. We will accept their commands. They cherish the 'bursting open of the living rock.' They whistle when they look on at our ceremonies. They whistle with impatience for the handing around of the medicinal herbs of the fields and mountains, and for the beneficial effects derived therefrom." The latter was probably *peyote*, obtained from the buttons of the mescal cactus, which is said to produce illusions of great beauty and happiness.

Landa narrates the following history: [212]

"It is believed among the Indians that with the Itzas who occupied Chichen Itza, there reigned a great lord named Kukulcan, and that the principal building, which is called Kukulcan, shows this to be true. They say that he arrived from the west; but they differ among themselves as to whether he arrived before or after the Itzas or with them." This Kukulcan, who was probably named for the god, although Landa declares that he was later deified because he was a "just statesman," is also credited with having built the beautiful city of Mayapan.

Tozzer [213] quotes from Seler's translation of an ancient manuscript of Motul: "Originally a god had been worshipped here who was the creator of all things, and who had his dwelling in heaven, but that a great prince named Kukulcan with a multitude of people, had come from a foreign country, that he and his people were idolators, and from that time the inhabitants of this land also began to practice idolatry, to perform bloody sacrificial rites, to burn copal, and the like."

According to Lizana, there were two invasions, one from the east called the "little descent," and one from the west known as the "great descent." [214]

In the Tizimin book, however, the two invasions were from the north and the west. Page 19: "They came sweeping down from the west. They came from the north. Many of the sons of God lost their lives. There was great dismay under the trees, beneath the branches."

---

[212] Tozzer 1941: 20-23.
[213] Ibid. 23; footnote 124.
[214] Ibid. 16; footnote 94.

The next sentence probably refers to the coming of the Spaniards: "Finally came the great, the excessive sorrow of the sons of our wretchedness, when the foreigners descended from the sea. That was a long time ago."

And on page 9: "The generations of the Itza! Once they came from the north, and once, later, from the west, the enemy in our midst. In great distress we were scattered among the forests and in the mountains. . . . The sorrows of those days!"

The adjective *nun* (Chumayel) or *num* (Tizimin) characteristically applied to the Itza is accepted by Roys in its meaning of "one who speaks brokenly; stammering." Although I have followed him in this interpretation, I should like to point out that both Pio Perez and the Motul Dictionary also give *num* the significance of "much, excessive." Hence the word could apply here to the *great numbers* of the Itza overlords who had to be fed and clothed by their unfortunate vassals. The use of the word "stammering" has led to the suggestion that the Itza may have spoken Chol or a similar Maya dialect, rather than an entirely foreign language such as the Mexican.

The statement on page 6, "The generations of the Itza will comprise three folds of katuns on 8 Kan the year-bearer which falls on 1 Pop in the eighth tun," seems to refer to the Katun 5 Ahau which began in 1594; but such a late date (1542) for the Itza invasion is manifestly impossible.

The proud Xiu leaders never became completely reconciled to the presence of the Itza lords in their midst, even when they made common cause against the Spaniards. Once, affairs reached such a crisis that the Xiu priests of the calendar, known as Ah Tem Pop and Ah Tem Zam, offered themselves as sacrificial victims by plunging into the sacred "Well of the Cavern," *u chenil ti yactunil.*

This great cavern appears to have been situated in the district of Mayapan, but caves in the limestone walls of the great *cenotes* or natural wells, were not uncommon. Landa's [215] description is of interest:

---

[215] Tozzer 1941: 188; and footnote 949.

"These cenotes have very nice water and are well worth seeing, for there are some of rock cut in the living rock down to the water . . . and within them are pretty vaults of living rock." Tozzer's footnote, quoting from the *Relacion* of Ciudad Real, is also important: " '. . . in the wall of this well there is a cave which reaches far within.' Edward H. Thompson, former owner of the ranch of Chichen Itza, often told the author that there is a tradition among the present natives of a cave connecting the two cenotes at Chichen."

The narrative of the remarkable occurrence at the Well of the Cavern follows:

Page 7-8: "Then the priest finally asks for a covering of green bark. Thirteen times he strips the flowers and leaves from branches. Then he binds the branches together . . . the face of the priest, when he is on the point of entering the Well of the Cavern. Once more we listen to their orations in the Cavern, when the priests of Pop and Zam, Ah Tem Pop and Ah Tem Zam, are about to destroy themselves on account of their grievous injuries, having come to the end of desire and to the end of being subjected to violence.

"Then they walk twice around the cave and around the well, stopping at the altars. One at a time, they rub their hands over the smooth stone and read the words: 'Justice exists. Heaven exists.'

"Thereupon the great priest Chilam replies, 'Perhaps so; perhaps not. True, for the present we must carry the highly ornamental sons of the Itza on our backs, maintaining them in our midst like a great stone, in our misfortune. But there will come a time when the white flowers will again be unsheathed in this land from the Island of Cuzamil to Mayapan. It will come to pass on account of the well, on account of the cavern in this land of magic.

" 'In the day of the overthrow of the Red Eagle, in the day of retribution, when it shall come to pass later over this beautiful land of billowing mountains, then quickly shall come the day of vexation, the vexation of the Itza.

" 'How, then, can we remember the prophecies, if there are no fathers of the days or of the festivals of the katun? How can the generations of the sons of the Itza tell us the days of the prophecies and the days of the tun? How can we celebrate the rites of Lord 5 Ahau in the twelfth tun, when he comes in benign holiness, in the katun of power and of the strength of the wooden idols, and the magic of the cup, and the magic of the plate, and the magic of the count of days, in Katun 5 Ahau, in the twelfth tun?

" 'When the festival of the katun is appointed throughout the province of the Itza and it comes to pass in the midst of the open country, it may be that the prophecies will deceive the sons of the day and the sons of the night. Perhaps they will come to pass. Perhaps they will not come to pass. The prophecies may deceive you, if you have contempt for the Ancestors.' "

The Itza overlords suffered with their vassals in periods of prolonged drought and famine, as will be seen from the following passage: (Page 9) "In the fourteenth tun . . . on the katun's day, the Itza recounted their grievances among themselves in great excitement . . . their burning needs, a tale of great distress, on the day in which they read their fortunes in the fangs of the fire. But after they assembled, they rejoiced to see the sky covered with clouds. On that day everyone saw it. Then the face of the sun was veiled, the face of the moon was covered. In the fourteenth tun the vegetation was fast disappearing owing to so much cropping. Too many mouths in our houses; too many mouths for the number of calabashes."

Gradually and inevitably as the katuns succeeded one another, there must have come about a blending of interests, even to the point of collaboration in the great calendar festivals of the people of Ix Toloch, and the rain ceremonies. We read on page 3 that the gizzards of birds and honey, the firstfruits of the hive, were offered to "the deity of the day, a god of the Itza; and there was a drawing of the days in silence to the very end."

Also on page 10: "The priests of the Itza take fruit from the receptacle. They take out grains of corn. They are suddenly interrupted by a rain-squall, by a tempest of wind. Then the face of the god is revealed to Ah Pop and Ah Zam. And as it appears overhead the people run among the trees, among the rocks. Take care that you recompense the idol for his protection!" Here the word for "priests" is not *kin,* which also signifies "sun or day," but *balmil,* "a master or priest (Motul)," apparently a shortened form of *balamil,* from *balam,* "jaguar."

And on the same page we learn that "the people have come to depend upon the cup and the plate," accessories of the katun ceremonies. "They lean upon their rulers (the Itza) who came long ago from the north and from the west."

As the Book of the Jaguar Priest is concerned chiefly with the spiritual history of a people, many concrete details are omitted. The only hint, for example, regarding a plan for recapturing Mayapan is a note that the hieroglyphic books were consulted for advice as to whether it would be best to attack the city from the north or from the south:

Page 11: ". . . according to the words of the katun, according to that which is set forth in the hieroglyphic books of the katun. The books tell whether we should go against Mayapan from the north or from the south; and when Ah Vuc Chapat shall reveal himself to us; and when little by little the vision of Ah Vuc Yol Sip himself shall be manifested unto us."

The narrative goes on immediately to describe a great celebration at which war-captives were sacrificed, but the purpose is to obtain rain and food, because "the food of the people of Ix Toloch has been entirely consumed." There is no mention of victory in battle. Finally, after an expression of resentment against the Itza overlords who were obviously responsible for the human sacrifices, we learn of a three-day festival in honor of "the return to the Well in the Cavern." This statement certainly implies that the sacred cave and well were situated in the district of Mayapan, and that Mayapan had been reoccupied by the Itza and Xiu warriors.[216] The narrative concludes as follows:

---

[216] According to the first record of the Chumayel, the Itza recaptured Mayapan in a Katun 4 Ahau; and according to the Tizimin page 34, the event occurred in a Katun 2 Ahau. The fall of Mayapan referred to in this section, however, is said to have taken place in a Katun 5 Ahau, in the eighteenth tun.

Page 11: "For three days we looked on at the ceremonies celebrating the return to the Well of the Cavern, while our gallant sons
entertained us with sports. O Thou who standest at our side and
fulfillest the rites of the sowing by sending the rains, how many
prophecies from on high have come true since the days of the return
of the Itza, the second descent!"

Nahau Pech voices the universal resentment against the Itza in
his statement on page 17 apparently written 80 years after the second descent: "In former times there was understanding of the
moon, in the time of our fathers. With compassion the government
redeemed us. That was four katuns ago. I will ask intercession of
the Holy Father (*kul yum*), if He will hear us, when you forget
the omens and neglect them. *When the Itza came to our country as
guests of our fathers,* they all together sowed discord among you."

This is one of the rare references to the fact that the Itza were
first introduced into Yucatan as mercenary troops by the Xiu fathers.
That was the "first descent"; but they liked the land so much better
than their own that after they had returned home they gathered
their families and possessions and returned to Yucatan to make a
permanent settlement.

Yabun Chan's statement on page 17 also concerns the Itza problem, particularly as it affected freedom of speech:

"In former times the priests of this country were allowed to
speak freely. Yes. Our fathers expected divine manifestations. And
the priests were the ones who cut the honey from the hives in olden
times. You will grant that they understood the good omens of abundance, when they sought for them in the fire. . . . You Itza are
altogether provoking, when you forget the Lord Ahau and sow discord among the holy ones." The "sowing of discord" may refer to
a conflict of ideologies between the followers of Kukulcan with their
human sacrifices and the peace-loving and philosophical "people of
Pop and Zam."

The third signed statement in these pages (17-18) is that of
the Jaguar Priest. Addressing the Itza directly, he adjures them
to accept Hunab Ku as their supreme deity. Indeed, he intimates
that the Itza are already "ignorantly worshiping" Hunab Ku under

the guise of Kukulcan, by interpreting the latter name as *ku u kul can,* "God the holy One of Heaven," a play on the name *kukul-can,* "Feathered Serpent":

Page 18: "These sacramental objects of yours, O Itza, these holy things of yours, derive from Kukulcan, 'God the holy One of heaven.' Find your holiness in truth and penitence. Find holiness with the people of God . . . and in the words of Hunab Ku, the one supreme God. He comes to you from heaven in the drops of rain. It is good, what I say to you assembled here, O Itza. Let the earth awaken when They tread upon it, and attend, in another katun later on. Sufficient unto themselves are my words, for I am Chilam Balam the Jaguar Priest. I repeat my words of divine truth: I say that the divisions of the earth shall all be *one!* This is the ninth year of Katun 1 Ahau."

What appears at first glance to have been a great natural catastrophe depopulated the districts of Chactenel (or Chactemal) and Sactenel. Described on page 19, the calamities apparently followed upon the great desire of the Thirteen gods for their rightful offerings in return for having produced "the sweetness of the honey, the bountifulness of the land." The story seems to start out as prophecy, but drops into the narrative tense:

Page 19: "The state of Chactenel must be abandoned. The forest trees shall be destroyed by fire, even the great roots at their feet. Then *they* shall come and scatter great quantities of grain, the staff of life, by the handful. . . . So sudden will be the violence of that day when it appears in the heavens, revealing the fleeing multitude! They shall grieve for Chactenel in its affliction. Then the state of Sactenel shall be depopulated. On a day 13 Ahau 9 Chen, the thirteen treasures of the Itza shall be shattered and swept away. Strong trees will be uprooted. A fire will be kindled in the very midst of the pueblo, when the prophecies shall be fulfilled amongst us."

Then the priests hurriedly turned the pages of the Books of the Katun to determine in what direction they should make their flight, while other priests, in order to preserve the sacred count of days intact, placed the various pouches of pebbles in pottery jars before they all escaped together into the night. "They search out the road in the pages of the book of the idols where the words are painted in many colors, telling the path which must be followed.

"As the priests were unable to tie up the bundles of the years, they placed them in pottery jars and carried them in their arms when they fled into the darkness. *And in the morning, when they worshiped the rising sun, they beat upon the jars with their hands, pretending that they were the drums of the inhabitants of the state of Chactenel.*" This realistic touch indicates that the Xiu calendar priests feared the presence of lurking human enemies who might be spying on their actions.

The narrative continues: "As the time approached for the katun to arrive, they were determined that the count should not become confused . . . and to put it in order, each one independently of the others. So when the time came to inquire into the pouch of the thirteenth katun and into the treasure of the country, they sought out a village in the heart of the forest, on an island, where the precious objects descended. When it came time to roll up the mat of the katun, we were wise by reason of our suffering. In adoration we lifted up our voices to the stars. With abuse and ridicule heaped upon our heads, the migration will arrive at Chacmitan; and at Chacmitan, we will take warning to lead better lives. At that time, the surface of the state of Chacmitan will extend a great distance."

One of the very few references to the legendary original habitat Suiva (the Chumayel Zuyua) occurs at this point: "The migration will begin like the last one from Suiva, as they lament for rain. . . . The state of Sactenel will be depopulated." Then comes a reference to the cruel tyrant of the Canul tribe who appears to be the cause of so much misery. During a protracted drought and famine the hapless Xiu were impressed as slave labor and forced to carry food from the mountains to feed the Canul. The seven years of famine had been foretold in their prophecy:

Page 20: "It chanced on 13 Ahau the katun-bearer, during the migration from Holtun-Suiva and the one from the Five Provinces also, that there should be no idols of carved wood. In those days the Lord of the Canul governed the five divisions of the country to our utter misery, to our degradation and to our sorrow. There was

Ah Canul in the midst of the country of the Canul, and the number of those who were severely punished by his government at Saclactun was legion.

"The pottery jars which were used for the storage of food were kept closed, and the food was sold for high prices, after it had been carried down from the mountains. Seven multitudes of bearers were engaged in this operation. Thus was fulfilled the prophecy of the katun that there should be seven years of drought in all. Seven times, the year of the waxing katun was changed in the usual manner. For seven years there was pestilence. But that which was to affirm the completion of the katun's treasure, they guarded there for seven years as if it were the very life of the Earth. For Saclactun is situated in the heart of the Island of Cuzamil and of them all.

"At the expiration of the period of the prophecy, there came the Sun of our life, and whichever one of the four Musencabs it was who measured the earth with his paces. And there was the utmost astonishment when the Lords of the Days, 13 Ahau and 1 Ahau, came to the festival, in spite of the fact that the enemy in our midst harassed us day and night."

The Tyrant of Ah Canul whose heartlessness surpassed even that of the Itza may have been the infamous Hunac Ceel, whose exploits are described at length in the Chumayel document. The Chumayel I Chronicle declares that Izamal fell to Hunac Ceel in a Katun 8 Ahau, which would have been possibly from 1102 to 1122 in the Tizimin calendar. The name *Hunac Ceel* appears in the Tizimin book only in the "borrowed" chronicle of the final pages, as on page 34: ". . . 8 Ahau. The Xiu, true men, abandoned Chichen Itza to the threatening words of Hunac Ceel. . . . Thirteen folds of katuns passed after they had abandoned the city to Hunac Ceel, because of the flayings they had heard about. Six Ahau, 4 Ahau: two score of years. Two Ahau in the beautiful citadel of Ichpaa, in Mayapan, because of the men of the Itza, the rulers of the country, on account of the sinful words of Hunac Ceel."

The first intimation that disaster was about to fall upon the city of Itzmal (or Izamal) arrived in the prophecy of Katun 8 Ahau:

Page 22-23: "Anciently on 8 Ahau we were the guests of our

blood-relatives, the people of Itzmal, because Sip (the warrior god) was there as the guest of the lords. When they opened the sealed katun in earlier times during the 17th katun, they pleaded for the satisfaction of our needs by the holy, heavenly Itzam-caan, and for his apparition as Lord of Heaven, and for the opening of heaven to our relatives, the people of Itzmal, by the god their guest, as in ancient times the sons of holy Itzmal declared it.

"When the lord of the katun (8 Ahau) appeared in the ancient kingdom of Itzmal, the people of Itzmal completed the count, absorbing the teaching even in the midst of afflictions. We had as our guest Yaxbolai. We had as our guests Chacbolai and Chacxibchac, three very unlucky spirits. Their gift when it descended in our midst proved to contain great suffering for our relatives here in Itzmal at the hands of that evil-doer, the King of the Canul.

"He ensnared our honorable sons into revealing the secret teachings to him. After he had learned from them the whereabouts of Kukulcan, he cut the throats of all of them and theirs. When the bodies of our noblemen lay stretched out upon the base ground, the heavens opened, and our leaders laid the frightful deed upon our oppressors.

"Then began the experiment of Itzam-caan to effect the reformation of the King of the Canul from his wicked ways. When the Lord of Heaven was manifested to the people of Chichen where Ah Canul had no power, they listened with careful attention."

The first explicit mention of the Spanish invaders occurs on page 15, as part of an exhortation to arouse the Maya people to anger against their oppressors, with the promise of eventual liberation and the return of justice to the land:

Page 15: "When that day comes, then with great vigilance we will enjoy the fruits of our heritage; but vigilance here below will gradually relax, *the more forceful becomes the heavenly anger directed against the Christians.* Justice must come. . . . This is the prophecy of the dishonorable katun: 'There will be no good purpose served by the Christian bishop when he arrives. He will seek to destroy this generation. Likewise, he will restrict your beliefs. He will destroy you. He will eradicate your true knowledge in the end. He demands that we shall accept the Christian teaching, as it is called.'"

In this final crisis of the Spanish invasion, Xiu and Itza joined forces against the Europeans. Page 22: "At the height of our afflictions, the stammering Itza called our sons to their aid, in order that together they might surpass the perfection of the powerful Christian warriors."

The heart-breaking struggle continued through Katun 11 Ahau (1535-1555). On Katun-ending day 9 Ahau (1575) a great conference was held for the purpose of asking the guidance and assistance of the Warrior God Sip, in the coming war to the death.

Page 24: "On this day at sunset, the men of responsibility met to consider the question of guidance, not only for the instruction of the chiefs and priests, but for the war-captains also, as well as the lords of Pop and Zam, all with one heart and mind.

"Then in company with Lord 9 Ahau descended the words of that wellknown Sip, the ancient Sip, the warrior of nobility and of days 9 and of the nine Zam, in the kingdom of Ah Vuc Chapat, the Seven-headed Serpent, whose shield is the sun. When this mighty warrior arrived, descending by the road of the Stars of the Abundant Life and of the living katun, on the day-sign of Sacvacnal, the faces of the lords were suffused with living tears, with tears like rain.

"When the battle for our lives was joined, our warriors looked very ferocious as if hungering for warfare, for a universal contest. They went into battle with high courage, first acknowledging the authority of the day 9 with a few words.

"It is the katun of the forcible withdrawal of the Hand, yes, from the granting of the prayers of warriors. The lords were vanquished, and there was much praying for their lives and shedding of tears at the end, as they lay stretched out on the mats trying to staunch the flowing blood, or lying flat on their backs in heaps. These are the words of the katun. So be it."

Then followed the long and wearisome years of learning to give outward submission to the Spaniards while preserving a measure of inward integrity. When the soldiers came to collect tribute for the Spanish Crown their contempt for their new subjects, their desecration of altars and temples and unrestrained ridicule of Maya customs, their avaricious prying into Maya homes and their brutal treatment of the women and girls—all these insults and oppressions made life intolerable for the high-spirited people who had preserved their self-respect and their erudition under centuries of subjection to the Itza lords. They were sustained only by the hope that when the land had been exhausted of its treasures, their insatiable rulers would depart.

Page 24: "The men of Katun 7 speak a great madness of words. They run to and fro in frenzy. In Ichcansiho they (the Spanish) will soon begin to take possession. They will bring to pass the final days and the end of all protection of the people, all. The nine magic rituals of life, the nine magic incantations for rain in abundance and for new growth in abundance were given us by the authors of our life.

"Whether by taking medicine or by eleven vomitings our daughters may become both good and beautiful, and whether they are beautiful or not, there will be no defenders to guard them in the days to come, in the seven days of collecting tribute. Men with trumpets are making the rounds of the country. Only seven days remain to our government. Then come the men to dig to the very bottom to fill their baskets. They lay waste the property of our people, making destitute the houses of our rulers.

"The holy symbols on the altars will allure them. They will covet the precious masks. These men will laugh in the faces of our countrymen and of the people of the province, and of our rulers and lords. Having at heart the welfare of Pop and Zam and of the government, true men will deny when they are asked, that they have any property. These avaricious rulers are the governing lords of Katun 7 Ahau."

Page 25: "The mouths of the white oppressors declare the things pertaining to the year to be only wind. They even go so far as say that there will not be a throne in the heavens, shining like the sun, to be adored in its majesty. But the dying lords of the land of Pop and Zam accept the eleven penances on faith, as they cut their throats on the altar of Pop and on the altar of Zam."

Page 29: "The bearded ones, the ones who shoot—this is the

signal of the white God—were arriving. Six sons of heaven, some aged and infirm, came shouting to announce the news, spreading it over the country. They were present in every clump of trees, behind every heap of rocks, the friars, all exactly alike in appearance, negotiating for our souls and haranguing us about the 'true God.'"

In the beginning the Xiu received the Christians in a friendly and pacific manner. "When you tried with all your hearts to emulate them they obstructed your efforts to protect the people. At our ceremonies, we prayed to the gods above, when asking intercession for our brothers, after *they* arrived. . . . Little by little we began to grow weary of the maiming of the people by the Christians, when I should have liked to protect the people and guard the country. . . . Gradually they began the hangings again for the second time, and they kindled the fire on the stone (a form of torture, perhaps). The offenses of the white people are all alike, even against those who surrender themselves or their relatives, everywhere they go. Brothers plead for justice in their throats. Gradually we discover that the Christians are great liars. Little by little we realize that they are great cheats."

But still there was hope that if the Xiu could be patient and submissive long enough, the invaders would eventually come to appreciate the fact that they were not ignorant barbarians, even as the Itza had done. Page 29: "This is the burden of Katun 7 Ahau (1575-1594): 'Little by little they will begin to esteem our learning and our knowledge of the unrolling of the face of the universe, for the protection of the fathers of the people from ruin and the descendants of our ancestors. The face of the squared stone of the mountains shall again be made beautiful.'"

The Maya priests and warriors were contemptuous of the manner of clothing worn by the Spanish gentlemen. Page 23: "On a day 9 Oc the first *strutting turkey-cocks* arrived. On that day came the quarrelsome strangers. On that day there were whippings at Chakanputun."

We can imagine their righteous indignation, therefore, when the friars began to coerce them into adopting European garments. Page 23: "Lest your visitor, the God of the White Face, make you change your manner of dressing and turn you into effeminate fellows, you must cut off the white, bearded strangers from Ichcansiho. Whip them from the land!"

Gradually and reluctantly the Maya people were forced to accept the often demonstrated fact: the White God was far more powerful than Hunab Ku and Ah Vuc Yol Sip and all the Bacabs and the Musencabs and Kinich Ahau and the lesser deities put together. The recognition of this incomprehensible superiority, the destruction of their sacred books, the loss of their fighting men, and the final horror of seeing their young children forcibly removed to the monasteries, to return years later thoroughly indoctrinated with the hateful religion of the Friars, these and the many other indignities which they suffered brought the Maya people to the abyss of despair.

Page 29: "Little by little, whether they take seven sacraments or not, their prayers are heard by their powerful God."

The desperate efforts of the Maya leaders to rally their flocks from the inertia of complete spiritual submission were soon cut short, however. Page 30: "Gradually, the hanging of the great men among us began to take place, the extinction of noble lineages. Gradually began our sorrow for our daughters, our sorrow for our sons, for the foolish behavior of our daughters and the foolish behavior of our sons, made purposely so.

"When they lifted up the necks and held in their hands the heads of nobles of high lineage, when they held up the neck of Chac Ahaucan of the lineage, when they began on the two priests of Zam and the two priests of Pop, and on Balam the Fox, Balam the interpreter of wonders, the Dog, then our hearts were broken when we heard the news."

Nothing was sacred to the conquerors. With force of arms behind them, they invaded the secret place where the pebbles of the days of the katun were being reverently counted. They questioned under torture in their determination to ferret out the sacred teachings of the centuries.

Page 30: "Little by little came the days of spying and lying, when we began to go hungry and our feet were bruised with much walking for the protection of the people. . . . The swindlers ridicule the year-count of the Jaguar. The white men invent a system of spying on our great ceremonials, on the cherished rituals of the Jaguar, *Balam.* . . . Now the priests begin the customary drawing of the katun days. Now they begin to name one at a time in their hands the great heap of small stones, passing them from hand to hand. Then there came into your dwelling, there came the men who want you to become Christians, into the midst of the ceremony. . . . The wretched men inquire minutely again and again as to how to be able to recognize the days of the moon-count, and the katun-bearer, and the prophecies of the gods above."

With their spiritual and intellectual leaders gone, the people had no one on whom they could rely for advice and guidance. In the despair and bewilderment which overwhelmed them, there came the final step in their degradation, the resort to devil-worship. This may have been a heritage from the Itza, the "sons of darkness," for we are told that in former days the magic of the katun-count had rendered the devils powerless:

Page 18: "The Thirteen gods hear the words of the devils, seven of them. For there are seven devils called *Satai,* and they are from the foundation of the heavens. Formerly they were the bearers of messages. At the time the heavens were established, there were seven inhabitants who caused discord. That was because foreigners came in great numbers in ancient times." Does this refer to the Itza or to the Spanish invasion? "But the government of the devils came to an end in ancient times, after we began counting within the folds of the days." [217]

And so, when the terrifying white foreigners arrived, it seemed as if the devils had regained the ascendancy. Page 22: "The seven devils (*vuc satai*) descend, bringing a condition of ruin, even utter darkness. But when they slit our throats and string us up by the neck, they are not reckoning with Hunac Sip and the prophecy of Ah Bobat, the Searchers. So be it."

The despair of the Priest of the Jaguar resounds in the lament

---

[217] See footnote 106.

on page 30: "The omens of the gods must go! The omens of Kavil must go, and those of the Sky-serpent, of Canhel the Sky-serpent, alas! Little by little began the offering of prayers to the Devil. . . . When you descend to covetousness and avarice and the invocation of the Devil, then you reach the lowest abyss of falsifying the words of Hunab Ku above."

The final haunting fear that the calendar would be destroyed and the very foundation of the revered teaching be taken from them seemed likely to be realized, as one by one the priests and leaders of the tribe were executed. According to their belief, as long as the katun-count continued to revolve in its customary cycles, the time must come when they would throw off the Spanish yoke. With the loss of the katun-count, the road would lie wide open for the complete annihilation of an ancient and noble people.

Page 32: "With regard to the internal affairs of the country, the omens appear black, indeed, *because of the entanglement of the katun.*" But hope was not yet extinguished. "The lords will take counsel together. They will cut the claws of those whom they will hang up in a row, when they scratch the bowed backs of the wolf and the foxes. They will burn fiercely on the altars. Then there will be no more foxes, no more wolves. Then there shall be the great Life, the Life of the Katun, the Spirit of the Katun, and a benevolent government. There will be rejoicing in the people's welfare. . . . Then the Katun, the flower of the Tree of Life, shall be established. . . . Malevolence shall be consumed. Secrecy shall be consumed. In the mouth of the sea are the words God in Heaven. The Perfect One will guard our backs. The Perfect One will guard our presence."

On the basis of a Katun 5 Ahau starting in 1594, the katun prophecies of the Book of Chilam Balam of Tizimin carry through 1791, but a change occurred in 1752 which can hardly be understood except on the hypothesis that the katun count had been broken. The change involved two innovations: *the katuns after 1752 contained 24 years instead of twenty tuns, and they were named for their beginning instead of for their ending days.*

The ancient manuscript ends on page 33. Then comes a curious statement which seems to indicate that the katun-count had become of secondary importance, the emphasis now being placed on the year-count: "Now, however, Ahau is subservient to the year-bearer of the south, 3 Cauac on the first of Pop, the year being 1752. The god Four is submerged on that very day, 4 Ahau." The author of this section apparently realized that the year-bearer was 3 Cauac, and that a katun-day 4 Ahau was due to fall during the year 1752. Knowing furthermore that 4 Ahau follows 3 Cauac in the tzolkin, he apparently jumped to the conclusion that a katun began on 4 Ahau 2 Pop. Since the New Year ceremonies began on 3 Cauac 1 Pop and lasted several days, the katun ritual on 4 Ahau 2 Pop would be "submerged" in the new year observances and would thus seem to be of secondary significance.

A comparison of the dates of the "old" and "new" katuns may be of interest, especially in relation to the violent uprising timed for 1849:

Year	Old Count	New Count
1752	4 Ahau ends	4 Ahau begins
1772	2 Ahau ends	
1776		2 Ahau begins
1792	13 Ahau ends	
1800		13 Ahau begins
1812	11 Ahau ends	
1824		11 Ahau begins
1832	9 Ahau ends	
1848		9 Ahau begins

The passage describing the advent of Katun 4 Ahau continues: "So it is with the katun. When finally they read the auguries of the katun, they explain to the people how it first originated. . . . And when they count, they are deceived as to the year-bearer of the teaching, like and old wound breaking out afresh, when they teach the three counts of the deceptive katun." It seems clear that by 1752 the Long Count and the month-days were lost and almost forgotten, and the position of the Maya year-bearer in the Christian year was unknown

A thin camouflage of Christianity overlies this part of the book; but there are frequent outbursts of the rebellious spirit which was to blaze forth in the rebellion of 1849. Underneath their submissive and resigned hopelessness, the Maya were secretly uniting against their oppressors, stirred by the memories kept alive in the Books of Chilam Balam, with their oft-repeated predictions of the eventual return of freedom and prosperity to the land of Yucatan.

At the end of the discussion of the katun on page 33 is interpolated the significant statement (page 34): "As each one of us pauses, those of us who have not forgotten [the ancient teachings], *they* are suspicious of our being together. Similarly on page 36: "In recompensing the white men, the bearded men, throughout their days the people will become united, likewise. So speaks the priest Chilam. The day will come when our elder brothers will themselves smooth away the obstacles." These statements fall within the section devoted to Katun 2 Ahau, the "united for a cause katun," which ran from 1776 to 1800 in the new and spurious katun-count.

The burning sense of injustice and resentment against the Spaniards burst out on page 36: "You shall again retain your food in your stomachs. You shall wear your accustomed clothing. . . . Shall we root up the small palms to make hats for them? You shall talk to me and I will talk to you. . . . All this wrangling over the buying and selling of merchandise!

"And in the season of the opening of flowers, when we yearn for the flowers and lie down on the flowers, no one of us is allowed to rest, while we weep for 11 Ahau. *The purpose of our uniting for a cause will unfold during Katun 11 Ahau.*"

In the ancient reckoning the long-awaited Katun 11 Ahau should have run from 1792 to 1811; *but if the katun were named for its opening day, it would* have been current between 1811 and 1831. In the spurious 24-year katun count, however, with the period named for the opening day, Katun 11 Ahau ran from 1812 to 1848. It was truly, therefore, a "uniting for a cause" katun, a period of secret preparation for the rebellion of 1849 which came within an infinitesimal margin of complete success. We quote from *The Temple of the Warriors:*[218]

---

[218] Morris, E.H. 1931: 26-27.

"In 1849 came the war of the castes. The Indian population rose against those who had tightened the yoke of slavery to the point of strangulation, and with the fury of the desperate they cut off one by one the towns and plantations, butchered the occupants and moved on to bathe again and again their racial wounds with the blood of their oppressors. . . . Finally Merida was surrounded by the horde that had laid waste the whole peninsula, stubbornly and hopelessly besieged. Day by day those who had found shelter within its gates fought valiantly to delay the doom that seemed as certain as the rising of the sun. It was near the end of the dry season, and the heat and drouth were almost insupportable. Then one night the sky turned black at sundown and like a gray curtain the cooling torrent fell. By morning the entire landscape was washed clean. Gone were the besiegers like the dust from the leaves of the plants. For centuries unnumbered the first rain of the season had been the call to begin the planting of the fields, a call to obey which had become an instinct against which reason could have no sway. The Corn God had spoken with the voice of the rain to betray the Maya army to its last great defeat."

The ancient Priest of the Jaguar would undoubtedly attribute the failure of the uprising on the very eve of its triumphant completion to the introduction of a fallacious katun-count.

How and where did the concept of a 24-year katun originate? Why does the author call it *lei katunob,* "spurious or deceptive katuns" on page 33? *Le* may also mean "to catch in a noose, to entrap," but the literal meaning is "to stretch" as a rope. Hence the phrase could also be read "the expanded katun."

A simple explanation for the construction of the new system may be deduced by Goodman's Tables.[219] By adopting a katun of exactly 24 Maya years, one can form a table in which the correct sequence of Ahau days is obtained by having the katuns always start in a Cauac year, as follows:

---

[219] Goodman, J.T. 1897. The Archaic Maya Calendar.

table of spurious or stretched Katuns

Year No.	Year-bearer	Day on which Katun began
4	6 Cauac 1 Pop	7 Ahau 2 Pop
28	4 Cauac 1 Pop	5 Ahau 2 Pop
52	2 Cauac 1 Pop	3 Ahau 2 Pop
24	13 Cauac 1 Pop	1 Ahau 2 Pop
48	11 Cauac 1 Pop	12 Ahau 2 Pop and so on.

The inference seems to be inescapable that the ancient reckoning of 7200-day katuns had been forgotten. The 18th century Maya who wished to reconstruct the katun-count knew the sequence of Ahau days, i.e., that each successive katun-ending day had a numerical coefficient *two less* than that of the previous katun. By experimenting he discovered that this result could be produced by assuming a katun of exactly 24 years. But he found that the ancient manuscripts listed only 20 "years" (actually they are *tuns* of 360 days). To explain this apparent discrepancy he drew upon his knowledge of the *year-count* and by analogy he arrived at two erroneous conclusions: (1) that the last four years of the katuns were "nameless," therefore not mentioned in the chronicles; and (2) that the katun was named, like the year, for its beginning day.

La Farge [220] has proved that there still exists in Central America an *intertribal tzolkin* agreeing with the Mexican date: 8 Ehecatl 9 Quecholli = November 8, 1519. It is entirely reasonable to suppose that in their reconstruction of the lost calendar the 18th century Maya adopted the Mexican tzolkin-days as their own at the time when the new katun-count went into effect.

That the author of page 33 and following of the Tizimin manuscript did not believe in either the new year-bearer or the new katun seems clear from the following statement (page 33):

"And when they count, they are deceived as to the year-bearers of the teaching, *like an old wound breaking out afresh,* when they teach the three counts of the deceptive katun."

---

[220] La Farge, Oliver: Maya Research II, No. 1. 1934 pp. 110-112.

CHAPTER THREE

Gods and the Calendar

SUN AND MOON STILL GOVERN CHURCH CALENDARS ALMOST
universally even in modern times. In Christian sects, for example,
the pattern of those festivals which depend upon the position of
Easter Sunday derives from the first full moon after the sun crosses
the equator on its way north in the spring, whereas Christmas is a
reminder of the ancient and time-honored rites associated with the
lowest altitude of the sun and the shortest days of the year around
the winter solstice.

The Maya were no exception to the general rule. On the con-
trary it may be said that the "cult of the calendar" reached its highest development in the Maya religion.

In general, primitive calendars began by reckoning the days of
the moon, as the moon's phases provide obvious advantages for
counts up to 30 days. The approximately 28 days of visibility of the
four phases suggested a division of the lunation into four seven-
day weeks, from the first appearance of the waxing crescent in the
west after sundown, to the last glimpse of the waning crescent in
the eastern sky at dawn. Although the ancient Egyptians employed
a ten-day division of the month, they worshiped the Moon-god as
the creator of numbers, counting, the alphabet, the art of writing,
literature and, finally, wisdom.

The sun completes his round of the seasons in approximately
365 days; and it was the incommensurability between the 29.53-day
lunation and the 365.24-day year which impelled our remote ancestors to try to make more accurate measures of the astronomical

137

constants in order to devise a more exact calendar, so that they might be forewarned of the approach of the natural phenomena produced by the changes of season, and possibly avert the rigors attendant upon them by appropriate ceremonies.

Days must be named or numbered in order to distinguish them from one another. The people of Mesopotamia chose to name seven days. The Maya calendar, being more formal, abstract, and aesthetically satisfactory than those of other ancient peoples, is based on the interplay of thirteen numbers and twenty day-names, with correspondences among the higher periods. In one respect only it resembled the Egyptian calendar: each considered the year to be composed of 360 + 5 days. In the Egyptian, the 360 days were divided into twelve 30's, whereas in the Maya calendar the division was into eighteen 20's. The Roman time-count modified the Egyptian calendar by distributing the odd five days among alternate months, and it is in this form with slight subsequent alterations that the calendar has come down to modern times.

Attempts have been made to account for the Maya twenty-day period by some natural phenomenon such as the days of the moon's visibility in the night sky from dusk to midnight, i.e., from the first crescent to the last quarter. Speculation as to a natural basis for the choice seems futile and inconclusive. Very likely, an esoteric mathematics beyond reach of present-day investigation forms the basic concept of the Maya calendar, in the form known to us. By adopting a formal count, the Maya ended the impossible struggle to reconcile the motions of the sun and moon with any kind of system. They very sensibly chose to maintain records of the sun's apparent revolution and the moon's irregular phases independently of the Long Count of days used in their chronology.

The Tizimin chronicle attributes to Yaxum, legendary progenitor of the tribe, the important achievement of establishing the calendar on an independent basis:

Page 12: "Yaxum our forefather cast aside the divisions of the katun pertaining to the moon. He was the first to make an arch. He was the first to carry an idol on his back. He was the first to concoct powerful drugs. And Ah Pilte, He-who-opens-the-eyes, appeared and accepted his offerings. Would that he might return from the west, uniting with us in commiseration over our present unhappy plight!" Certainly to some early intellectual leader must be attributed the erudite achievement of raising the calendar above the eternal contest of the sun and moon over the possession of the days and giving it the perfected form which it possessed in the time of recorded history. It was the calendar in fact which made recorded history possible.

With its interaction between the numbers 13 and 20, carried from the lowest level, the tzolkin, into the higher periods of katuns, baktuns, pictuns and so on (7200, 144,000, and 2,800,000 days, respectively) the calendar also constituted the framework of the Maya religion and one cannot be understood apart from the other.

On the terrestrial side, the time-periods were inextricably interwoven with the agricultural groundwork of Maya economics, involving, as it did, the necessity for knowing the correct times for preparing the soil, for planting and harvesting the various grains and vegetables, for bending the cornstalks over, for burning the milpas, for cutting honey from the hive, for hunting, trapping and fishing, for renovating the houses and their furnishings against the violence of the rainy season, and for all the other activities of normal life in Central America, as well as for the need of averting or ameliorating the effects of the elements over which they had no control and of which they lived in constant terror. Such enemies were drought and flood, hurricanes, epidemics, the burning of the forests by lightning, earthquakes and plagues of insects, and they called for frequent invocation and propitiation of the gods by ceremonial magic and sacrifices to insure against the ever-threatening devastation and annihilation.

On the celestial side, the calendar led to observations of the sky to determine the motions of sun and moon and presumably of planets, comets and meteors, the aspects of the constellations, as well as the various types of weather indicators and auguries. Closely associated with the esoteric side of the calendar was the reading of the great and small prophecies concerning the course of future events, and the casting of lots to find the propitious days for every form of activity.

It must be inferred that a rather formidable hierarchy of priests was required to regulate and interpret the calendar and advise and order the lives of the Maya people. The priests who had charge of the counting of the days were called Ah Pop and Ah Zam, which can be rendered "he who represents authority (pop)" and "he who works wonders (zam)." Pop and Zam were the calendar gods, and the Tizimin manuscript sometimes writes the titles of the priests as Ah Tem Pop and Ah Tem Zam, "he of the altar of Pop" and "he of the altar of Zam." There seem to have been at least two of each of these, and there is one reference to "nine Zams."

The highest order of priesthood was probably the *Chilam Balam*, the priests or prophets of the Jaguar-god. There were several of these at any given time. Still another order was *ah bobat*, "the searchers," or "the prophets," whose duty it is to determine the road of the future; also *ah miscit*, "the sweepers."

The common term for Maya priest was *ah kin*, usually accompanied by the name of a person, as Ah Kin Napuctun, Ah Kin Hun Uitzil Chac, Ah Kin Chelyaxnak who were apparently *chilam balam*. It is possible that *ah kin, ah bobat* and *ah chilam* may all be synonyms rather than separate orders of priests. A section beginning on page 17 is given the title *u tzol tzan ah kinob*, "The Interpretation of the Priests." The subtitle contains three distinct words for priests or prophets in a single line: *u bobat tzan noh ah kinob ah miatzob profeta;* literally "their prophet words great the priests their wisdom the prophets," or "the great prophetic words of the priests, the wisdom of the prophets." The casual use of the Spanish *profeta* is interesting in view of the fact that the passage appears to have been written as early as 1523, eight years after the beginning of Katun 13 Ahau;

"The great prophetic words of the priests; the wisdom of the prophets: Hear ye their commandments! So let it be done! The prophet of the Jaguar, Chilam Balam, shall be Ah Xupan Nauat during Katun 13 Ahau. Ah Xupan is his name. In the eighth year of

Katun 13 Ahau, the priests proclaim to their listeners their judgments concerning the arrival of the foreign visitors." Such judgments could have been based on the expeditions of Valdivia in 1511, Cordoba 1517, Montejo and Grijalva, 1518, and of Cortes in 1519. The passage was probably written in hieroglyphs and was transcribed in script in the early 17th century.

The Maya word for the Spanish friars was *yum*, "father," according to the Tizimin manuscript.

A number of the functions and duties of the Maya priests are listed below:

to impersonate and invoke the deity
to offer food and drink to the idols
to effect the drawing of the pebbles of the days and regulate the calendar
to read weather and other omens in the clouds
to study the night sky and interpret the appearances of the celestial bodies
to determine the lucky and unlucky days for various mundane activities by the casting of lots
to perform the numerous rituals of the cup, the plate, etc.
to work miracles
to concoct medicinal herbs into ceremonial drinks
to predict the future
to announce the times for various agricultural and other activities
to insure adequate rainfall
to avert or bring to a timely end famine, drought, epidemics, plagues of ants and locusts, earthquakes
to distribute food to the hungry in time of need
to cut the honey from the hives
to determine the compensations to be placed on the crossroad altars
to read from the sacred scriptures the future road of the katun
to design and supervise the carving of stelae, the manufacture of wood and clay idols, and the construction of temples
to construct tables of eclipses and heliacal risings of planets such as are found in the Dresden Codex

The following citations from the Tizimin manuscript vividly illustrate many of these varied activities:

Page 4: "Then the priests performed seven enchantments with the cup, affirming the magic of the mat and interpreting it to the people. Since it was the month of Pop, the priests effected the exchange of years, and there was dancing among you as well as contests of courage. Then prayers were offered to remind the Seventeen [gods] of their responsibility."

Page 5: "The day of 6 Ix fell, and they totaled up the pebbles of the days, after they had divested themselves of breeches and other garments, before the drawing of the days." Extreme care was taken to prevent a pebble from being lost in a fold of clothing in case it was accidentally dropped. "At that time Ahaucan the Rattlesnake (a constellation) was lifted high on the back of the Leopard, Chacbolai. They sum up the days in order to determine how much recompense is due to the altar of Pop and to the altar of Zam, when they come to the crossroads to devour the offering, stretching out their arms for it."

Page 7: "Eleven Cauac came on the first day of Pop in the eleventh tun. Our two priests of Pop and our two priests of Zam set the drinking-vessels firmly beside the idols. The people recompense the idol of the Bacab, Ah Cantzicnal, who is seated upon the stone of the eleventh tun of the Katun. Then Ah Cantzicnal made his presence known to us. . . . Moreover Ah Tem Pop and Ah Tem Zam interpreted the future road of the katun, after removing their breeches and other clothing in the presence of heaven and the lords. They read the auguries by the paths of Chacbolai the Leopard and Bolai Can the Fierce Serpent and Chacbolai Ul." These are undoubtedly names of constellations.

Page 11: "It is customary for the priests, the Chilam, Ah Kin Napuctun and Ah Kin Hun Uitzil Chac, to read from the teachings of the six eternal books at Uxmal." This may be a reference to the inscriptions on stone. "This is the revelation of the hieroglyphic writings of the prophecies. And Ah Kin Chel Yaxnak is he who looks into them to see by what road guilt will be brought home to us. This is the expectation according to the Jaguar Priest, the Chilam

Balam, coming from Hunab Ku the One God and from the Thirteen gods. . . . The people feel forsaken when the lords stir up discord and the auguries fail. When good rulers come, will not the people again place reliance on the cup and the vestments, even in times of the most rigorous discipline? Those who whistle in derision shall paint the wooden idols . . . on 11 Ahau, when Balam and Pop shall make a recompense to the wooden idols. The idols would wither away in close confinement because of the rainy weather."

Page 13: "Eight Muluc came on the first day of Pop and we lodged the square-cornered stone in its place, we who are called Ah Kauil Chel, Ah Napuctun and Ah Xupan Nauat, priests and brave and true men, and Hun Uitzil Chac, the Tutul Xiu of Uxmal."

Page 14: "Here in our houses, however, such injuries will be done that the priests will look at the faces of the people to see if they really desire to listen to their speeches. For the people grieve deeply for their homes and their property. Consequently they interrupt with lamentations over the loss of all their possessions, whenever the priests attempt to speak with confidence about the future. Then they make such a clamor that, when the priests of our company who are trying to restore faith in the prophecies, go about the country teaching out of their own knowledge, the people close their ears. They do not cooperate, although they should trust in the important teachings of our forefathers, according to their words.

"When there are enemies in the land, and the prophet Chilam begins to teach out of his own knowledge concerning the cup of the first katun and the cup of the dishonorable katun, and the footsteps of the Seven Subjugated Ones and about the baseness, not of our fathers, but of the descendants of Yaxum, then nobody pays any attention to him. On that day they must choose representatives from among their own number when the priests arrive, lest there be no one to listen to them after they have come."

Page 16: "What good can it do to wail childishly in loud voices on account of these men who are spreading everywhere? Where is your faith? Daily at noon I press my hands on the head of the well. After sprinkling the sacred objects of our religion and the holy products of the sea, I look upward at the divine face of the heavens.

Standing on the stone pavement at the mouth of the well, I look for the guide-posts on the face of the sky, to see whither they navigate. No man speaks to me without a grievance. *My part is to interpret to you. Your part, later, as well as my own, is to be born again.* . . .

"Even if they publish seven sacred books our priests will read them. The priests Ah Xupan, Ah Kin Chel and Napuctun, will make themselves known in three scrolls. Gradually the priests of the Jaguar will compose seven holy books for our altars, in which we will explain the manner of offering invocations, so that finally the katun will arrive as in ancient times with no diminution in the power of the prophecies."

Page 17: "The prophecy of Yabun Chan: In former times, the priests of this country were allowed to speak freely. Yes. Our fathers expected divine manifestations. And the priests were the ones who cut the honey from the hive in olden times. You will grant that they understood the good omens of abundance when they sought for them in the fire."

Page 18: "Sufficient unto themselves are my words, for I am Chilam Balam, the Jaguar Priest. I repeat my words of divine truth: I say that the divisions of the earth shall all be one. . . . Pay attention, all of you! Your sins have become heavy burdens. It is almost time for Lord 1 Ahau to come down from above: 1 Ahau in the heavens, 1 Ahau in the earth, according to the ancient prophecies. . . .

"Xupan Nauat, as he is called, is he who will explain the order of the world. Ah Kin Chel, Nahau Pech, Napuctun, the war-captain Balam, and the prophet Chilam Balam—these are the priests who know the future, and the order of the world and of the katuns."

Page 19: "These are the words spoken by the Thirteen gods through their prophet, Ah Kin Chilam, who carries in his pouch the lottery of life. A little more, a little less—and what are your chances? He who impersonates the god casts lots to determine the final outcome of the country's affairs such as: when the needs of the land shall be supplied; when there shall be many ceremonies to gaze upon; the time of abundance all through the mountains; the time when malevolent men in the land shall be apprehended; the times of confused agitation; the times for unrolling the scrolls of the many genealogical trees of our lineage; the times for standing firm; the times for attaching three seals to the Tree of Life; the times for completing the three bundles and distributing the excess; the time when whispering between the teeth shall be brought to an end; the time for delving into the drawing of the days; and the times for scattering underneath the trees and under the branches," in famine.

The number of these quotations could be greatly extended, but two more should suffice. The first explains the advisory functions of the priesthood in some detail; the second lists the various offices at the time of katun-ending celebrations.

Page 23: "The women singers must chant invocations to Yaxal Chuen, the First-born Chuen, for the protection of the people. Great numbers were assembled and they all sang together to the gods. There was he who advises about new moons; and he who advises about attaining man's estate; and he who advises about buying and selling; and he who advises about the prime of life; and he who advises on the problem of marriageable daughters." It should be remarked that the Tizimin manuscript does not expressly state that these advisers belonged to the priesthood.

Page 26: "Ten will interpret the opening of the sealed katun of 10 Ahau. One looks at the face of Citbolon or at the face of the sky of Citbolon, one at the sun, one at the forests, one at the trees, to determine what kind of remedy the heavens will provide, to be written down in the Book of the Katun for future years: 'The business of life will be difficult, and retaining the breath of life full of sorrow.'"

the Maya Pantheon

The deities of the Maya pantheon were legion. There were gods of the numbers one to thirteen, usually grouped under the title "The Thirteen." There were the nine Wisemen, the Bolon Tzacab, probably identical with J. E. Thompson's "Lords of the Night." There were the lords of the days 1 Ahau to 13 Ahau, and probably of all the other 247 days of the tzolkin, certainly of those which served as year-bearers. There were the four Bacabs who stretched out the earth and planted *imix*-trees at the cardinal points, and the four Musencabs who measured the earth by their paces. There were the various Chacs, associated with the wind and rain, but these do not figure prominently in the Tizimin chronicle with the exception of Chacbolai and Chacxibchac. There was Kinich Ahau, the marvelous Kinich, the Sun-god. There was Ku Mitnal, god of the underworld, and various gods and goddesses of the crafts and occupations, the gods of the katuns and other time periods, and the lesser spirits of the mountain and forest. There were gods of inanimate objects, such as the spirit of the great katun-stone, and even deities of abstract qualities, among whom Mother Terror, Mother Despair, and Mother of Lies are shining examples.

Supreme over this vast array the Maya recognized the "One God," Hunab Ku, nameless, remote, formless. He was invoked in times of crisis, but usually, among the people whose trials and sufferings are recorded in the Timizin manuscript, worship was directed toward the lesser deities, the Bacabs, the Thirteen, the Nine, the Eight, or the Seventeen, as they are often alluded to in the chronicle.

Some of the names are undoubtedly duplications. For example, Kinich the Sun-face, Kinich Chan, Ah Chaante the Wonderful, and Kinich Kakmo which Roys interprets as "Kinich the Fire-macaw, are probably all appellations of the Sun-god, whom the Maya recognized as the source of life. Page 9: "O Sun, with thy eagle's eye, look down upon our pleading before thy throne! O rolling sun, our Deliverer, and the Ripener of our Fruit!"

Kukulcan, the dominant god of the Itza, is mentioned several times in the Book of Tizimin but invariably as a god of the Itza. The Xiu were not above addressing a petition to him, however, particularly when they begged him to remove the Itza far, far away, because they were tired of having to support them. This prayer was offered to Kukulcan in Katun 8 Ahau, because that was the katun during which the Itza first settled in Yucatan, and it was therefore considered to be an appropriate time for them to move on.

The Maya priests were the representatives and impersonators of the gods. Ah Kin Pop and Ah Kin Zam who presided over the calendar, were the vicegerents of Pop and Zam above. The Chilam

Balam were the agents of the Jaguar-god, but they summoned deities of all varieties to attend their ceremonies.

Landa describes the four Bacabs who governed the four types of year and were stationed at the four points of the compass. The Tizimin refers to them as a group, but only Cantzicnal, ruler of the *Cauac* years, is mentioned by name. Landa characterizes Cantzicnal as the most benevolent of the Bacabs, "best and greatest of the Bacabs," but assigns to him the *Muluc* years.

The following list contains the names of deities which are found in the Book of Chilam Balam of Tizimin, together with the numbers of the pages on which they are mentioned. As some names are given both with and without the prefix *Ah* or *Ix*, it seems advisable to ignore these particles in determining the alphabetical position of the names.

Maya Gods listed in the Book of Chilam Balam of Tizimin

	Name of Deity	Page
1.	Ahaucan the Rattlesnake, constellation god	3, 5
2.	Ahau, with numbers 1 to 13	3, 4, 12, 20, 22
3.	Bacabs in general	12, 21, 26, 27
4.	Bacab Cantzicnal	7, 10
5.	The Bacab of the North	27
6.	Balam the Jaguar	14, 19, 23, 26, 30, 46
7.	Bolai-can, Fierce Serpent, constellation god	7
8.	Ah Bolon Kanan, He-of-the-nine-gifts	1
9.	Bolon, the Nine, probably identical with 10	15, 20, 22
10.	Bolon Tzacab, Nine Wisemen (or "God of 9 generations")	21
11.	Ah Bolon Yocte, He-of-the-nine-paths	1
12.	Canhel, the Sky-serpent	20, 30
13.	Ah Cantzicnal, see Bacab	
14.	Ah Chaante. See also Kinich Chaante	1
15.	Ah Chac, the four rain-gods	4
16.	Chacbolai the Leopard, constellation god	5, 7, 22
17.	Chacbolai Ul, constellation god	7
18.	Ix Chac, wife of a Chac?	12
19.	Chac Vayab the Bat. See also Zotzil	21

[221] These are names of Yaxal Chuen.

54.	Vaxac, the Eight	12
55.	Ah Vuc, Lord Seven	2
56.	Ah Vuc Chapat, "the Seven-headed Serpent"	1, 2, 11, 24
57.	Ah Vuc Yol Sip	3, 4, 11, 30
58.	Vuclahun, "the Seventeen"	4
59.	Yax Ah Cocaimut, "Green Firefly Herald" (a star?)	28
60.	Yaxal Chuen, First-born Chuen	23, 31
61.	Yaxbolai, constellation god	22
62.	Yaxum, the Ancestor	1, 12, 14
63.	Zam, a Calendar god	5, 8, 24, 25, 27, 28
64.	Zotzil the bat	5, 25, 26, 27

The following passages contain significant information concerning these various deities:

1. Page 3. "They say it will rain when Ahaucan the Rattlesnake is lifted high above the trees." I am assuming, perhaps unjustifiably, that the same name may apply both to the visible constellation in the sky and to the deity of which it is the manifestation.

1 and 16. Page 5: "At that time Ahaucan the Rattlesnake was lifted high on the back of the Leopard Chacbolai."

2 and 44. Page 20: "At the expiration of the period of the prophecy, there came the Sun of our life and whichever one of the four Musencabs it was who measured the earth by his paces. And there was the utmost astonishment when the Lords of the Days, 13 Ahau and 1 Ahau, came to the festival in spite of the fact that the enemy in our midst harassed us day and night."

3 and 64. Page 27: "They are agitated by the drums. The Bat is awakened by the drums. The four Bacabs ride to earth on the back of a green rainbow. One by one the stars fall."

4. Page 7: "The people recompense the idol of the Bacab, Ah Cantzicnal, who is seated upon the stone of the eleventh tun of the katun."

6. Page 14: "In the twelfth tun, as it is called, the Jaguar should be the head. So many ill-advised turtle-doves that pass for men!" Page 19: "At the time of the great pestilence they will worship as lord of the sky the Jaguar war-god."

7, 16 and 17.   Page 7: "They read the auguries by the paths of Chacbolai the Leopard and Bolai Can the Fierce Serpent, and Chacbolai Ul."

8 and 11.   Page 1: "We are agitated by these sharp blows. We are moved to sorrow, sending up our pleas to Ah Bolon Yocte of the Nine Paths, and to Ah Bolon Kanan, of the Nine Precious Gifts."

10.   Page 21: "Eleven Ahau was the day of the descent of the words of the Bolon Tzacab, the Nine Wisemen, and the prayers which were folded within the bundle of Katun 9, the bundle which descended on the day 4 Kan. When the bundle was completed, when it descended, the time arrived in the heart of the heavens for the second birth of the Nine. Searching for resting-places, the Nine descended in a company and were not consumed." According to Landa, Bolon Dzacab was a single god, who was worshiped in Kan year ceremonies.

12.   Page 20: "When Canhel the Serpent destroyed the cornfields and ground them into powder, then they created the new growth from the old, lest the divine vigor waste away, lest our gains crumble away." Page 21: "Once there was truth, which we drew from the Serpent in ancient times, from the clear unclouded heavens to the evil-knotted earth beneath."

12 and 37.   Page 30: "The omens of the gods must go! The omens of Kavil must go, and those of the Sky-serpent, of Canhel the Sky-serpent, alas!"

14 and 38.   Page 1:"We poured ourselves out in supplication. We entreated Ah Chaante the Wonderful, Kinich Chaan who dwells in the heavens, that he be kind." Page 9: "When we pray thus from our roots, Kinich the Sun-face, Kinich Chaante the Marvelous Kinich, will manifest himself in speech."

15.   Page 4: "Being without strength, the country would have been in grave danger in the past, had it not been for the thousands of the lineage of Ah Chac. Perhaps they will come to our aid in the future."

18 and 22.   Page 12: "In another part of the cave where they interpret the movements of the heavens and the movements of the earth, quietly went the wooden idols Ix Chac and Ix Chuah into

the well of the Cavern, into the midst of the waves, because they have the power of bestowing wonderful nocturnal visions. Such are the instructions given by the katun of sufficiency."

19. Page 21: "Chac Vayab the Bat, he it is who sucks honey from the flowers."

20 and 49. Page 26: "There are some who smooth the way, who placate and seek to calm the angry words of Katun 1 Ahau by the authority of the altar of Pop and the altar of Zam, when the words of Chacvenco and the many Sacvencos dart forth." The Motul Dictionary defines both chacvenco and sacvenco as "refined villains." They were probably mischievous nature spirits.

21. Page 22: "In response to the fervent prayer of the Lord of Uxmal, Chacxibchac came carrying animals on his back."

23. Page 26: "Ten will interpret the opening of the sealed katun of 10 Ahau. One looks at the face of Citbolon or at the face of the sky of Citbolon." Landa classifies Citbolon with the gods of medicine.

24. Page 24: "The opening of the sealed katun of 7 Ahau took place at Mayapan. Katun 7 Ahau belongs to Ek Chuuah." *Ek Chuah* is listed by Landa as a god of merchants, travelers and cacao-growers.

25. Page 30: "At the opening of the sealed Katun [of 3 Ahau] Ek Cocaimut showed himself in the presence of the lords. There was watchfulness on their faces. There was courage on their faces." In the Chumayel the name is spelled Cocahmut. *Cocay* is given the meaning "firefly" in the Motul, hence the Tizimin version might be freely translated as "Black firefly Herald," or, since *ek* also signifies "star," as "Firefly-star-herald." *Mut* is literally "news."

26, 33, and 41. Page 21: "For five days Ix Haunab, Mother Despair, Ix Huznab, Mother Terror, and Ix Kuknab, Mother of Lies, eat from the red-painted bowl, from the white-painted bowl, from the black-painted bowl and from the yellow-painted bowl. After a while they cease from smelling the *yol*-flowers and from eating them by the handful. Then they perform a rite against sterility, including the penance of blood-letting by cutting, and they sip from the hollow hearts of the *yol*-flowers and from the bellies of the *yol*-flowers. Let the flowers spring forth from the bowl!"

27.   Page 7: "The summer will be so dry that you will entreat Hunab Ku to have compassion upon you, lest the commonwealth be destroyed." Page 13: "This is the recollection of the ancient things as they descended from Hunab Ku the One god, and from the Thirteen gods, and from the One Thousand gods, as found in the words of the priests and prophets of Chilam Balam." Page 31: "There will be three breaks in the lineage, three hindrances to speech, to the speeches of the fathers in the houses of grief . . . and to the pride of the fathers, the pride of the house of the One God, Hunab Ku, when they plead with him, lamenting the Tree of Abundance to the people of Pop." Page 25: "The ancient people strove to attain perfection. In olden times they recognized the miracles performed by the heavenly Hunab Ku." Page 30: "When you descend to covetousness and avarice and the invocation of the Devil, then you reach the lowest abyss of falsifying the words of Hunab Ku above."

6, 28, 29, 30 and 60.   Page 26: "In Saclactun is held the opening of the sealed katun of 12 Ahau, the katun of Yaxal Chuen, First-born Chuen. The lords watch for the coming of Hunac the Knower, Hunac the Artist, Hunac the Enchanter. He will teach the priests the complete magic of Zam and Pop. And Balam the Jaguar will measure out the six magic formulas of government."

31.   Page 14: "In time of pestilence let them hide themselves in the forest, who have become indifferent to Pop and to the words of Hun Sip, and to the katun of Sip and the three divisions of life, and the three-fold flowery katun." Page 22: "The seven devils descend bringing a condition of ruin, even utter darkness. But when they slit our throats and string us up by the neck, they are not reckoning with Hunac Sip and the prophecy of Ah Bobat."

32.   Page 36: "The coils of Hun Yapotik restrict the bread of life; they compress the bread of life one-half." The word "coils" suggest that Hun Yapotik is a serpent-deity.

34 and 51.   Page 22: "Anciently on 8 Ahau we were the guests of our blood-relatives, the people of Itzmal, because Sip was there

as the guest of the lords. When they opened the sealed katun in earlier times during the seventeenth katun, they pleaded for the satisfaction of our needs by the holy Itzam-caan, and for his apparition as Lord of Heaven, and for the opening of heaven to our kindred, the people of Itzmal, by the god their guest, as in ancient times the sons of holy Itzmal declared it." Page 23: "Then began the experiment of Itzam-caan to effect the reformation of the King of the Canul from his wicked ways."

9, 35 and 45.   Page 20: "When they came down and ranged to and fro over the earth, the Thirteen gods and the Nine gods, they put in order that which they had created, and that which Itzam-cabain, Itzam the Earth-monster, had put in order. . . . Even when the Thirteen gods once had their beginning in ancient times, when there was rigorous discipline upon the earth and the Earth-monster tore up great trees by the roots, still the prophecies of the Katun-folds were fulfilled, even when he once threatened to shake the earth. The prophecies of the katun shall be fulfilled! And the Nine gods, when they cut the throat of Itzam-cabain and created the island out of his body, had no desire to destroy the works of his hands or his books. Nevertheless, we do not invoke him by name or burn incense to him, when the lords bind up the face of the tun at the present time."

36.   Page 17: "One [priest] goes forth as ambassador. Another awakens Itzamna Kauil in the west. The lions' whelp come, the Itza fathers. The people come. The enchanters work their magic with the precious stones." Itzamna Kauil is mentioned by Landa as one of the gods to whom sacrifice was offered at the beginning of a Kan year.

37.   Page 12: "There is the life of the katun to be considered, and it incites us to blood-letting and to our responsibilities, and it calls upon Kauil, when the day 7 Kan arrives in the avaricious katun." Page 21: "Now the wizards vie with one another in taking the shapes of the blue heron and of the humming-bird. Then flowers descended from the Source and from the folds of the Hand (Kavil), nine flowers. When the hearts of the flowers appeared, the priests placed four branches of flowers on the burning altar of

the Sun." Roys [222] states that *kauil* is an obsolete word for "food." However, since it is also written *kavil* (or *kabil*) in the Tizimin manuscript, I derive it from *kab*, "hand." For *kabil*, the Motul Dictionary gives, "one who is adept with the hands," with the further amplification "one who has a good hand for such tasks as sowing grain or setting up beehives." In the second passage here cited, the "folds of the Hand" may be a poetical allusion to the sky, from which descend food-bringing rains as from the folds of a great hand. The *sky* is undoubtedly referred to in the following lines from page 30: "The omens of the gods must go! The omens of Kavil must go, and those of the Sky-serpent, of Canhel the Sky-serpent, alas!"

39.   Page 27: "When Kinich Kakmo shall descend in majesty, then those of other lands shall descend also, when they can be set free straightway from the insolent and lawless men, and from those who look with scorn upon our ancestors and upon our noble lineage." Page 32: "When the sealed katun was opened in the presence of our guests, once more the Shield descended, and the arrows descended above Chakanputum where the Garden of Sculptured Stones stands within its walls, the fulfillment of the desire of Kinich Kakmo, at the opening of the sealed katun."

40.   Page 16: "Presently Baktun 13 shall come sailing, figuratively speaking, bringing the ornaments of which I have spoken from your Ancestors. Then God, (*ku*) will come to visit his little ones." Page 33: "If they have failed to keep the commandments of God (*ku*), but increasingly, without noise, without agitation, without writing it down, our kindred on the road of love desire with all their hearts to change back, in order to satisfy their yearning [for the ancient practices] at the times of the great festivals, may they then be preserved from all evil!"

42.   Page 12: "Thus it came to pass that at the mouth of the sea the lords made sport with much good-humored chaffing. Then for five days they all confessed their sins to Kukulcan." This passage probably refers to the Itza overlords who worshiped Kukulcan as their supreme deity. Page 22: "Then when Kukulcan, He who causes

---

[222] Roys, R. L. 1933: 165.

the flowers to open, descended they petitioned him to remove the
Itza far away, saying that when the Itza arrived without warning
and settled on our soil, they overran us. They picked the ears of
corn, and their feet trespassed against us. Lord 8 Ahau was our
guest then, also." Page 23: "He (the Lord of the Canul) ensnared
our honorable sons into revealing the secret teachings to him. After
he had learned from them the whereabouts of Kukulcan, he cut the
throats of all of them." The reference here may be to a human leader,
rather than to the god or his idol.

43.   Page 21: "The penances dear to the heart of Ku Mitnali,
God of the Underworld, did not arrive, either, when Bolon Tzacab
descended for the penance of the flowers."

44.   Page 20: "On 11 Ahau when Ah Musencab arises, they
bind up the faces of the Thirteen gods and they do not even know
the names of the deities." This passage apparently refers to the efforts of the Itza priests to imitate the religious observances and rituals of the Xiu with insufficient knowledge and understanding.
" 'Holy elder brothers!' These are the names which they invoke. Nor
do they observe their faces either, when the gods direct their feet
upon the earth. Nor do they know when they are being greatly deceived." The "rising" of Ah Musencab indicates that it may be the
name of a constellation as well as of a god.

45.   Page 19: "These are the words spoken by the Thirteen
gods through their prophet, Ah Kin Chilam, who carries in his
pouch the lottery of life." Page 20: "But when the Thirteen gods are
rightly called by name and the Nine gods, then corn descends, salt
descends, precious stones descend, trees descend. Then come the
carvers in wood and stone, and then come the treasures of the Thirteen gods, even with a great crash of drums. And their faces are
seen, even when they are covered up."

46 and 62.   Page 12: "Yaxum our Forefather cast aside the
divisions of the katun pertaining to the moon. He was the first to
make an arch. He was the first to carry an idol on his back. He was
the first to concoct powerful drugs. And Ah Pilte, He who opens
the eyes, appeared and accepted his offerings."

47 and 63.   Page 5: "They sum up the days in order to deter-

mine how much recompense is due to the altar of Ah Pop and to the altar of Ah Zam when they come to the crossroads to devour the offerings." Page 8: "Once more we listen to their orations in the Cavern, when the priests of Pop and Zam, Ah Tem Pop and Ah Tem Zam, are about to destroy themselves on account of their grievous injuries, having come to the end of desire and to the end of being subjected to violence." Page 26: "He will teach the priests the complete magic of Zam and Pop. And Balam the Jaguar shall measure out the six magic formulas of government: these involve good chiefdoms, a good aristocracy, good men, and good sons throughout the earth." According to this interesting passage Yaxal Chuen instructed the calendar priests in their calculations and ritual concerning the counting of time, whereas the Jaguar priests were instructed in the various phases of political science. Page 28: "They die, he who is of Pop and he who is of Zam. If true men cut their own throats, to the people will be left only what resembles the approach to a blank wall, a being left on the outside. Since no one ever arrives who travels by an evil road, the people weigh their words, whatever they may be, lest there be almost no end to lies."

47 and 63.   Page 28: "Three times for government they will have the authority of Zam, three times the authority of Pop. . . . The gods give us the bread of heaven in their mercy. Let there be obedience to their laws. Is not the desire to obey, is not obedience itself, the duty of the lords? Their throats will be silent when the life of abundance comes to an end, and with it esteem for one blood-relationship. And there will no longer be obedience through veneration for one western tongue in the land of Pop and Zam."

4 and 48.   Page 7: "Then Ah Cantzicnal made his presence known to us . . . and Ah Sac Tzin was manifested to us."

45 and 50.   Page 18: "The Thirteen gods hear the words of the devils, seven of them. For there are seven devils (cisin) called Satai, and they are from the foundation of the heavens. Formerly they were the bearers of messages. At the time the heavens were established, there were seven inhabitants who caused discord. That was because foreigners came in large numbers in ancient times. But the government of the devils came to an end in ancient times,

after we began counting within the folds of the days." Although *satai* bears a close resemblance to the name *Satan*, it may derive from *saat*, "loss or ruin," or be connected with *zata*, "discord."

51 and 52.   Page 6: "On the name-day of the katun the Seven Sons of Suhui Sip came down. Then there was the prophecy of Sip, the ancient Sip, who can play musical instruments on earth and whose jingles resound through the heavens." Page 22: "The priests of Sip are here, of the mighty Lord Sip. The warriors of Sip are here. All these evils shall cease when [our enemies] are overwhelmed, when they are all overthrown by the Guardians, when they are all overthrown by the Anointed ones." Page 24: "Then in company with Lord 9 Ahau descended the words of that well-known Sip, the ancient Sip, the warrior of the nobility and of days 9 and of the nine Zam in the kingdom of Ah Vuc Chapat, the Seven-headed Serpent, whose shield is the sun."

53.   Page 22: "May the drunkards be torn up by the roots! Ix Tab shall carry them dangling from her hands, even before we have tied up the face of the katun. They shall be punished in our midst."

64.   Page 5: "Then the men of Zotzil the Bat (written sozil) are strong because of the coming of the sons of the deity." Page 25: "The opening of the sealed katun of Zotzil the Bat, Katun 5 Ahau. The faces of the lords will be clear and shining." Page 27: "They are agitated by the drums. The Bat is awakened by the drums."

54.   Page 12: "Famine shall be turned aside. This shall be the witness of the Eight who ask for offerings, when the days of the katun are drawing to a close." The Eight (*vaxac*) may be the four Bacabs and the four Musencabs, or possibly the four Chacs.

55 and 56.   Page 1: "Above the twisted earth we invoke Ah Vuc Chapat the Seven-headed Serpent, asking him to carry his seven bundles as an extra burden during the next two tuns; also for the same period, the vestments." During the migration following the abandonment of Mayapan, no count of the days was possible for two tuns. Page 2: "Has this generation forgotten the emptying of the towns the entire length of the land? Then the sons of Ah Vuc, the Seven, availed themselves of the eleven penances. . . . In the

seven mouths at that time there was abundance of bread. They took heart, because Ah Vuc, Lord Seven, is powerful, Ah Vuc Chapat, the Seven-headed Serpent."

56 and 57.   Page 11: "Day and night Ah Chapat lies overhead. If we do not smear ourselves with soot in mourning for our lives, we shall lament for food because of this grievous fault, according to the words of the katun, according to that which is set forth in the hieroglyphic books of the katun. They tell whether we should go against Mayapan from the north or from the south; and when Ah Vuc Chapat shall reveal himself to us, and when little by little the vision of Ah Vuc Yol Sip himself shall be manifested to us."

57.   Page 3: "When 9 Muluc fell on the first of Pop there came the tun which is known as 5 Ahau, as it is spoken in our language. Ah Vuc Yol Sip came to the festival as was his custom. When he arrived we experienced a burning sensation, afterwards extreme cold. He caused our sons to tremble and the mothers of our sons to shake violently." Page 4: "Ah Vuc Yol Sip will take charge of the fire. In that day of deliverance from the covetous ones, from bewilderment and vexation, there will come salvation by reason of his authority and by reason of their departure." Page 30: "And you, my brothers, mourned for the casting of lots and lamented the coming of the intruders, when you learned the divisions of the road which we are to follow in the genealogical tree, when we receive the gifts of Ah Vuc Yol Sip." The name of this deity may be rendered "he of the seven generations or lineages of Sip." Zip was the name of the third month, and three important festivals were celebrated during Zip, according to Landa: on 2 Zip the fiesta of the physicians and sorcerers; on 7 Zip the feast of the hunters; and a few days later, that of the fishermen. Tozzer remarks: "Sip, according to Redfield and Villa (117-8), is a supernatural being of the Mayas today who protects the deer from the hunter. If not placated he causes the hunter to miss his shots." [223] Some authorities write the

---

[223] Tozzer 1941: 154, 155 and footnote 781.

name as Dzip. As the word dzip means "to flay," there is probably a connection between the Maya Sip and the Mexican god Xipé.

58.   Page 4: "Since it was the month of Pop, the priests effected the exchange of years, and there was dancing among you as well as contests of courage. Then prayers were offered to remind the Seventeen of their responsibility."

59.   Page 28: "At Chichen one-half the katun shall be good; one-half shall be without good. There will be the majesty of the throne of him who speaks the magic language of the stars of heaven submerged in blue water, Yax Ah Cocaimut is his name." The name may be rendered "Green-firefly-herald" and it may refer to a bright star or planet. One of the names for the planet Venus is said to have been *Xux Ek,* "Wasp Star." Landa states that Yax Cocahmut was a regent of the Muluc years. See also Ek Cocaimut.

60.   Page 23: "The women singers must chant invocations to Yaxal Chuen, the First-born Chuen, for the protection of the people." Page 31: "Twelve Ahau was the seventh katun since the new count was begun, and it arrived at Saclactun, at the opening of the sealed katun of Yaxal Chuen."

16, 21 and 61.   Page 23: "We had as our guest Yaxbolai. We had as our guests Chacbolai and Chacxibchac, three very unlucky spirits."

62.   Page 1: "Now in those days when Mayapan was captured in battle, they confronted the katun of affliction. During the migration of the remnant of the descendants, the remnant of the descendants of Yaxum, good fortune should have come to generation after generation of his sons; but instead there came all at once castigation, oppression, vigilance in the night. That was a long time ago."

47 and 63.   Page 28: "Finally a day will come when there will be no more uprooting in the land, when it has been overthrown once again. There will be no more festival days to honor the authority of Pop and the authority of the Zams." Page 4: "No longer will our priest, Ah Kin, have to conceal himself here and there in the village. For the first time, his hiding and his silent misery will be a thing of the past. We will face our father squarely once more: Ah Zam is his name, to whom is given authority for eternity."

CHAPTER FOUR

The Count of Katuns

THE TIZIMIN CHRONICLE PROVIDES MUCH NEW AND SPECIFIC information regarding the practical observances of the significant days of the katun count, thus helping to bridge the gulf between modern ways of thinking and the Maya philosophy of life. Even so, it is extremely difficult to understand the deep veneration which the Maya held for these calendar cycles and the tremendous solemnity which surrounded the ceremonies of the counting of the days. The katun count brought together religion and science, government and economics, faith in the future and bondage to the eventful past. It was thrilling drama; it was life and death.

During a period of famine and distress, the voice of Katun 12 Ahau spoke as follows, the year being 1673:

Page 31: "Twelve Ahau was the seventh katun since the new count was begun and it arrived at Saclactun. At the opening of the sealed katun of Yaxal Chuen, the faces of the lords were in mourning for the teachings of the day and the teachings of the night. *This is the burden they shoulder, to dig to the bottom of the food baskets.*

"When the power descended with great force sprinkling the faces of fierce warriors, they trembled and shuddered with fear. Immediately their hearts were grieved at the condition of affairs here on earth in the katun of perplexity, in the majesty of the katun, the lordship of the katun, the words of the katun, the food of the katun, the holiness of the katun, the march of the katun, the occupation and purpose of the katun, the great sons of the katun, the great daughters of the katun, the children of the katun, the warriors of the katun, the young men of the katun."

160

Is it not evident that the katun was something more significant than a mere period of 7200 days?

And later on page 31: "One-half the remainder of the katun will be lucky, one-half will be unlucky—six years of misfortune and six years of good fortune. When all the mourning of the eternal katun 12 Ahau has been placed on high, when the seven lineages are exalted after the custom of the country, when the sacred prophecies regarding the conditions of domestic affairs in our land have come to pass, then you will [again] receive your replies by the casting of lots. There will be a laying down of burdens. There will be a shout of joy."

Each of the thirteen katuns of the cycle had a distinct character, as was pointed out in the first chapter of the commentary, and each period was governed by a particular deity. Not all of the latter are named, but we are told that Katun 7 Ahau belonged to Ek Chuuah, Katun 5 Ahau to Zotzil the Bat, Katun 12 Ahau to Yaxal Chuen and Katun 6 Ahau to Kinich Kakmo.

We may be sure that every precaution was taken in counting the pebbles of the days to avoid error or confusion. Page 29 sheds a little light on the method: "On 9 Ahau (1575), we put the katun in order when we counted in four different ways the established katun."

A simple method of preserving a record of the passing days would be to have four receptacles. In the first, a pebble would be placed each day. When these totaled 20, a larger or differently colored stone would be placed in the second receptacle. Then the process would be repeated, a new pebble being inserted in the second container every twenty days, until after the expiration of 360 days, the second receptacle would contain 18 pebbles. These would then be removed and a still larger stone or one of a third color would be placed in a third pouch. Thus the first receptacle would contain the kins or days, the second the uinals of 20 days each, and the third would hold the tuns of 360 days. When twenty such 360 day periods had elapsed, the katun would be complete, and this event would be indicated by inserting a single large stone in the fourth container. The progress of the days, uinals and tuns could be ascertained at any time by counting the stones of each color which still remained outside the four receptacles, providing they were kept in exact numbers in suitable repositories.

The difficulty with this method is that there would be only the twenty tun-stones to count at the end of the katun. From the descriptions in the Tizimin manuscript, it is clear that a much more elaborate and impressive method of counting was used on the last day of the katun. The record was made by at least four priests, two representing Pop and two representing Zam, the gods of the calendar. The count was made in the presence of all the people, after the priests had removed all their clothing in order to prevent even the suspicion that a pebble had been lost in the folds. The pebbles were passed from hand to hand in plain view of the assemblage, and not a sound was heard except the voices of the naked priests, as they named the successive days of the katun, pebble by pebble.

Page 30: "Now the priests begin the customary drawing of the katun-days. Now they begin to name one at a time in their hands the great heap of small stones, passing them from hand to hand." This clearly indicates that all 7200 pebbles were counted at a katun drawing, each one being given the name of the day it represented. These solemn ceremonies which included also the taking of the auguries from the sky and the reading of the prophecies from the Books of the Katun, as well as various other rituals, must have consumed many hours. Perhaps they began at sunset and lasted until the sun rose above the morning horizon.

Page 12 describes the observance of the 19th tun of Katun 5 Ahau, in 1613, the year-bearer being 7 Kan. "Good and virtuous shall be 7 Kan and a day of great rejoicing. The people assemble to hear Ah Pop and Ah Zam interpret the path of the katun, after they have concocted the cup of honey and water, on account of our afflictions during this katun. Famine shall be turned aside. This shall be the witness of the Eight who ask for offerings, when the days of the katun are drawing to a close. Thus they loudly declare the path by which it shall come in the heavens, as they divide the honey among themselves.

"Then the aspect of the sustaining heavens changes, with the apparition of the Sun in the eastern sky, the Ruler of the Kingdom. The people draw together to contemplate his majesty. When the bundle of the katun shall be completely filled, they will tie it up. . . . The people must rely upon Zam. The people must rely upon Pop."

The completion of Katun 5 Ahau and the inauguration of 3 Ahau are described on page 13: "From the land of Mayapan they came to see the taking of the plate of Lord 3 Ahau, in the hope that they might thus perhaps observe the engraving of the words upon the stone and see the drenching rain, when in all honesty and integrity I counted the pebbles of the days from the pouch of the katun as whole-heartedly as when I first counted the katun here in Bakhalal."

There are many references in the Tizimin manuscript to the folds, *vuz*, of the katun and the expression puzzled me very much when I tried to apply it to the receptacles in which the katun pebbles were kept.

Page 13: "Thirteen Oc should be the day for measuring the katun, and 4 Cauac should be the day *for taking a turn in the folds of the katun*. These are the days which Pop and Zam declare." The meaning of the day-sign Oc is "a foot," or "to measure by feet or paces." Note that the *tun* is thought of as completed on *cauac*, indicating that the following day, *Ahau*, is looked upon as the day on which the *new tun began,* by analogy with the year-bearer.

Page 20: "Even when the Thirteen gods once had their beginning in ancient times, when there was rigorous discipline upon the earth and the Earth-monster tore up great trees by the roots, *still the prophecies of the katun-folds were fulfilled*."

Page 21: "Eleven Ahau was the day of the descent of the words of the nine Wise Men and the prayers *which were folded* within the bundle of Katun 9, the bundle which descended on the day 4 Kan."

It was not until I realized that the word *folds* must apply to the pages of the Book of the Katun from which the prophecies were read year by year, that these passages became clear. "Taking a turn in the folds of the katun" became equivalent to turning a page of the *fan-folded book.*

The oft-mentioned "katun-day" was the tzolkin-day of the same name as the katun and it occurred every 260 days. It received especial remark when it was likewise a tun-beginning day. The recurring name-day of the katun and the annual year-bearer were observed with appropriate ceremonies. The following examples are taken from the early pages of the manuscript during the regency of a certain Katun 5 Ahau:

Page 6: "Five Ahau shall be the day of the apportionment of food at your wells."

Page 3: "When 10 Ix came on the first of Pop, at the time when the ruler of the katun, Lord 5 Ahau, descended along the celestial road, we smelled the fragrance of heaven. From the beginning, the ruler interprets his government to the people and declares it to the people, and prepares the people for the march." This was written during one of the periods when the tribe wandered homeless through forest and mountains.

Again in the 13th tun when 13 Muluc was the year-bearer we read on page 8: "On the katun's day, on 5 Ahau, a great mound of cayman meat will appear, because of the cup into which the lords draw their blood with the flint knife of the katun."

Several of the rituals associated with the calendar ceremonies are alluded to in the following passages:

Page 7: "In the twelfth tun when the day 12 Kan arrived on the first day of Pop, there was a folding up of the days and the speeches of the festival and the interpretation of the prophecies . . . and the fulfillment of the true sayings to the sons of the day and the sons of the night, which in due time shall take place on earth, shall take place in the heavens."

Earlier on page 7: "Eleven Cauac came on the first day of Pop in the eleventh tun. Our two priests of Pop and our two priests of Zam set the drinking vessels firmly beside the idols. The people recompense the idol of the Bacab, Ah Cantzicnal, who is seated upon the stone of the eleventh tun of the katun. Then Ah Cantzicnal makes his presence known to us. . . . On the day of the katun, when Cantzicnal took us under his protection, the people performed the figures of the dance known as Ix Toloch. At the time of the magic ceremonies of the aforementioned katun, when the eleven penances had come to an end, the other rituals were then presented and the other heavens of the Moon were honored by appropriate dances to the gods on high, on whatever days should prove to be fortunate, according to the teaching. Moreover, Ah Tem Pop and Ah Tem Zam interpreted the future road of the katun, after removing their breeches and other clothing in the presence of heaven and of the lords. They read the auguries by the paths of Chacbolai the Leopard and Bolai-can the Fierce Serpent and Chacbolai Ul." These were probably constellations.

When famine followed drought and the food situation became acute, the Itza lords insisted upon an offering of human sacrifices to the gods. Page 11: "When Lord 5 Ix, the bearer of the days, arrives in the eighteenth tun near the end of the katun, and the day 5 Ahau comes carrying his burden, then the war-captives with collars about their necks and in great distress, are led to the stone of life. The drums set up a loud clamor. Words are spoken telling the important purpose of the ceremony, the reason being that the food of the people of Ix Toloch has been entirely consumed.

"When the beat of the drums is changed, the lords settle themselves expectantly. The seven war-captives are stretched out on their backs, naked. This is the record of the eighteenth tun, after the return to the province: 'The Itza shall feel retribution!'"

The counting of the pebbles of the days was expected to produce precipitation. Page 13: "From the land of Mayapan they came to see the taking of the plate of Lord Ahau . . . and the drenching rain." Page 32: "The spirit of Katun 12 Ahau was certainly expressed in the numerous rainbows. Rainbows arched over the island."

Page 6: "On the name-day of the katun the Seven Sons of Suhui Sip came down. . . . When the count of the pebbles of the katun was taken, they estimated the [remaining] length of the katun cycle. When the pebbles had been completely separated and taken out one by one in this manner, then we saw before our eyes that which was heaped up in the sky, the multitude of clouds over the face of the Sun, over his face."

The importance of the rain-bringing characteristic of the ceremonies is borne out in the lament on Page 9: "There is no one left
with sufficient understanding to set in order the days of the katun.
And so there will be no great abundance of water."

In ancient times it was customary to commemorate the passing
of a katun by the erection of a stela, engraved with hieroglyphic inscriptions of great beauty and we are told in the Tizimin narrative
that people traveled from other provinces to view the work of making the engraving upon the katun-stone. It is possible that the following statement refers to the actual carving of the inscription
rather than to the proper selection of words and phrases: Page 18:
"Three years to the day we were accustomed to spend in polishing
our words to awaken the gods above, we prophets." To the unlet-
tered populace the hieroglyphic writing must have appeared to be
a very potent magic.

There is a curious reference to the suffering of the *spirit of the
katun-stone.* Page 7: "It was at this time that the Itza betook themselves almost into the heart of the forest and along its borders where
it was customary for the soul of the great stone to wander on the
day of the katun in misery and torment by reason of its afflictions."
This seems to indicate that part of the actual carving of the inscription was carried out on the katun-day.

In addition to the pouch for holding the bright pebbles of the
days and the high stela or "squared stone" with its ornamented
faces, the property of the katun also comprised: a plate for offerings,
a cup for libations, bowls for catching blood from the self-inflicted
wounds, a flint knife, a fan, a mat, a bench, a stone seat, and the
elaborate vestments of the god impersonator. There was also the
katun-idol which was carried on the back of one of the priests. Most
of these articles have already been mentioned in the various quotations. Others follow:

Page 3: "The people are well grounded in the liturgy, and in
the ritual of the chocolate cup and in the working of miracles, and in
the ceremony of the mat and of the square-cornered bench of the
god, today and in all future times, when they shall make their libations from the cup, that the people may be set free, delivered."

Page 8: "How shall we celebrate the rites of Lord 5 Ahau in the twelfth tun, when he comes in benign holiness in the katun of power and of the strength of the wooden idols, and the magic of the cup, and the magic of the plate, and the magic of the count of days, in Katun 5 Ahau, in the twelfth tun?"

Page 10: "The people have come to depend upon the cup and the plate. They lean upon their rulers who came long ago from the north and from the west. Furthermore, in the sixteenth tun they go about the island searching for the lords of the katuns, particularly for the current ruler, Lord 5 Ahau."

Page 13: "The people assemble. The cup follows the mat, and the miracle-working follows the cup. Then come the lords, carrying Lord 5 Ahau in a pack, *looking backward,* after he has accepted the offerings. The cup has gone. The mat has gone. The prophet has gone with his oration. If they arrive at the Pueblo of the Sleeping Earth, at the Tree of Life, at the divisions of the pierced Earth, they will witness the completion of the katun bundle."

The purpose of the fan is indicated in the following sentence on page 16: "Are you not accustomed to raise your voices in song when you fan the katun upon its arrival, when you sound the flutes for your sins as the ancient day approaches?"

There is an unusual prophecy about the end of the world on page 16: ". . . in the final days of misfortune, in the final days of tying up the bundle of the thirteen katuns on 4 Ahau, then the end of the world shall come and the katun of our fathers will ascend on high." It is entirely possible that there is a copyist's error here and that thirteen *baktuns* was intended, since the katun cycle began and ended with 11 Ahau, we are told elsewhere, and the thirteen baktun cycle ran from 4 Ahau to 4 Ahau.

The prophecy continues: "These valleys of the earth shall come to an end. For those katuns there shall be no priests, and no one who believes in his government without having doubts. . . . Pay heed to the truth which I present to you in the katun of dishonor. Shall my intercession, my pleading be in vain? I speak to you! I Chilam Balam, the prophet of the Jaguar! I recount to you the words of the true gods, when they shall come."

There are several illustrations in the Dresden Codex which depict the headfirst descent from the sky of a god and of a beast carrying torches in his claws. It is therefore very interesting to find a reference to such a descent in the Tizimin chronicle.

Page 10: "From the milpa of the Dragon (perhaps the Milky Way) Cantzicnal comes down to fulfill his promises to the people. When the day of 2 Cauac arrives over this great land, then comes the descent of the katun headforemost, the Katun of Ix Toloch, the playful katun to soften the hearts of anger. The priest declares the auguries to be of good fortune from the remote places of the spirit." The headlong precipitation perhaps symbolizes the falling rain.

Landa describes the practice of covering the body with soot, as part of the penance during the period of fasting which always preceded such solemn ceremonies as the New Year's festival: "Here now the men come, clean and ornamented with their red ointment, after having cleansed themselves of the black soot with which they covered themselves when they fasted." [224] There are illustrations in the Maya codices which show men with blackened bodies.

One of the authors of the Tizimin manuscript emphasizes the necessity for covering the body with soot, as if he feared that the ancient practice was falling into disuse. Page 11: "If we do not smear ourselves with soot as a sign of mourning for our lives, we shall find ourselves lamenting for food because of this grievous fault, according to the words of the katun, according to that which is set forth in the hieroglyphic books of the katun."

There was a spontaneity about the Maya ceremonies which proves them to have been genuine expressions of a definite philosophy of life. In the curious incident on page 5, when the Itza were holding a festival in honor of the earth while the Xiu, at the same time, were celebrating the New Year's day 4 Kan, and "leopards with burnished skins came one by one out of the forest," earthquake and tempest followed the dual arousing of the forces of Nature. "After the fiesta the heavens were moved. The earth also was moved. The priests were deeply disturbed. The lands throughout the

---

[224] Tozzer 1941: 152.

province were greatly annoyed. Fierce warriors were among those who were dubious about the outcome, and they felt that further observances were required to celebrate the festival of the katun when 5 Muluc came, and the time of his taking office. Fruit was falling from the trees, and the elder brothers collected it in great quantities to save what they could.

"Then when 5 Ahau arrived on his day within the year 5 Muluc, there was a crescent moon, omen of life. In another part of the province there was a flood of water. In great abundance it silently spread over all creation. The people begged to be told in what way they had offended against the law, whether in not speaking the words of truth, or in the silent rites, or in the magical incantations, or in the casting of lots. . . . From everywhere, by day and by night, they came one by one to see the solemn casting of lots."

Dancing was a prominent feature of the festivals according to Landa, but only one dance is mentioned by name in the Tizimin manuscript. It is called the "dance of Ix Toloch," and the instance in which it is referred to is associated with the benevolent Bacab, Cantzicnal (Page 7). The name has survived in the modern *Xtol* dance. The same passage in the Tizimin contains the line "And the other heavens of the Moon were honored with appropriate dances to the gods on high."

As an astute observer and the first European historian of the "Cosas de Yucatan." Diego de Landa left an invaluable guide to posterity. Many of his statements have been proved true; very few have been definitely proved to be incorrect; but some have been misunderstood and misinterpreted. His interesting description of the Maya katun is found on pages 166-9 of Tozzer's version:

"Not only do the Indians keep track of the year and the months . . . but they had a certain way of counting the periods of time and their affairs by *ages,* which they did by periods of twenty years, counting thirteen twenties by means of the twenty letters (the names of the days) of the months called Ahau, not in regular order but inverted. . . . They call these *katuns* in their language, and by them they kept the account of their ages marvelously well. . . .

"Whoever put in order this computation of katuns, if it was the devil, he did it, as he usually does, ordaining it for his own glory, or, if it was a man, he must have been a good idolater, for with these katuns of theirs, he increased all the principal trickeries, divinations and delusions with which these people, beside their mysteries, were entirely deluded, and thus this was the science to which they gave the most credit, and that which they valued most, and not all the priests knew how to describe it. The order which they used in counting their affairs and in making their divinations, by means of this computation, was this,—they had in the temple two idols dedicated to two of these characters. They worshiped and offered homage and sacrifices to the first . . . as a remedy for the calamities of their twenty years. But for the ten years which remained of the twenty of the first idol, they did not do anything for him more than to burn incense to him and show him respect.

"When the twenty years of the first idol had passed, he began to be succeeded by the destinies of the second and (they began) to offer him sacrifices, and having taken away that first idol, they put another in its place, in order to worship that for ten more years."

This scheme is clarified by an example: the katun which ended on 11 Ahau ran from 1541 to 1561, according to Landa. But the idol of Katun 11 Ahau was placed in the temple in 1531, ten years before the katun actually began, and it "shared the government" with Katun 13 Ahau during that period. When the katun-ending day 13 Ahau arrived, the latter was removed. Then the idol of Katun 11 Ahau reigned in solitude for ten years until, in 1551, the idol of Katun 9 Ahau was introduced to share the honors with him until 1561, when the idol of 11 Ahau was withdrawn. It should be noted perhaps that Landa's katun-ending days do not agree with those which are derived from a Katun 5 Ahau starting in 1594, as given in the early pages of the Tizimin chronicle.

There is only one passage in the manuscript which has any bearing on the arrangement of shared katun "governments" described by Landa. In the sixteenth tun of Katun 5 Ahau the people are represented as turning to the Lord 3 Ahau, whose katun did not actually commence until four years later. How long before the sixteenth tun the authority of Lord 3 Ahau began one cannot conjecture.

It is also worthy of mention that 1531, the year in which the idol of Katun 11 Ahau was placed in the temple according to Landa, was just four years before Katun 13 Ahau ended and 11 Ahau began in the Tizimin sequence of katuns.

Page 10: "In the sixteenth tun, 3 Kan shall come on his day on 1 Pop, in the rain-bearing katun and the lords of the land shall be present also (the Itza). They shall bind up the faces of the lords at that time, and no one shall speak for the jesting katun at the festival of 3 Kan. They shall despoil the trees of their black and red and white coloring matter. The priests of the Itza take fruit from the receptacle. They take out grains of corn. They are suddenly interrupted by a rain-squall, by a tempest of wind. Then the face of the god is revealed to Ah Pop and Ah Zam. And as it appears overhead, the people run among the trees, among the rocks. Take care that you recompense the idol for his protection!

"In confusion the people turn to authority. *They go to the seat of power,* to Lord 3 Ahau, for the interpretation of the path. When the other lords arrive, they place reliance on their words and upon their priests. They lean upon the warriors among their own number. The people have come to depend upon the cup and the plate. They lean upon their rulers who came long ago from the north and from the west (the Itza). Furthermore, in the sixteenth tun, they go about the island searching for the lords of the katuns, *particularly* for *the current ruler, Lord 5 Ahau.*"

CHAPTER FIVE

Omens and Prognostications

WITH THE OMISSION OF THE OBVIOUSLY CHRISTIAN
references, the Saints' days and holy days, as well as the days of the
"Burner period" and those days on which the months entered the
calendar, the following list contains the prognostications which accompanied specific tzolkin-days, as enumerated in the final pages of
the Tizimin manuscript. The majority of the days are designated
utz, "good," or *lob*, "bad," but only those which have some additional characteristic are reproduced here:

January

1 Ix	unlucky	In which death comes to men.
9 Ik	unlucky	There will be sickness.
1 Manik	lucky	The guilt of our sons unites us.
6 Eb	lucky	Searching the forest for deer.
1 Ahau	unlucky	Rain appears in Chacmitan.

February

7 Cimi	lucky	In which there is much rain.
12 Chuen		The culpability of our priests.
1 Ben	unlucky	Sickness; heat.
5 Caban		Blame falls on the seers.
8 Ahau	unlucky	Then comes our enemy Satan.
11 Akbal		The sin of our religion.
12 Kan		The sin of eating men.

172

March

4	Muluc	lucky	The day of great purification.
6	Chuen	unlucky	They unite in disorder.
12	Caban	unlucky	The great sunset is here.
13	Eznab		A handful of food. The first rain comes.
6	Kan	lucky	On which the rain begins.
7	Eznab	lucky	A handful of food on this day.

April

9	Ahau	lucky	God the Creator, Himself.
11	Ik		New growth appears in profusion, from days of rain.
13	Kan		The kernels of corn which God asks for.
4	Imix	unlucky	A handful of food.

May

13	Oc	lucky	A day of rain.
2	Eb	unlucky	A handful of food.
3	Ben	unlucky	Searching through the forest.
4	Ix		Recalling the sins of our rulers.
6	Cib	unlucky	Perchance going into the forest [for food].
7	Caban	unlucky	Luring the deer with good things [into the traps].
8	Eznab	unlucky	When men sing.
9	Cauac	lucky	For the lords of the land.
11	Imix	unlucky	For the caciquedom.
12	Ik	unlucky	A spirit in the hearts of men.
1	Kan	unlucky	A calm upon the spirits. The moon is completed.
2	Eznab	lucky	The count of strong suns.
6	Muluc	lucky	For people to visit on this day.

June

1 Oc	lucky	The day of a very great event.
4 Cimi	lucky	The Holy Spirit.

July

12 Ix		The festival of the Jaguar Year.
13 Men	lucky	Rewards are multiplied.
3 Eznab	lucky	Now is the time to call for a measure of the stores of food.
9 Kan	lucky	For giving presents.
12 Manik	lucky	For the crops.
1 Muluc	lucky	Calm skies for the crops.
4 Eb	lucky	For one's desires.
5 Ben		The spirit recalls the sharp pain of the
12 Ahau		flint knife.
	lucky	On which wise men are born.

August

1 Ik	lucky	For the nobility.
10 Chuen		Sudden death while in full vigor. There will be a tempest.
1 Men		All kinds of sudden death.
5 Cauac	unlucky	A storm.
6 Ahau		Cutting appears at Chacmitan.[225]
1 Lamat		The fire causes the Jaguar pain.

September

10 Caban		The strength of our rulers.
13 Ahau	lucky	There will be wind.
3 Akbal	lucky	Now there is much rain.

---

[225] Sacrificial blood-letting?

4 Kan	lucky	Now there is much rain.
6 Cimi	lucky	In the power of the god of life.
8 Lamat		The one Lord eats corn by the mouthful.
1 Ix	unlucky	On which rulers are born.
3 Cib	lucky	For the honey harvest.
9 Ik		The feathered flint knife. There is sickness.

October

11 Kan	lucky	Floods of water.
13 Cimi		Great vigor.
1 Manik		The guilt of our children falls upon us. There is sickness.
6 Eb	lucky	For going hunting in the forest.
12 Eznab		There will be very terrible death.
1 Ahau	unlucky	Cutting will appear at Chacmitan.
7 Cimi	lucky	Great vigor.

November

4 Cib		Guilt falls upon the seers.
11 Akbal		Guilt falls upon [the seers].
12 Kan		For the death of rulers.
4 Muluc	lucky	There will be a great stirring.
6 Chuen		Memories of ancient times are confused.
13 Eznab		Great handfuls of food arrive from the harvest.
1 Cauac	unlucky	There will be cold weather.
2 Ahau	unlucky	There will be cold weather.

December

6 Kan	lucky	Rain begins.
7 Eznab	lucky	Great handfuls of bread.

9 Ahau	God the Creator Himself.
11 Ik	The Great Festival.
13 Kan	The corn of the Kingdom of God.

■■■■■■■■

Many of these prognostications are so frankly seasonal that one is forced to conclude that the tzolkin-day plays very little part in them. Rain or other weather phenomena, for example, is predicted on the following dates:

January	31	1 Ahau	unlucky	rain
February	6	7 Cimi	lucky	rain
March	16	6 Kan	lucky	rain
April	3	11 Ik	new growth from days of rain.
May	1	13 Oc	lucky	rain
July	19	1 Muluc	lucky	calm skies
August	10	10 Chuen		tempest
August	18	5 Cauac	unlucky	storm
September	11	3 Akbal	lucky	much rain
September	12	4 Kan	lucky	much rain
November	26	1 Cauac	unlucky	cold weather
November	27	2 Ahau	unlucky	cold weather
December	1	6 Kan	lucky	rain

Clearly there is no systematic relation between the day-name or number and the type of weather indicated in this list. Cauac is the only repeated name, but the predictions are not the same. No rain is predicted for June or October; but "much rain" is expected on September 11 and 12, in the hurricane season around the equinox.

That the calendar on which this list of 365 days is based belongs to the Julian, not the Gregorian count, is proved by the fact that the year is said to start on July 16. Hence September 21 or 22 would appear as September 11 or 12 at the time of Landa.

Certain important festivals are clearly established at strategic points in the tropical year, i.e., at the equinoxes and solstices. They are:

(a) March   9 12 Caban   The *Great Sunset* is here.
(b) June   10 1 Oc   The day of a *very great event*.
(c) September 14 6 Cimi   In the power of the God of Life.
or September 16   8 Lamat   The One Lord eats corn by the mouthful.
(d) December 19 11 Ik   The *Great Festival*.

(a) Landa describes a *five-day festival* [226] which ended on the first day of Yaxkin and, in the Makemson correlation, included the day of the Vernal Equinox, March 22. In the Julian calendar of Landa's day the festival occurred between March 6 and 12, thus including in the period the day March 9. The phrase "Great Sunset" indicates that an important event associated with the sun was taking place, and may well refer to the passage of the sun through the Vernal Equinox. It suggests that observations of the setting sun were made.

(b) On 7 Ahau 17 Zac occurred a "very great festival" according to Landa,[227] perhaps the "very great event" of June 10 listed in the Tizimin year-count. In the Makemson correlation, 7 Ahau 17 Zac fell on June 25 Gregorian in 1553. Assuming that this eventful day climaxed a five-day ceremony from June 20 to 25 in honor of the longest days of the year when the sun passes through the summer solstice, the dates in Landa's time would have been written June 10-15. They would thus have coincided in their beginning with the time of the great event listed in the Tizimin chronicle.

(c) Landa [228] does not specify the exact date in Pax on which was held the great five-day celebration of *Pacum Chac*, "Recompense to the Rain-gods (Roys)," which compared in scope and solemnity with the *Chic Kaban* festival at the time of the vernal equinox. The month *Pax* fell between September 17 and October 7

, [226] Tozzer 1941: 157-8.
[227] Tozzer 1941: 162.
[228] Tozzer 1941: 164-165.

Gregorian, or between September 7 and 27 Julian, in Landa's day. It is hence entirely possible that one or both of the September dates from the Tizimin list may belong to the observance of the sun's passage through the Autumnal Equinox.

(d) Landa describes a fourth important ceremony, the *Pocam* or "Washing (Roys)" which fell in Uo, sometime between December 11 and 31 Gregorian, or December 1 and 21 Julian, in the Makemson correlation. There is therefore reason to believe that this notable occasion on which "the prognostications of the year were read," was associated with the Winter Solstice. As the Christian dates previously discussed from the Tizimin calendar seem clearly to be given in the Julian calendar of 1553, one would expect the time of this "great festival" to lie between December 9 and 14. It cannot be intended to represent the celebration of *Christmas,* as that is expressly given on the correct *Gregorian* date: "December 25, 4 Lamat, lucky. The Nativity of Jesus."

The Gregorian shift of 1582 must have greatly mystified the Maya, if, indeed, they ever heard of it. At any rate it would not be surprising to find an error of ten days in a "double date" of this nature.

■■■■■■■■■

Like most people who lived before the scientific era, the Maya envisaged portents of the future in all unusual natural phenomena as well as in many common-place events. Like the Polynesians they saw coming events in the shapes and colors of clouds and in various types of rain, and they probably rivaled the ancient Babylonians in interpreting the appearances of sun, moon, comets, meteors and other phenomena of the heavens.

Even a shower might bring a message if it came on a particular day. Page 10: "On that day (the year-bearer 4 Muluc) at the end of a Jaguar year, a gentle rain presaged that we would be greatly afflicted by ghosts."

A downpour was always anticipated when ceremonies of great solemnity were held, especially on the occasion of a count of the pebbles of the days. Page 12: "From the clouds they collect the auguries as to the earth, and there is almost rain in our presence." Page 9: "But after they had assembled, they rejoiced to see the sky covered with clouds. On that day everyone saw it. Then the face of the sun was veiled and the face of the moon was covered." "There is no one left with sufficient understanding to set in order the days of the katun. And so there will be no great abundance of water."

In the calendar of 365 days which closes the Tizimin manuscript, 3 Cauac is characterized as a day of good fortune. In the text, moreover, this day is said to be particularly favorable to travelers:

Page 2: "Afterwards comes 3 Cauac, the day of activity at the wells throughout the land. The people will travel by good roads asking alms. They will travel in safety, even when going by night."

The day Oc had a special significance. In the section on the *Creation of the Uinal,* in the Book of Chilam Balam of Chumayel,[229] it is stated that *13 Oc* was the inventor of the 20-day period. Likewise the day 12 Oc, *lahca oc,* is credited with having measured off the earth by paces. There is a play on words here, the phrase being read as if it were *lah cab oc.* In the Book of Tizimin, on the other hand, one of the four Musencabs is said to have measured the earth by his paces, and the day Oc is concerned with the katun-count:

Page 13: "Thirteen Oc should be the day for measuring the katun, and 4 Cauac should be the day for taking a turn in the folds of the katun. These are the days which Pop and Zam declare."

The occasion for this remark was the completion of the count of Katun 5 Ahau. The day 13 Oc falls 70 days before 5 Ahau or 190 days after it in the tzolkin. Since Landa informs us that preparations for celebrating a new year's festival began three uinals or 60 days in advance of the event, it would not seem unusual if they began to make ready for a katun-ending celebration 70 days before the completion of the period. The interval, however, appears to have no significance, for in the case of the completion of Katun 11 Ahau, a day 3 Oc was selected for special observances:

---

[229] Roys, R.L. 1933: 116.

Page 21: "Similarly the folds of the katun were made on the day 3 Oc; and on the day 1 Cimi the prophecy of the katun was afterwards completed." The day 3 Oc is 190 days *before* or 70 days after the day 11 Ahau, which is just the reverse of the example previously cited. The day 1 Cimi falls 114 days before and 146 days after 11 Ahau.

It would seem safe to conclude from these passages that on a day Oc, some months before the final day of the katun, a preliminary check or count of some description was made, perhaps to determine when the long period of abstinence should commence. Perhaps an entry was made in the Book of the Katun and the page folded back against its predecessors, ready for the final entry on the day of completion.

Another reference to auspicious days is found on page 7: "The other rituals were then presented, and the other heavens of the Moon were honored by dances to the gods on high, on *whatever days should prove to be fortunate*, according to the teaching."

■■■■■■■■■

Certain numbers appear to have had a mystical significance. Hun, "one," occurs in proper names with the implication of uniqueness; Hunab Ku, the Supreme God; Hunac the Artist, Seer and Enchanter; and that barbarous Mexican warrior Hunac Ceel whose name might be rendered "Unique Terror." The literal meaning of *ceel* is "cold," and the derived meaning "cold chills," of fear. The name of Hunac Ceel appears only in the late part of the Tizimin manuscript. There was also Hun Uitzil Chac, "One Great (or Red) Mountain," the Tutul Xiu or ruler of Uxmal.

The mystical use of the word *ox*, "three," is illustrated by the following passages: "Three earthen walls were wholly demolished. Three symbols of the fatness of the Tree of Life failed." The ramparts belonged to the ancient city of Mayapan, which was undoubtedly centuries older than the one Landa wrote about which had two walls only, the inner one surrounding the inclosure where the temples and pyramids stood. This was "a very broad stone wall, laid dry, of about an eighth of a league, leaving in it only two narrow gates." [230] And Tozzer adds in a footnote: "In addition to the small walled enclosure here described by Landa, within which were the temples and the houses of the lords, there was a wall surrounding the city." It was reported that 60,000 persons were housed within the larger wall. Modern archaeology indicates the truth of the statement, according to S. G. Morley: "The Institution's survey established that the wall surrounding Mayapan is 5½ miles in circuit, enclosing a rough oval about two square miles in area. The wall varies from 9 to 12 feet in thickness at the base and from 6 to 7 feet in height outside." There is no mention of a third wall, but Mayapan was undoubtedly razed and restored several times in the course of many centuries. The importance of the site to the People of Ix Toloch appears to have been due to the great *chenil ti yactunil*, "The Well of the Cavern," which was held in veneration as a sacred place for ceremonies.

To continue with the use of the word "three": Page 4: "Have you forgotten the downpour on the day when you carried the idol called Kan? Three symbols of the thickness of the Tree of Life; three clusters of fruit from the tree of nourishment." "Clusters of fruit" suggests the pendent *cumulus* clouds with their treasures of rain.

Page 22: "I do not speak the words of the Thirteen gods when they despatched three different groups of men upon the earth in order that they might fold the katun three times." The expression "three-fold katun" occurs frequently.

Page 11: "Death will consume the fathers of the three-fold katun. In bewilderment they will dwell underneath the trees; for such is the purport of the prophecy of the day, the words of memory for the seventeenth tun."

Page 30: "Katun 1 Ahau was the sixth katun and it arrived in the pueblo of Emal. At the opening of the sealed katun there descended both recompense in the form of *yol*-flowers and at the same time, alas, three prophecies, three precepts, three hindrances to

---

[230] Tozzer 1941: 24-25.

meditation, three hindrances to seeking the wisdom of the Sculptor of the Squared Stone."

Page 32: "At the opening of the sealed katun of 10 Ahau, in the presence of guests from the pueblo of Chable, they will violently break the thongs which fasten the ladders of wood over the heads of the lords of the land. Three lives, three lives are consumed by fire."

Page 31: "This is the burden of the katun: there will be three breaks in the lineage, three hindrances to speech, to the speeches of the fathers in the houses of grief during the katun."

In some phrases the word *ox* seems to be used as a kind of prefix to enhance the meaning, rather than in the numerical sense of "three." The following examples illustrate this theory:

kokol, to be manifested	ox kokol, a phantom
numut kuil, miserable.	ox numut ku, very wretched
	ox numya, misery
	ox numul ti yail, misery.

No ready explanation of the expression "three-fold katun" occurs to me, nor of the seals attached to the Tree of Life as in the words: Page 19: ". . . the times for attaching three seals to the Tree of Life; the times for completing the three bundles and distributing the excess."

The number six is found less frequently than three, but it occurs in some interesting connotations:

Page 31: "One-half the remainder of the katun will be lucky, one-half unlucky—six years of misfortune and six years of good fortune. When all the mourning of the eternal katun 12 Ahau has been placed on high, when the seven lineages are exalted after the custom of the country, when the sacred prophecies regarding the conditions of domestic affairs in our land have come to pass, then you will [again] receive your replies by the casting of lots."

Page 11: "It is customary for the priests . . . to read from the teachings of the six eternal books at Uxmal. This is the revelation of the hieroglyphic books of the prophecies."

Page 26: "He (Hunac the Knower) will teach the priests the complete magic of Zam and Pop. And Balam the Jaguar will measure out the six magic formulae of government; these involve good chiefdoms, a good aristocracy, good men, and good sons, throughout the land."

The significance of the number *seven* is illustrated in the following quotations:

Page 6: "Seven Cauac arrives on his day in the seventh tun on the first of Pop, [the anniversary of the day] on which the lord of the day, the god of the katun, created writing."

There were seven devils who caused havoc. Page 18: "At the time when the heavens were established, there were seven inhabitants who created discord. That was because foreigners came in large numbers in ancient times." This may be a reference to devil-worship on the part of the Itza "sons of darkness." "But the government of the devils came to an end a very long time ago, after we began counting within the folds of the days." The calendar, particularly the katun-count, was the panacea for all ills.

There are many other uses of the number *seven:* There are the well-known deities, Ah Vuc Chapat, the Seven-headed Serpent; and Ah Vuc Yol Sip, He of the seven lineages of Sip. There are also the Seven Sons of Suhui Sip who descended on the day of the katun 5 Ahau. There are the seven enchantments which the priests performed with the cup on a certain new year's day. There were the seven sacred books which the priests of the Jaguar set out to compose for the guidance of future generations who had lost the art of reading the hieroglyphs, lest the ancient teachings perish from the face of the earth. There were the seven years of drought and pestilence, and the "foot-steps of the seven Subjugated Ones."

The number *nine* occurs occasionally in such phrases as *bolon ti ku*, "the nine (of) gods," and *bolon tzacab*, "the nine wise men," which Roys following Landa interprets as the name of a single deity, Bolon Tzacab. It is also found in the names of two deities who are mentioned only once, *ah bolon yocte*, "Lord of the nine paths," and *ah bolon kanan*, "Lord of the nine precious gifts."

Also, on page 24: "The nine magic rituals of life, the nine magic incantations for rain in abundance, for new growth in abundance, were given by the authors of our life."

Lahun, "ten," is found in the following situation, probably with no esoteric significance. Page 27: "Eight Ahau is the katun of settling down [in a new place], as of old Mayapan was depopulated. In the south, at the opening of the sealed katun of 8 Ahau, we were in the presence of *ten statues,* representations of the forms of the Lords of the Abundant Life."

Buluc, "eleven," appears to be a mystic word of peculiar power. The phrase, *buluc chabtan,* "the eleven penances," is found frequently in the manuscript in connection with the painful procedure of the Maya warriors when they opened their veins with the flint knife, so that their blood might be caught and offered to the idols.

Similarly on page 24: "Whether by taking medicine or by eleven vomitings our girls may become both good and beautiful. . . ."

The phrase *bulucte ti chuen,* "the eleven Chuens," whose faces are said to be "in agony" is puzzling.

Lahca, "twelve," appears in one esoteric setting. Page 33: "There are twelve enchantments, of course, to meet all sorts of needs."

There were thirteen gods of the numbers one to thirteen, as well as thirteen heavens. The thirteenth tun was the occasion for rejoicing and special ceremonies. Page 19: "There was great desire on the part of the Thirteen for their offerings, in return for having produced the sweetness of the honey, the bountifulness of the land, so that all who looked upon it might wonder."

Page 20: "But when the Thirteen gods are rightly called by name, and the Nine gods, then corn descends."

Page 8: "When the thirteenth tun arrives on his day and 13 Muluc falls on the first of Pop, on the day 1 Oc there will be majesty, when Pop shall descend, when Zam shall descend in Tun 13. At the ceremonies there will be overwhelming grandeur, the impressive majesty of the heavens. As always there will be the cup; there will be the plate which they will heap up with great quantities of food, from the abundant rains. They will break up the mountains of food into portions and distribute them. The heap of food left over will be enormous."

Page 20: "When the Bolon Tzacab, the first Nine Wisemen in the thirteenth level of the heavens, heap up everything in abundance including quantities of jewels, and when the path leads straight to the heart for the sake of the Thirteen gods, there shall be no more pain or suffering."

The Maya believed in the significance of visions, both waking and sleeping. There are frequent allusions to the apparition of various deities when the priests, with fervent invocations, summoned the gods from the heavens. Different gods were implored on various occasions and we read on page 11 that the hieroglyphic books tell the days "on which Ah Vuc Chapat shall reveal himself to us, and little by little the vision of Ah Vuc Yol Sip shall be manifested.

Even the lowliest who looked on in open-eyed wonder at the great spectacles participated in the visions along with the priests and aristocrats. Page 10: "Then the face of the god is revealed to Ah Pop and Ah Zam. And as it appears overhead the people run among the trees and [hide] among the rocks."

Page 22: "In response to the fervent prayer of the Lord of Uxmal, Chacxibchac came, carrying animals on his back. Then when Kukulcan, He-who-causes-the-flowers-to-open, descended they petitioned him to remove the Itza far away."

Page 27: "When Kinich Kakmo shall descend in majesty . . . when our rulers shall presently fulfill all their obligations, perhaps there will descend arrows, perhaps there will descend shields to shelter the homeless ones. . . . Ah Kinich Kakmo having revealed himself as cause during Katun 8 Ahau will be recompensed on the threshold when he comes, cleaving the heavens, darkening the earth. Then as in ancient times parting the sky, Sip will arrive."

Page 30: "At the opening of the sealed Katun [of 3 Ahau] Ek Cocaimut showed himself in the presence of the lords. There was watchfulness on their faces. There was courage on their faces. There was intelligence on their faces."

Two goddesses, Ix Chac and Ix Chuah, were associated with the transmission of messages through the medium of night dreams.

Page 12: "In another part of the cave where they interpret the movements of the heavens and the movements of the earth, quickly went the wooden idols Ix Chac and Ix Chuah into the midst of the waves, because they have the power of bestowing great nocturnal visions. Such are the instructions given by the katun of sufficiency."

Page 5: "Then the men of the Bat [tribe] are strong because of the coming of the sons of the deity. . . . They told about a vision of the earth and its four quarters, how great activity came from the north and a great stirring from the west. On the name-day of the katun the Seven Sons of Suhui Sip came down."

A hint that the waking visions at the spectacular ceremonies were stimulated or produced in part at least by the drug *peyote,* derived from the mescal cactus is found in the passage on page 6: "They whistle [with impatience] when they look on at our ceremonies. They whistle with impatience for the handing around of the medicinal herbs of the fields and mountains, and for the beneficial effects derived therefrom." It was the ancestor Yaxum, we are told, who was the first to concoct powerful drugs.

Page 16: "The days foretell events through visions, whether in the day-time or in the night-time."

The significance of omens derived from a variety of sources is illustrated in the following citations.

Page 16: "These valleys of the earth shall come to an end. For those katuns there shall be no priests, and no one who believes in his government without having doubts. They are broken, the omens, because of the katun of dishonor."

Page 3: ". . . we were guilty in the eyes of our rulers. When a sufficient number of prayers had been offered in the presence of the Maya people, above the faces of the children, we started out early in the morning upon the road. We traveled by day, so as to see the omens in the sky." This probably refers to cloud formations.

Page 17: "I will ask intercession of the Holy Father, if he will hear me, when you forget the omens and neglect them. . . . In former times, the priests of this country were allowed to speak freely. Yes. Our fathers expected divine manifestations. . . . You will grant that they understood the good omens of abundance when they sought for them in the fire." Perhaps the Xiu learned to read auguries in the flames from their guests, the Itza, for we read on page 9: "The Itza recounted their grievances among themselves in great excitement . . . on the day in which they read their fortunes in the fangs of the fire."

After the Spanish conquerors forbade the ancient practice of divination on the pain of death, there was deep sorrow and sense of loss. Page 30: "The omens of the gods must go! The omens of Kavil must go, and those of the Sky-serpent, of Canhel the Sky-serpent, alas!"

Other references to omens follow:

Page 28: "The omens of the great ones are of toil and wretchedness, and the gnawing of bark for food to preserve the holy people lest they close their eyes in death."

Page 32: "With regard to the internal affairs of the country the omens appear black, indeed, because of the entanglement of the katun."

Page 36: "There are omens of a famine at Chacmitan, a restriction on bread and a stringency on the bread of life."

Page 14: "When Mayapan was named, the heavens were filled with omens of good luck, as they have appeared in other skies and in other katuns."

the prophecies

The Maya prophecies were many and varied. Hardly a page of the Tizimin chronicle is without one or more predictions of events to come. In this chapter will be presented a few examples classified according to the time-period involved in the subject-matter.

1. *The Tun Prophecies.* Page 8: "When the thirteenth tun arrives in its day . . . there will be majesty. . . . There will be the plate which they will heap up with mountains of food from the abundant rains."

Page 10: "In the seventeenth tun . . . a drought will sweep the province bringing a pestilence in its wake in the days of bitter hunger. There will be no rain, and even the springs will become dry in this land of the south."

Page 11: "This is the word of the eighteenth tun after the return to the province: The Itza shall feel retribution. The great idols are men of vigilance and they delight in the words of prophecy even in the very midst of the rains."

Page 12: "This is the fulfillment of the prophecies of Katun 5 Ahau: the pottery jars shall be shattered into dust, when Tun 19 arrives. At that time there will be imprisonment among the lords, when the prophecies have come true. There will be vigils in the overburdened katun. So be it."

2. *Year Prophecies.* Page 11: "This is the expectation according to the Jaguar Priest, coming from Hunab Ku and from the Thirteen gods: They will preserve a resting-place for us to stretch out in during the Balam or Jaguar year, and for almost a whole month later."

3. *Katun Prophecies.* Page 18: "Sufficient unto themselves are my words, for I am Chilam Balam. . . . I say that the divisions of the earth shall be one."

Page 23: "And the priests of the living God (Hunab Ku), the true God, shall write in the sacred book of the universe concerning the earth, when He descended and His effulgence grew brighter and brighter. Gradually in this land there shall be no more sculptured temples of the Jaguar for you, when these men extend their sway among the heavens, when they reach the Source, the origin of the three-fold majesty of the heavens. . . . This is the burden of Katun 11 Ahau."

Page 26: "According to the omens above the earth and the prophecies, the disturbers of our land shall eventually turn back, after the years of avarice have passed and our sons have used concealment after concealment. The hearts of men are sorrowful when they hear the piercing words which are the burden of Katun 1 Ahau. . . . When good men are oppressed and their towns destroyed, there will be no more mountain-lions in the land, no more foxes, no more ferrets in the ravines. There will be no niggardly king. There will be no deliverer to save his kingdom. There will be no licking [of the feet] of rulers. No longer will the theft of our idols continue. This is the burden of Katun 12 Ahau: There will be majesty. There will be the nobility. There will be the religion.

"When an end finally comes to the troublesome days of the troublesome katun, He who crushes the rocks will bring to pass six good years followed by six bad years, in order that once more there may be an intercessor in our midst. The wicked knife of the warrior will wound grievously and destroy. We look forward to the good things of holy 10 Ahau, when happiness will finally come to the land. There will be no more foxes, no more ferrets in the ravines. There will be no more noble descendants adorning the lions' den. It will be better if the world comes to an end. It will be better if our land comes to an end, in the thirteenth fold of Katun 13 Ahau. Vale."

4. *Baktun Prophecies.* Page 15-16: "When the original thirteen baktuns were created, a war was waged which caused the country to cease to exist. Little by little, however, our enemies came to hear the prophecies of Ahau; but finally even the hope of hearing Ahau is brought to an end, because of the words of opposition. When the need arises for the high authority at the head of the mat to safeguard our children, then we will feel deeply the tragedy of being captives in war; also when we are ordered to obey. . . . Presently at the arrival here below of a cross of iron, I will suddenly come into your presence. I will be a companion to you in prison. The Nine shall arise in sorrow, alas. . . . And when over the dark sea I shall be lifted up in a chalice of fire, to that generation there will come the day of withered fruit. . . . The face of the sun will be extinguished because of the great tempest.

"Then finally ornaments shall descend in heaps. There will be good gifts for one and all, as well as land, from the Great Spirit wherever they shall settle down. Presently Baktun 13 shall come sailing, figuratively speaking, bringing the ornaments of which I have spoken, from your ancestors. Then the god will come to visit his little ones. Perhaps 'After Death' will be the subject of his discourse."

A division of the prophecies according to subject-matter follows:

1. *Prophecies of Rain or Drought.*   Page 7: "The summers will be so dry that you will entreat Hunab Ku to have compassion on you, lest the commonwealth be destroyed. For seven years there will be drought. The living rock will be burst asunder." The last statement seems to be a reference to human sacrifice in times of extreme distress. "The sacred pebbles will be consumed by fire," a reference to the repeated casting of lots in order to find a solution of the problem. "Finally, the *Hand* will begin to use gentleness in order to save the fields and mountain valleys."

Page 17: "Upon you, Hunab Ku inflicts the penalty of stripping the bark from trees [for food]. . . . In the last days, learn about the Tree of Life. Remember your blessings."

Page 36: "When Mayapan itself negotiated the katun, there descended soothing things from heaven. There descended gifts. Now there will descend the sorrow of pestilence," which always followed a drought, "and great heaps of rocks and skulls. . . . The coils of Hun Yapotik restrict the bread of life; they compress the bread of life one-half."

2. *Prophecies concerning the Itza.*   Page 11: "The Itza shall feel retribution." This sentence always follows a description of human sacrifice, and it appears to voice the Jaguar Priests' disapproval of the practice. "The great idols are men of vigilance, and they delight in the words of prophecy. . . . The people feel forsaken when the lords stir up discord and the auguries fail. When good rulers come will not the people again place reliance on the cup and the vestments even in times of the most rigorous discipline?"

Page 19: "The thirteen treasures of the Itza shall be swept away. Strong trees shall be uprooted. A fire will be kindled in the very middle of the pueblo, when the prophecies shall be fulfilled amongst us."

Page 6: "The rule of the Itza shall be completely established over us. We will accept their commands."

Page 8: "True, for the present we must carry the highly ornamental sons of the Itza on our backs, maintaining them in our midst, like a great stone in our misfortune. But there will come a time when the white flowers will again be unsheathed in this land, from the Island of Cuzamil to Mayapan. In the day of the overthrow of the Red Eagle, in the day of retribution, when it shall later come to pass over this beautiful land of billowing mountains, then quickly shall come the day of vexation, the vexation of the Itza.

3. *Prophecies as to the Advent of Europeans.* Page 6: "Five Ahau shall be the day of apportionment of food at your wells. Mountains shall descend. They shall descend in your midst, kindling the fire of great brightness. Foreigners shall descend from the sea as of old. Why do they come? They come to harass us!"

4. *Prophecies regarding Christianity.* Page 15: "When that day comes, then with great vigilance we will enjoy the fruits of our heritage, but vigilance here below will gradually relax, the more forceful becomes the heavenly anger directed against the Christians. Justice must come, and our plots of land will be enlarged when suspicion has dried up and the country has been put in order. There will be great grief until the fulfillment of the katun of dishonor. Nobody will keep his promise when the foundation itself happens to be blameworthy. And so, great trees which formerly towered to the sky over the whole country are no more. This is the prophecy of the dishonorable katun: There will be no good purpose served by the Christian bishop when he arrives. He will seek to destroy this generation. Likewise, he will restrict your beliefs. He will destroy you. He will eradicate your true knowledge in the end. He demands that we shall accept the Christian teaching, as it is called. When there are beatings, when finally the rulers shall make an end of good things among you, then shall arise vigilance against lascivious guests who call upon your wives by name."

Page 16: "At this time I speak to you of 'Justitia' for the purpose of vexing the Christians. Nine souls shall be baptized by the dishonorable men, and shall be asked questions by them which not even the nobles in the pueblo would be able to answer. When they shall appear in this land of trees, in this land of rocks and shall settle down in the towns, there will be no one to understand these things. Then sorrow and misfortune will follow."

5. *Prophecies regarding the End of Spanish Rule.* Page 22: "All these evils shall cease when *they* are overwhelmed, when they

are all overthrown by the Guardians, when they are all overthrown by the Anointed Ones. The number of men here in our land shall be increased ten-fold, and when they arrive they shall fulfill the words of the warriors of the katun. May the drunkards be torn up by the roots! May Ix Tab carry them dangling from her hands even before we have tied up the face of the katun.

"They shall be punished in our midst, wounded in many places by our lances and by the flowers of death of the priests and the wisemen and the lords and the warriors. The prophecies shall be made manifest in the current katun, in the ninth tun, when it shall come to pass that the government shall be cut off by the lords and nobles and the priest Ah Kin Chilcoba, and the Sweepers."

Page 27: "The warrior will employ his prowess on nobody. When they are taught about the abundant life, they will have compassion on the fields. They will have compassion on the mountains. They shall be followed for the benefit of everyone, so that there shall be no more sorrow in the fields, no need for distress in the mountains, because the whole province and the entire earth were stretched out by the Bacabs.

"When Kinich Kakmo shall descend in majesty, then those of other lands shall descend also, when they can be set free straightway from the insolent and lawless men, and from those who look with scorn upon our ancestors and upon our noble lineage. This is the offense of the lords of Chichen, the lords who came from the sea. . . . Then as in ancient times parting the sky, Sip will arrive. Now let true men be revealed to the people! They will break the necks of the lords of creation, because they secretly scoff at the altar of Zam and at the altar of the Pops."

Page 28: "When trees grow in the land, when rocks grow in the land, when it happens for the third time that they dwell in peace and serenity of life in Chacmitan, then there will come a recompense for the ancient hunger. Three times for government, they will have the authority of Zam, three times the authority of Pop. In the fourth tun they shall see an increase in the prosperity of the state and in the prosperity of the lords. Finally a day will come when there will be no more uprooting in the land, when it has been overthrown once again. There will be no more festival days to honor the authority of Pop and the authority of the Zams. . . .

"When discord comes among the rulers, may the gods forbid that true men among the people shall perish! . . . The day will come when you shall withhold the bread of life from these white-skinned effeminate fellows, from their very teeth. Our descendants shall pierce them with the lance. Our ancestors shall pierce them with their hands tied together. The chanter of news shall pierce them. The horse shall strike them down with despair. The horse shall pierce them in secrecy. It is decreed."

Page 4: "When we have been set free throughout the land, on the day when *they* abandon the government, we will wash the chocolate cups. We will cleanse everything, in that day of goodwill in government. As soon as they have departed, we will no longer need to speak exceedingly softly when we cast our lots. And in that day there will be no more violent disputes. Our good fortune will unite us. We will be able to look at ourselves in the mirror without sadness. We will amuse ourselves once more when that day comes.

"Ah Vuc Yol Sip will take charge of the fire. In that day of deliverance from the covetous ones, from bewilderment and vexation, there will come salvation by reason of his authority and by reason of their departure. No longer will our priest have to conceal himself here and there in the village. For the first time, his hiding and his silent misery will be a thing of the past. We will face our father squarely once more: Ah Zam is his name, to whom is given authority for eternity. We will then unburden ourselves to him. He will look upon our eleven penances. These are what exalt the soul during great affliction. In those times, there will be some who clamor for 'Just one shot! Why not?' But our good elder brothers will turn them back upon the road. Our guide will ask intercession for them in that day when they put their trust in authority."

6. *Prophecies as to the End of the World.* Page 16: "In the final days of misfortune, in the final days of tying up the bundle of the thirteen katuns on 4 Ahau, then the end of the world shall come and the katun of our fathers will ascend on high." In the Makemson

correlation, which is amply corroborated by the katun and tun sequences of the Tizimin chronicle stemming from a Katun 5 Ahau beginning in 1594 in a year 1 Muluc, the Long Count date of 4 Ahau is 13.0.0.0.0 4 Ahau 3 Kankin, which fell in 1752. Hence the passage quoted would have more force if we assumed that the author had intended to say "the tying up of the bundle of *thirteen baktuns* on 4 Ahau." The end of the world is more likely to come at the completion of the great cycle which began with 13.0.0.0.0 4 Ahau 8 Cumhu (3373 B.C.) and contained all the historical dates of the Maya civilization.

"These valleys of the earth shall come to an end. For those katuns there shall be no priests and no one who believes in his government without having doubts. They are broken, the omens."

Page 33: "Thirteen Ahau is the thirteenth katun and they shall count it in Cabal. In the assemblage of people they shall open the sealed katun. At dusk they will smell the fragrance of flowers. Day shall be turned upside down. Their faces shall be disturbed. The genealogical tree shall descend. Stones shall descend and Heaven and Earth shall be universally consumed by fire."

Page 34: "A time will come when the katun-folds will have passed away, when they will be found no longer, because the count of tuns is reunited." In other words, separation of time into periods will be no more.

Page 36: "These are the words which must be spoken: The prophecies are a solemn trust from ancient times. They are the first news of events, and a valuable warning of things to come."

CHAPTER
SIX

Astronomy, Philosophy
and Mythology

ASTRONOMY IS GIVEN NO MORE THAN A PASSING THOUGHT
in the Book of Chilam of Tizimin, yet the meager glimpses afford
a provocative view of the heavens through the eyes of the old Maya
priests and make one fervently wish that an astronomical treatise
of post-conquest times would come to light. I should explain at the
outset that I am not making a distinction between astronomy and
astrology in these pages. When considering primitive teachings in
which astronomy and religion are practically inseparable, it should
suffice to define astronomy in such broad and inclusive terms as:
"that which is observed in the sky or deduced from such observations." If much that we now consider irrelevant was deduced from
the observations, it must be accepted for its great historical value
and for the light it throws on the evolution of the thought of early peoples. In modern astrology, if I am not mistaken, it is not necessary
to be able to recognize or identify a single star or planet by name in
the sky.

We have seen that the skill of the Itza priests as star-gazers and
prognosticators excited the admiration of the Xiu wisemen. "Wherever
they live, whether in the north or in the west, they study the aspect
of the heavens. They say it will rain when Ahaucan the Rattlesnake
is lifted high above the trees, above the rocks, above the houses, and
above everything else." Page 3.

Nevertheless, the Xiu also must have been well versed in the

195

science of celestial phenomena if they were the originators of the Maya calendar and the authors of such astronomical treatises as the Dresden Codex. It may be that their methods were less spectacular and more scientific than those of the more barbarous Itza.

The priest of the Jaguar declares (page 16): "Daily at noon I press my hands on the head of the well. After sprinkling the sacred objects of our religion and the holy products of the sea, I look upward at the divine face of the heavens. Standing on the stone pavement at the mouth of the well, I look for the guide-posts on the face of the sky, to see whither they navigate. No man speaks to me without a grievance. My part is to interpret to you." Here the observations may include the meridian altitude of the sun, the time being noon; but it is probable that they refer principally to cloud formations. On page 3 we read: "We traveled by day so as to see the omens in the sky." And on page 12: "From the clouds they collect, among themselves, the auguries as to the earth."

Rainbows were among the celestial phenomena which served as "guide-posts." Page 25: "The circles of a double rainbow adorned the blue sky of Ichcansiho for three days." A rainbow lasting continuously throughout a whole day is, of course, impossible, since rainbows cannot form unless the sun is within 42° of the horizon. Page 32: "The spirit of Katun 12 Ahau was certainly expressed in the numerous rainbows. Rainbows arched over the Island. Rainbows stood in the midst of the land."

Observations of the night sky comprised part of the ceremonies for speeding an old katun on its way and welcoming the new ruler. Page 26: "Ten will interpret the opening of the sealed katun of 10 Ahau. One looks at the face of Citbolon or at the face of the sky of Citbolon, one at the sun, one at the forests, one at the trees, to determine what kind of remedy the heavens will provide, to be written down [in the Book of the Katun] for future years." Citbolon, god of medicine and magic, may have had his representative among the constellations or planets. "They are agitated by the drums. The Bat is awakened by the drums. The four Bacabs slide to earth on the back of a green rainbow. *One by one the stars fall.*" The last statement is a clear reference to a meteor shower, such as the great Leonid showers which used to occur every 33 years, in the autumn, and which were most intense within the tropics.

The moon was considered an important astronomical body in the period of Old Empire greatness. Speaking as a Priest of the Moon, Nahau Pech declares (page 17): "In those days there was understanding of the moon, in the time of our fathers. . . . This saying came from the mouth of Nahau Pech, *the priest of the lunar calendar.*"

Long ago, before the Maya time-count was perfected, the days of the moon were considered more important than they became at a later date. The numerous lunar series in the inscriptions on the monuments, however, indicate that moon-ages and lunations continued to be assiduously observed and recorded, although they had no connection with the Long Count or the year. In the following statement from page 12, the word "katun" should probably be interpreted in the broad sense of "calendar": "Yaxum our forefather cast aside the divisions of the *katun* pertaining to the moon."

The Polynesians believed that the waning crescent or "dying" moon journeyed to a far-off heaven where it bathed in the water of Eternal Life and was restored to vigor, during the days of invisibility. Some such idea may be conveyed by a statement on page 5: "When 5 Ahau arrived on his day within the year 5 Muluc, there was a crescent moon, omen of life." The association of the new moon with rain is suggested in the next lines: "In another part of the province there was a flood of water. In great abundance it silently spread over all creation. . . . At new moon they prayed for the remnant of the days, for the remnant of the katun afterwards."

Other associations with the moon are found in the following passages:

Page 23: "When the invasion came, during Katun 11 Ahau, even the Heavens pitied themselves. They blamed it on the Moon when our warriors cut their own throats. . . . Great numbers were assembled, and they all sang together to the gods. There was he who advises about new moons," doubtless a priest of the lunar count, like Nahau Pech.

On page 19 there is what may be considered an example of the ancient custom of recording the moon's age as in the Old Empire inscriptions: "The state of Sactenel will be depopulated [on] the tenth [day] of the moon."

That the astronomical skill of the Maya excited the curiosity of their Spanish conquerors is brought out in the following excerpt from page 30: "The wretched men inquired minutely again and again as to how to be able to recognize the days of the moon-count, and the katun-bearer, and the prophecies of the gods above."

One of the duties of the nobles appears to have been to study practical astronomy. At the opening of the katun bundle of Lord 6 Ahau at Uxmal, the god Kinich Kakmo addressed the assembled people (page 28): "In the appointed union, the faces of the lords express their appreciation of his words, when he enters. . . . Suffice it that they learn the true nature of the stars. And if they should misunderstand, they ask that they may be corrected promptly."

The quotation of the Itza that rain would fall when Ahaucan the Rattlesnake was high in the sky proves beyond reasonable doubt that this was the name of a constellation. (See footnote 18.) Wherever similar names of animals are associated with Ahaucan in the proper context, we may expect to find other constellations, as for example in a passage from page 5: "At that time Ahaucan the Rattlesnake was lifted high on the back of the Leopard, Chacbolai." The Leopard was very probably a constellation situated below Taurus in a certain part of the sky. If observations were made in the eastern sky where the stars were rising, as seems reasonable, the Leopard must have been the conspicuous configuration which we call Orion.

The date referred to in this paragraph on page 5 was the new year's day 6 Ix, in the Katun 5 Ahau which began in 1594. According to the Makemson correlation, the year 6 Ix in the sixth tun of Katun 5 Ahau began on November 1, 1599, Julian. Between sunset and midnight on this day, the Taurus group rises in the east and ascends toward the zenith in the latitude of Yucatan. Below it and slightly to the south follow the brilliant stars of Orion. Hence it could be said of these two star-groups that "Ahaucan was lifted high on the back of Chacbolai."

Other possible constellation names include Bolai Can and Chacbolai Ul, which are associated with Chacbolai on page 7: "Moreover, Ah Tem Pop and Ah Tem Zam interpreted the future road of the katun. . . . They read the auguries by the paths of Chacbolai the Leopard and Bolai Can, the Fierce Serpent, and Chacbolai Ul, the Leopard Lodge." There can be little doubt that these were all the names of stellar configurations—"Leopard Lodge" suggests the Square of Pegasus—and they were probably also the names of deities associated with the star-groups.

Another likely constellation name is Yaxal Chuen, a Maya god and lord of Katun 12 Ahau, according to the Tizimin chronicle. In the Chumayel book, on the other hand, he is explicitly connected with the sky: "Katun 12 Ahau is the seventh (emended) katun of the count. The katun is established at Zaclahtun (Saclactun in the Tizimin). Yaxal Chuen is his face. Buleu-caan-chac is his face to the rulers. He shall manifest himself. He is in the sky by day; he is in the sky by night. The great artisan (hunac ah menil), the wise man shall come." [231]

Roys adds in an instructive footnote: "Yaxal Chuen appears to be an important deity and probably a constellation as well. The name might be translated as the 'green or first artisan.' We find on pages 23, 24 of the Codex Peresianus a glyph composed of the elements *yax* and *chuen*, which may refer to this deity (Gates 1910, p. 30). These are the pages containing the figures which represent the thirteen divisions of the Maya Zodiac."

Ah Musencab, Yaxbolai, and Chacxibchac may also be names of stellar configurations or planets as well as the names of deities who inhabited the heavens, as may be inferred from the following passages:

Page 20: "On 11 Ahau when Ah Musencab rises. . . ."

Page 23: "We had as our guest (at the opening of Katun 8 Ahau at Itzmal) Yaxbolai. We had as our guests Chacbolai and Chacxibchac." If Chacbolai is a constellation-deity as was inferred earlier in the chapter, it is probable that Yaxbolai and Chacxibchac are stellar configurations, also.

---

[231] Roys, R.L. 1933: 158.

The Seven Sons of Suhui Sip may be associated with the seven stars of the Big Dipper.

Ah Chapat or Ah Vuc Chapat, the Seven-headed Serpent, may be the name for the Milky Way, as well as for the deity who dwells in the sky. Page 11: "Day and night, Ah Chapat lies overhead." Page 24: "Then . . . descended the words of that wellknown Sip, the ancient Sip . . . in the kingdom of Ah Vuc Chapat, the Seven-headed serpent whose shield is the sun." The next passage possesses the beauty of poetry:

"When this warrior arrived, descending the road of the Stars of the Abundant Life, and of the living katun, on the day-sign of Sacvacnal (the sixth day of the month Zac?), the faces of the lords were suffused with living tears, with tears like rain."

Canhel the Sky-serpent suggests either the Milky Way or the band of the Zodiac.

Two other deities may prove to be associated with bright stars or planets: Yax Cocaimut and Ek Cocaimut. An unusual statement on page 28 indicates that part of the ritual at the well may have consisted in reading the aspect of the stars as reflected in the smooth water of the cenote: "At Chichen, one-half the katun (of 4 Ahau, 1732-1752) shall be good; one-half shall be without good. There will be the majesty of the throne of him who speaks the magic language of the stars of heaven submerged in blue water, Yax Ah Cocaimut is his name."

Landa lists Yax Cocahmut as a regent of the Muluc years, an honor he also assigns to Cantzicnal. Another reference to studying the stars at the water-surface level of a cenote, a practice which has the great advantage that the walls cut off the diffused sky-light and enhance the brilliance of celestial objects, is found on page 12: "In another part of the cave where they interpret the movements of the heavens. . . ."

Ek Cocaimut, companion of Yax Cocaimut, was associated with Katun 3 Ahau: Page 30: "At the opening of the sealed katun, Ek Cocaimut showed himself in the presence of the lords. There was watchfulness on their faces." Both Yax Cocahmut and Ek Cocahmut are mentioned in the Chumayel manuscript.

Finally, Balam the Jaguar may have been a constellation or a planet, Page 19: "At the time of the great pestilence they will worship as lord of the sky the Jaguar war-god.

philosophy

As the Maya of Yucatan staggered under the repeated onslaughts of the Spanish adventurers, as they saw one ship after another washed to their shores and men armed with weapons more deadly than the thunder-bolt pour out of them, they became painfully aware that their gods were fighting a war to the death, a losing war, against the powerful gods of the white men. Their desperate prayers and blood-sacrifices prolonged the struggle, perhaps, but the end was inevitable. The old gods, dishonored, were forced to make room for the new ones.

A similar dislodgment had happened once before, at the time of the Itza invasion, the "second descent," and the memory of those far-off times was kept fresh in the Books of the Katuns. The suffering would not be forgotten as long as the Books still lived. But as the katuns passed, the Xiu had found it possible to dwell in peace and mutual respect beside their Itza conquerors, and to depend upon them for protection against attackers. The Itza had adopted their writing and calendar, and had become active participants in the great festivities which marked the changes of the year and seasons and the ending of a katun. The exchange of knowledge had undoubtedly proved beneficial, and it had enabled the Xiu to maintain their self-respect in such adverse circumstances.

The ancient Maya gods had not made room for the gods of the Itza without a bitter struggle. Page 23: "There were many idols of wood, and their duplication caused quarrels and bloodshed." This state of affairs was the exact opposite to that which prevailed when the long migration had started from the original habitat, the legendary Holtun Suiva, as well as in the more recent evacuation, when the merciless Ah Canul ruled the five provinces of Yucatan. Page 20: "During the migrations both from Holtun Suiva and from the five provinces also, it chanced that there were no idols of carved wood." The absence of idols during the ancient migrations has been interpreted as proof that the Maya were not originally idolators; but at the period of Ah Canul, they were most certainly the worshipers of idols. Hence it would seem that some other reason must be found to account for their absence in the latter instance, such as confusion due to haste, or a general conflagration.

The time had come when the Itza priests had insisted on officiating at the counts of the pebbles of the days, to the evident dismay and stern disapproval of the Jaguar Priest, who wrote down his thoughts in the following entry (page 6): "At that time, there was only one count to be made. A single straight shot it should have been, but nobody was frank and honest. You who despise your mothers, you who despise your fathers, are *you* fit to make the count of the katun cycle?"

These hard words may be compared with a description of the Itza, found in a footnote to the Chumayel:[232]

"They (the Itza) were feared and hated, but at the same time regarded as holy men. Their customs were certainly different from those of the rest of the people of northern Yucatan, for they are called rogues, people without fathers and mothers and people who are disobedient to their fathers and mothers. Indeed this last epithet was a very mild statement of the facts in the case, for Avendano tells us that they had the custom of beheading the older men when they passed the age of fifty, 'so that they shall not learn to be wizards and to kill; except the priests of their idols, for whom they have great respect.'"

When the Maya people suffered through drought and famine, the gods sorrowed in sympathy. Page 10: "A drought sweeps the country bringing pestilence in its wake in the days of bitter hunger. There is no rain, and even the springs become dry in this land of the south. There is much blood-letting . . . there is blood-letting by way of appeasement. They will clamor for jars and basins when they perform the eleven penances. The Eleven Chuens wear an aspect of agony. . . . *The gods shall mourn.*"

---

[232] Roys, R.L. 1933: 178.

In times of distress and calamity the Maya had a deep sense of guilt, and did what they could to make amends for their sins, even to paying with the sacrifice of their own lives, as when the priests of the Calendar threw themselves into the well of the Cavern, or the warriors cut their own throats on the altars of Pop and Zam, probably offering themselves for the sins of all the people. When a flood spread over the land, the people went to the priests to ask in what way they had sinned against the gods, "whether in not speaking the words of truth, or in the silent rites, or in the magical incantations, or in the casting of lots."

In another instance of prolonged drought and famine (page 11): "Ah Kin Chelyaxnak is he who looks into the hieroglyphic books to ascertain by what road *guilt falls upon us.*"

Landa informs us that the Maya were in the habit of confessing their sins when they thought they were going to die, with sometimes embarrassing consequences when they unexpectedly recovered. In the Tizimin manuscript, the lords confessed their sins to Kukulcan in a great purification ceremony held "at the mouth of the sea," in the 19th tun of Katun 5 Ahau (page 12).

It seems surprising to find so strong a sense of the "conviction of sin" and its dire consequences among the ancient Maya. Page 16: "Are you not accustomed to raise your voices in song when you fan the katun upon its arrival, when you sound the flutes *for your sins,* as the ancient day approaches?"

Page 25: "A wave of disgust sweeps through the house of the gods because you forget Life, you forget your own ancient teachings. Within your very doors, the avaricious lords (the Spaniards) *are your punishment* in the living katun."

Page 18: "Pay attention, all of you! Your sins have become heavy burdens! . . . *The soul shall dwell in goodness. All the vile qualities within us are washed away by sorrow. These are within everyone.*"

Sometimes the Xiu gods were self-sacrificing and compassionate, as in the passage on page 6 in which the priests exhort the people to renewed courage after a prolonged drought and famine: "The heavens will increase the supply of provisions. They will increase them according to their promises. When you are assembled together, dry your tears. Without breeches, without clothing, the idols our patrons though they are even without food, *demand nothing for themselves.*"

At other times, the gods showed an all too human greediness and cupidity at least for that which they considered their just dues. Page 19: "Then there was a great desire on the part of the Thirteen for their offerings, in return for having produced the sweetness of the honey, the bountifulness of the land, so that all who looked at it might wonder."

Page 22: "They are words of great mischief when the Lords of the Days complain without the sacred food, when they desire to eat their food according to the time-honored custom. They look at the foot of a bird and complain of their food to the god Sip, and their words are noted by Sip in his mind."

The belief in a scape-goat may have been strengthened by the teachings of the friars. At any rate it has persisted into post-conquest times. The sacrifice of the daughter of Franco Cocom in 1629 during a plague of locusts demonstrates the tenacity of the belief in the efficacy of vicarious atonement. Tozzer cites a number of examples of the practice in his invaluable notes to Landa's *Relacion.* The priest of the Jaguar, however, expressed stern disapproval (page 42):

"And all the people did not die, but blessed their benefactress for their food, because she took upon herself the guilt of the locusts which were destroying that which they had sowed. *O wretched people! Why are you so agitated by hunger, all of you?*"

The people of Ix Toloch prized learning to a remarkable degree. Twice in their history, most of their wonderful books had been destroyed, first by the Itza, later by the Spaniards. In the pages of the Tizimin, the loss of the records of the katuns and the sacred teachings was mourned with as poignant a sorrow as that of human life and of the food supply:

Page 1: "With rivers of tears we mourned the sacred writings amid the delicate flowers of sorrow in the days of the katun. . . . Should we not lament in our suffering, grieving for the loss of our maize and the destruction of our teachings concerning the universe of the earth and the universe of the heavens?"

Page 2: "They pray that the eyes of their children may read the writings." This was written at a time when the children had been forcibly taken into the monasteries and were being taught the Spanish writing, and the elders realized that knowledge of the hieroglyphic books and inscriptions was threatened with immediate extinction. "We are pierced with a great longing to read the books of wood and the writing on stone, now in ruins. *They contain the seven wellsprings of life.* They were burned before our eyes at the well."

Truth came from Heaven, from the Sky-serpent, which may represent the Zodiac, in which sun, moon and planets have their motions. Page 21: "Once there was truth, which we drew from the Serpent in ancient times, from the clear, unclouded heavens to the evil-knotted earth beneath." Religion embraced all branches of knowledge, and ritual ennobled even the meanest of tasks. Page 3: "Our wonder-working religion is the foundation of everything."

From earliest times, the followers of the One God appear to have been idealists: Page 25: "The ancient people strove to attain perfection. In olden times, they recognized the miracles performed by the heavenly Hunab Ku, the One God. . . . The security of our land, the security of the province shall return! Our faces shall be set free! Our hands shall be set free! Our feet shall be set free!" And later on the same page: "The lust of the belly, the lust of carnal sin, the lust for noble family, the sin of arrogance, all these are vices which come quickly, the evil desires of our rulers in Katun 1 Ahau. So be it."

Perfection was the high objective for which they strove; but with the arrival of the Europeans, "It came to pass that the true men (*halach vinicil,* which has the derived meaning of "government officials"), the lords of the Itza, pleaded with lamentations, asking, 'With whom will perfection rest among dishonorable men?' These nine lords, when they build a wall to defend worthy men and provide canes for arrows, will prevail against the enemy by means of the magic of the Book."

Page 27: "When the country is on the point of being turned upside down, the humiliation of the overturning is a great evil in itself, the denial of perfection."

In the period of deepest humiliation when they were conscripted to carry food from the mountains to feed the people of Ah Canul, there was no thought of vengeance; but instead, the heavenly Itzam set out to bring about a change of heart and character in the treacherous and cruel ruler. Page 23: "Then began the experiment of Itzam-caan to effect the reformation of the King of the Canul from his wicked ways. When the Lord of Heaven was manifested to the people of Chichen where Ah Canul had no power, they listened with careful attention."

Love of truth, humility and compassion were qualities to be assiduously cultivated. Envy was to be condemned. Page 15: "Among the great things which those who speak the exact truth have taught us, is the covering of our bodies with soot in deep humility and true knowledge."

Page 17: "It shall come to pass that you will adore the divine truth, and the government of our ancestors will stand always in readiness forever. . . . Do the humming-birds take unfair advantage of one another? Do the humming-birds envy one another? . . . With compassion the government redeemed us. That was four katuns ago."

Freedom of speech was another important factor of the old way of life which had become lost in modern times. Page 17: "In former times, the priests of this country were allowed to speak freely."

These ancient seers even envisaged a time when there would be "One World," and war would be a thing of the past. They may well have been the first people on earth to foresee such an eventuality. Page 18: "I repeat my words of divine truth. I say that the divisions of the earth shall all be one!"

Page 27: "The warrior will employ his prowess on nobody. When they are taught about the abundant life, they will have compassion on the fields. They will have compassion on the mountains. They shall be followed for the benefit of all concerned, so that there shall be no more sorrow in the fields, no need for distress in the mountains, because the whole province and the entire earth were stretched out by the Bacabs. When Kinich Kakmo shall descend in majesty, then those of other lands shall descend also, when they can be set free straightway from the insolent and lawless men, and from those who look with scorn upon our ancestors and upon our noble lineage. This is the offense of the lords of Chichen, the lords who came from the sea."

The Spanish concept of justice as dispensed by the Inquisition, was something quite unknown in the native ideology. It is always referred to in the Latin form *Justitia,* as having no Maya equivalent. Page 31: "There will be agitation in the midst of the land when Justitia descends upon the teaching of our sacred religion, and upon the words of the true God, and our obligation to protect the people from the abyss." The protection of the people from attack was the moral responsibility of the lords or warrior caste.

A stable, trustworthy and benevolent government was a prime necessity if they were to live the "abundant life," but "the people feel forsaken when the lords stir up discord and the auguries fail. When good rulers come again, will not the people again place reliance on the cup and the vestments," symbols representing the authority of the Lords of the Katuns, "even in times of the most rigorous discipline?"

Obedience to the will of the gods from whom all benefices derive was the duty of the ruling class as well as of the common people. Page 28: "The gods give us the bread of heaven in their mercy. Let there be obedience to their laws. Is not the desire to obey, is not obedience itself the duty of the lords? Their throats will be silent when the life of abundance comes to an end, and with it esteem for one blood-relationship. And there will no longer be obedience through veneration for one western tongue in the land of Pop and Zam."

The elements of good government are enumerated in a passage on page 26: "The Jaguar will measure out the six magic formulae of government: these involve good chiefdoms, a good aristocracy, good men, and good sons, throughout the earth."

A love for nature breathes through the pages of the **Book of** Tizimin. Page 25: "The Jaguar, the mountain-lion, the innumerable *sacbob* and *chacbob* all love the native lords." Page 26: "When good men are oppressed and their towns destroyed, there will be no more mountain-lions in the land, no more foxes, no more ferrets in the ravines. . . . There will be no more foxes, no more towns, no more ferrets in the ravines. There will be no more noble descendants adorning the lion's den. It would be better if the world came to an end." Page 28: "The horse shall strike them down with despair," referring to the Spaniards. "The horse shall pierce them in secrecy. It is decreed."

mythology

There are a few incidental and incomplete allusions to ancient myths in the Tizimin manuscript which leave much more to be desired. The world was created in a Katun 5 Ahau, or at least the sky was quite new at that time, and too close to the earth for comfort. In the following passage, there may be an implied thrust at the cupidity of the Spanish conquerors: Page 4: ". . . it was also in a certain Katun 5 Ahau long, long ago that the sky was new, having just been created. And it was so close to the earth that certain crafty fellows made a loud outcry, from amid the branches of the Tree of Life, entreating Lord 5 Ahau that he make an end to the drunken begging, an end to covetousness on the part of our rulers."

The Bacabs who stand at the four cardinal points and watch over the earth, "with their faces twice as high as the Tree of Life," [233] who stretched out the earth and planted the "trees of abundance," the *imix*-trees, at the four corners. Page 21: "Now it should be said of the four gods, the four Bacabs, that they stretched out the earth, and when they had finished stretching out the earth, they planted the red *imix*-tree. They should receive a handful of offerings as a token of their having stretched out the earth. These Bacabs shake the tree. Perhaps the Moon germinates the plants.

"And they planted the white *imix*-tree in the north. Perhaps they will grant us a sign, a symbol of the stretching out of the earth. Although they place a black *imix*-tree at the west of our land as a sign

---

[233] Page 12 of the manuscript.

of their having stretched out the earth, the black face of this black
imix-tree in our midst will frighten the multitude. The yellow *imix*-
tree stands to the south of the land as a sign of the stretching out
of the earth. It stands there, yellow, to tell the news. Finally there is
the green *imix*-tree in the middle of the country to commemorate
the stretching out of the earth. The people are instructed concerning the origin and existence of the katun. So be it." The green tree
of abundance in the middle of the earth is the Tree of Life, the
yaxche.

In the Tizimin manuscript, one of the four Musencabs is credited with having measured the earth. Page 20: "At the expiration of
the period of the prophecy, there came the Sun of our Life, and
whichever one it was of the four Musencabs who measures the earth
by his paces."

The earth was then divided into four quarters. Page 6: "They
told about a vision of the earth and its four quarters, how great activity came from the north and a great stirring from the west." But
eventually, in the last days, there was to be a reuniting of these
divisions and a return to unity. Page 18: "I say that the divisions of
the earth shall all be one."

Allusions to the Tree of Life are plentiful. Page 4: "Have you
forgotten the downpour on the day when you carried the idol named
Kan? Three symbols of the thickness of the Tree of Life! Three clusters of fruit from the tree of nourishment!" The three symbols of
abundance or "clusters" suggest three heaps of cumulus clouds, full
of life-giving rain, such as one sees in the hieroglyph Cauac.

Page 17: "In the last days, learn about the Tree of Life. . . .
Remember your blessings. Lean upon the protection of the Tree.
Yes, this sign is your assurance that they come from heaven." Page
19: "He who impersonates the god casts lots to determine the final
outcome of the country's affairs such as . . . the times for attaching three seals to the Tree of Life."

A reference to the belief that the first period of the earth's existence was shrouded in darkness before the creation of the sun, is
found on page 17: "There will be abundant rains to record during

Katun 9 Ahau. The heavens will shield themselves with darkness, *as in the first division of world history.*"

The discovery of the art of writing was attributed to Lord 7 Cauac, who was apparently the god of the katun as well as of the year-bearer. Page 6: "Seven Cauac arrives on his day in the seventh tun on the first of Pop, when the lord of the day, the god of the katun, created writing."

Itzam-cabain the Earth-monster (or Earth-crocodile according to Roys) played an important role in putting the world in order. The name stands in antithesis to Itzam-caan, the heavenly Itzam, a sky-deity. Itzam-cabain also wrote books, it appears. Page 20: "When they came down and ranged to and fro over the earth, the Thirteen gods and the Nine gods, they put in order that which they had created, and that which Itzam-cabain, Itzam the Earth-monster, had put in order. The knife of the Sun protects his people. When the heavens cease to be, we shall all die and four-footed creatures will destroy the land.

"Even when the Thirteen gods once had their beginning in ancient times, when there was rigorous discipline upon the earth and the Earth-monster tore up great trees by the roots, still the prophecies of the katun-folds were fulfilled, even when he once threatened to shake the earth. The prophecies of the katun shall be fulfilled! And the Nine gods, when they cut the throat of Itzam-cabain and created the island out of his body, had no desire to destroy the works of his hands or his books. Nevertheless, we do not invoke him by name or burn incense to him, when the lords bind up the face of the sun at the present time."

CHAPTER SEVEN

The Correlation Question

PAGES 1 TO 13 OF THE BOOK OF CHILAM BALAM OF Tizimin present the calendrical framework of a single period of 7200 days comprising a certain Katun 5 Ahau, in such a way as to furnish an almost perfect criterion for any *Ahau Equation,* as the correlation between the Maya and Christian calendars is sometimes called. The structure of year-bearers and tuns is clearly delineated, and the katun is anchored in the Christian calendar. Only the Long Count is missing, but that defect is supplied on page 16 of the manuscript.

The opening sentence, "Thirteen Kan on the first of Pop: Katun 5 Ahau follows along its path, the year being 1593, save that one year still remains to be checked off before the bearer of the future katun arrives," makes it clear that a Katun 5 Ahau is about to commence in 1594.

The statement that a Maya year 13 Kan fell during 1593 is supported by abundant evidence from independent sources and need not be challenged. The figure *1593* is clearly inscribed. Several corroborating combinations of year-bearer and tun are supplied in the text, as if the coincidence of their numbers struck the author as significant:

Page 6: "Seven Cauac arrives on his day in the seventh tun on the first of Pop. . . . The generations of the Itza will comprise three folds of katuns on 8 Kan, the year-bearer which falls on 1 Pop in the eighth tun."

Page 7: "Eleven Cauac came on the first day of Pop in the eleventh tun. . . . In the twelfth tun when the day 12 Kan arrived,

211

there was the folding up of the days, and the speeches of the festival and the interpretation of the prophecies."

Even the *tzolkin* is not neglected, being represented by the "katun's day" 5 Ahau, the name-day of the katun, which occurred every 260 days.

No ambiguity is involved, therefore, in reconstructing the calendar of this section of the chronicle, if one avoids an occasional repetition and recapitulation. Table 1 exhibits the reconstructed calendar just as it is given in the text, except that the gaps have

Table 1

Calendar of Katun 5 Ahau; pages 1-13 of the Tizimin

Year	Year-bearer	Tun No.	Katun
1593	13 Kan	(20)	(7 Ahau)
(1594)	1 Muluc	(1)	5 Ahau
(1595)	(2 Ix)	(2)	
(1596)	3 Cauac	(3)	
(1597)	4 Kan	(4)	5 Ahau
(1598)	5 Muluc	(5)	5 Ahau
(1599)	6 Ix	(6)	
(1600)	7 Cauac	7	
(1601)	8 Kan	8	
(1602)	9 Muluc	"5 Ahau"	
(1603)	10 Ix	(10)	5 Ahau
(1604)	11 Cauac	11	
(1605)	12 Kan	12	
(1606)	13 Muluc	13	
(1607)	(1 Ix)	14	5 Ahau
(1608)	2 Cauac	15	5 Ahau
(1609)	3 Kan	16	
(1610)	4 Muluc	17	
(1611)	5 Ix	18	
(1612)	6 Cauac	19	
(1613)	7 Kan	(20)	5 Ahau
(1614)	8 Muluc	(1)	3 Ahau

been filled for the sake of continuity. All such additional data are inclosed in brackets.

Table 2 presents evidence that the Makemson correlation produces Long Count dates in agreement with the data of Table 1, as far as they go. The year-bearers and tun numbers also appear to be consistent, when it is seen that a year 1 Muluc, for example, runs from 1593 November 2 through 1594 November 1 and contains the critical date, 1594 September 29, on which 7 Ahau fell, the day which brought Katun 7 Ahau to a close and ushered in Katun 5 Ahau. Table 2 contains the following data:

Column 1: the Long Count dates of the successive tuns of Katun 5 Ahau, according to the 12.9.0.0.0. correlations.

Table 2

the equivalent dates in the Makemson correlation

The Long Count Date			Date Julian			Year-Bearer		
12.11.19.0.0	11 Ahau	18 Kayab	1593 Oct.	4	13 Kan	1592 Nov.	2
12.12. 0.0.0	7 ”	13 ”	1594 Sep.	29	1 Muluc	1593 ”	2
12.12. 1.0.0	3 ”	8 ”	1595 ”	24	2 Ix	1594 ”	2
12.12. 2.0.0	12 ”	3 ”	1596 ”	18	3 Cauac	1595 ”	2
12.12. 3.0.0	8 ”	18 Pax	1597 ”	13	4 Kan	1596 ”	1
12.12. 4.0.0	4 ”	13 ”	1598 ”	8	5 Muluc	1597 ”	1
12.12. 5.0.0	13 ”	8 ”	1599 ”	3	6 Ix	1598 ”	1
12.12. 6.0.0	9 ”	3 ”	1600 Aug.	28	7 Cauac	1599 ”	1
12.12. 7.0.0	5 ”	18 Muan	1601 ”	23	8 Kan	1600 Oct.	31
12.12. 8.0.0	1 ”	13 ”	1602 ”	18	9 Muluc	1601 ”	31
12.12. 9.0.0	10 ”	8 ”	1603 ”	13	10 Ix	1602 ”	31
12.12.10.0.0	6 ”	3 ”	1604 ”	7	11 Cauac	1603 ”	31
12.12.11.0.0	2 ”	18 Kankin	1605 ”	2	12 Kan	1604 ”	30
12.12.12.0.0	11 ”	13 ”	1606 July 28		13 Muluc	1605 ”	30
12.12.13.0.0	7 ”	8 ”	1607 ”	23	1 Ix	1606 ”	30
12.12.14.0.0	3 ”	3 ”	1608 ”	17	2 Cauac	1607 ”	30
12.12.15.0.0	12 ”	18 Mac	1609 ”	12	3 Kan	1608 ”	29
12.12.16.0.0	8 ”	13 ”	1610 ”	7	4 Muluc	1609 ”	29
12.12.17.0.0	4 ”	8 ”	1611 ”	2	5 Ix	1610 ”	29
12.12.18.0.0	13 ”	3 ”	1612 June 26		6 Cauac	1611 ”	29
12.12.19.0.0	9 ”	18 Ceh	1613 ”	21	7 Kan	1612 ”	28
12.13. 0.0.0	5 ”	13 ”	1614 ”	16	8 Muluc	1613 ”	28

Column 2: the corresponding date (Julian) given by the Makemson correlation.

Column 3: the year-bearer sequence and the order of the tuns as given in the Tizimin chronicle.

Column 4: the Julian date of the year-bearer in the Makemson correlation.

Note that in the Tizimin manuscript the *tuns* were numbered, not in *elapsed*, but in *current* time. Tun 1, for example, ran from 12.12.0.0.0. to 12.12.1.0.0.

On page 3 of the manuscript is found the statement: "When 9 Muluc falls on the first of Pop, there will come the tun which is known as 5 Ahau, as it is said in our language." According to Table 2, the year-bearer 9 Muluc fell on October 31, 1601, whereas the tun date 5 Ahau arrived 61 days earlier, on August 23. Strict agreement between the table and the manuscript requires, therefore, *that the tun, like the year, be named* for its initial day. This practice is consistent with the numbering of the tun in current time, pointed out above. Since the tun so closely parallels the vague year, it would seem more logical to name them both for the beginning day, or for the ending day. There can be no doubt, on the other hand, that the katun was named for its ending day, in this period; but it has been shown in an earlier chapter that even the katun was named for its initial day in 1752.

A statement on page 14, in the midst of the exhortation which follows the enumeration of the events of a certain Katun 5 Ahau, makes the needed connection between the current Katun 5 Ahau which began in 1594 and the Long Count: "In the twelfth katun, as it is called, the Jaguar should be the head." Table 2 indicates that Katun 5 Ahau began on 12.12.0.0.0 and ended on 12.13.0.0.0 in the Makemson correlation. Another possible connection with the Long Count will be discussed later.

Table 3 exhibits the same data as Table 2, except that the dates have been computed according to the Goodman-Thompson correlation for the Katun 5 Ahau nearest to 1594.

Table 3

the dates in the Goodman-Thompson correlation

The Long Count Date			Date Julian			Year-Bearer		
11.18.19.0.0	11 Ahau	18 Chen	1597 Dec.	29	4 Kan	1597 July		5
11.19. 0.0.0	7 "	13 "	1598 "	24	5 Muluc	1598	"	5
11.19. 1.0.0	3 "	8 "	1599 "	19	6 Ix	1599	"	5
11.19. 2.0.0	12 "	3 "	1600 "	13	7 Cauac	1600	"	4
11.19. 3.0.0	8 "	18 Mol	1601 "	8	8 Kan	1601	"	4
11.19. 4.0.0	4 "	13 "	1602 "	3	9 Muluc	1602	"	4
11.19. 5.0.0	13 "	8 "	1603 Nov.	28	10 Ix	1603	"	4
11.19. 6.0.0	9 "	3 "	1604 "	22	11 Cauac	1604	"	3
11.19. 7.0.0	5 "	18 Yaxkin	1605 "	17	12 Kan	1605	"	3
11.19. 8.0.0	1 "	13 "	1606 "	12	13 Muluc	1606	"	3
11.19. 9.0.0	10 "	8 "	1607 "	7	1 Ix	1607	"	3
11.19.10.0.0	6 "	3 "	1608 "	1	2 Cauac	1608	"	2
11.19.11.0.0	2 "	18 Xul	1609 Oct.	27	3 Kan	1609	"	2
11.19.12.0.0	11 "	13 "	1610 "	22	4 Muluc	1610	"	2
11.19.13.0.0	7 "	8 "	1611 "	17	5 Ix	1611	"	2
11.19.14.0.0	3 "	3 "	1612 "	11	6 Cauac	1612	"	1
11.19.15.0.0	12 "	18 Tzec	1613 "	6	7 Kan	1613	"	1
11.19.16.0.0	8 "	13 "	1614 "	1	8 Muluc	1614	"	1
11.19.17.0.0	4 "	8 "	1615 Sep.	26	9 Ix	1615	"	1
11.19.18.0.0	13 "	3 "	1616 "	20	10 Cauac	1616 June		30
11.19.19.0.0	9 "	18 Zotz	1617 "	15	11 Kan	1617	"	30
12. 0. 0.0.0	5 "	13 "	1618 "	10	12 Muluc	1618	"	30

Although 1593 is the only Christian year expressed in the section of the Tizimin chronicle under discussion, the figures are so clearly written that they cannot be mistaken for any other year, in my opinion. Consequently there seems to be no ambiguity about the time of the beginning of Katun 5 Ahau. The manuscript also gives the correct year-bearer for 1593, which serves as a check on our conclusions. Later, the seventh tun is correlated with a year-bearer 7 Cauac, the eighth tun with 8 Muluc, and so on throughout the greater part of the katun. The whole body of data is consistent, and all point to a Katun 5 Ahau beginning in a year 1 Muluc, in 1594.

Thus we are forced to conclude that the whole structure of the calendar as found in these pages is harmonious in all its parts, and it is in agreement with what is known from independent sources regarding the year-bearers in the Christian years.

In Table 2, the katun ends on a day 12.13.0.0.0 5 Ahau 18 Ceh in a year 8 Muluc. Such a combination of katun-ending day and year-bearer can occur only once in 18,720 vague years, this number being the least common multiple of 13 katuns (93,600 days) and 52 vague years (18,980 days). The katun-ending day 5 Ahau occurs only once in 13 katuns. The year-bearer 8 Muluc comes once in 52 years. Hence we can hardly attribute the close-knit agreement to chance.

In Table 3, on the other hand, Katun 5 Ahau begins in 1598, in a year 5 Muluc. The seventh tun falls, therefore, in a year 11 Cauac. One can easily find when the Goodman-Thompson correlation will give a katun-ending day 5 Ahau in a year 8 Muluc by computing a few dates:

11. 7.0.0.0 5 Ahau 18 Kankin falls in a year 2 Kan.
12. 0.0.0.0 5 Ahau 13 Zotz　　 ” 　” ” 　 ” 　12 Muluc.
12.13.0.0.0 5 Ahau 13 Ceh 　　 ” 　” ” 　 ” 　 8 Muluc.

The third date, which is the one we are looking for, coincides with December 15, 1874 (Julian). It must be conceded, therefore, that the Goodman-Thompson correlation fails to meet the following requirements:

(a)　a Katun 5 Ahau commencing in 1594;
(b)　a Katun 5 Ahau commencing in a year 1 Muluc;
(c)　there is no agreement between the tun-number and the numerical coefficient of the year-bearer;
(d)　Katun 5 Ahau is not the twelfth but the nineteenth katun of the current baktun.

With regard to (d), a glance at Table 3 shows that the day 12.0.0.0.0 would have ended *Baktun 11* on June 30, 1618 in the Goodman-Thompson correlation. If this had been the true situation, would such an important and significant event have passed without some mention, when the pebbles of the days were solemnly counted, on the day 5 Ahau?

In the Makemson correlation, on the other hand, *Baktun 12* came to an end in 1752, on a day 13.0.0.0.0 4 Ahau 3 Kankin. This day is recorded as belonging to the "katun for remembering knowledge and writing it down in histories." Is it not probable that "Books of the Baktun" were written at the close of one of these 400-year periods in the same way that the Book of the Katun was compiled at the end of each 7200-day period?

The word *baktun* is a modern synthesis and does not appear in the Motul dictionary or the vocabulary of Pio Perez, to my knowledge. *Bak* has a variety of meanings such as "flesh; to twist, as rope; to inclose in a circle; to embrace; and finally a count by 400's." In compounds, *bak* has the significance of "many things together." *Bakxoc* is "to sum up," for example.

The phrase *oxlahun bak*, 13 bak," occurs in both the Chumayel and the Tizimin manuscripts in passages which have points of similarity. Roys[234] has translated the sentence *Likom katun Habana oxlahun bak chem lae,* as "An army shall come forth from Havana [with] a fleet of thirteen ships," literally "thirteen 400's of ships." It is part of the prophecy of Katun 1 Ahau which treats of war, the Inquisition and violent death.

The passage in the Tizimin which contains this phrase follows the detailed account of the events of Katun 5 Ahau of the first thirteen pages, and occurs in the midst of a long exhortation urging the people to a passive resistance of the Spanish rulers. The following passage, containing two mentions of *oxlahun bak,* is found on pages 15 and 16 of the Tizimin manuscript:

"When the original thirteen baktuns were created, a war was waged which caused the country to cease to exist. Little by little, however, our enemies came to hear the prophecies of Ahau; but finally, even the hope of hearing Ahau is brought to an end, because of the words of opposition.

"When the need arises for the high authority at the head of the mat to safeguard our children, then we feel deeply the tragedy of being captives in war; also when we are ordered to obey. . . .

[234] R.L. Roys 1933: 95 and 158.

Presently, at the arrival here below of a cross of iron, I will suddenly come into your presence. I will be a companion to you in prison." Is this the god speaking through the prophet of the Jaguar? "Go you to the war-captain. I will protect your trembling backs.

"The Nine shall arise in sorrow, alas . . . and when over the dark sea I shall be lifted up in a chalice of fire, to that generation there will come the day of withered fruit. There will be rain. The face of the sun shall be extinguished because of the great tempest.

"Then, finally, the ornaments shall descend in heaps. There will be good gifts for one and all, as well as lands, from the Great Spirit, wherever they shall settle down. Presently *Baktun 13* shall come sailing, figuratively speaking, bringing the ornaments of which I have spoken from your ancestors. Then the god will come to visit his little ones. Perhaps 'After Death' will be the subject of his discourse."

The Tizimin sentence corresponding to the one quoted from the Chumayel is: *ca tu sihsah u chun oxlahun bak, ca tu liksah katun hauana u lumil.* I have rendered it: "When they created the original thirteen baktuns (or Baktun 13), then a war was raised which caused the country to cease to exist." It seems to me that this is a genuine reference to the invention of the calendar and to the legendary date 13.0.0.0.0 4 Ahau 8 Cumhu. Since the Chumayel version was obviously written after complete conversion and reconciliation to Christianity, while the Book of Tizimin preceded that state, there can be no doubt that the Tizimin is the much older document.

Note that the word *chem,* "ship or to navigate," is not found in this first statement in the Tizimin. That this is not a mere oversight is corroborated by the fact that there is no numerical classifier for ships, such as *ac,* for example. I have construed hauana (Roys, Havana) as the participial form of *haual,* "to cause to cease," with the enclitic *a.* It is not difficult to understand how the passage could have been modified to the Chumayel version in the course of a century or two.

Page 15 concludes with the prophecy of marvelous gifts which are to descend in the future. And when are they to arrive? "Presently Baktun 13 shall come sailing, figuratively speaking, bringing the ornaments of which I have spoken, from your ancestors."

The Maya text is: *licutal oxlahun bak chem, ti u cenic u tzan a ceni ciac aba yum texe.* Here, as in the Chumayel, *oxlahun bak* is followed by *chem,* but as the numerical classifier is absent I have taken *chem* as the verb, "to sail or navigate." There is no other word in this clause which could be a verb. The next phrase is of special interest. Pio Perez gives the following meanings:

cen, cenil, ornaments

cen, centi, to say

ciac, I say

ti u cenic u tzan, as they say it in their language.

Having translated the passage in accordance with all these definitions, I believe that it refers to the tremendously important event of the arrival of 13.0.0.0.0 4 Ahau 3 Kankin in the not too distant future, rounding off the long cycle of baktuns which began with 13.0.0.0.0 4 Ahau 8 Cumhu in 3374 B.C.

There is another reference to the same 4 Ahau on page 16 in a somewhat confused passage: "Later, then, they must all profess my teachings when that day comes . . . without forsaking them, in the final days of misfortune, in the final days of *tying up the bundle of the thirteen katuns on 4 Ahau,* then the end of the world shall come, and the katun of our fathers shall again ascend on high." There are two reasons for believing that this passage refers to the end of a cycle of thirteen *baktuns,* and that an ignorant copyist has read *katuns* into it erroneously: (1) the cycle of thirteen *katuns* began and ended on a day 13 Ahau, as is clearly stated in another part of the manuscript; and (2) the katun-ending day 4 Ahau must have come in 1752 according to the calendar of the first pages of the chronicle, and this is 13.0.0.0.0 4 Ahau 3 Kankin, in the Makemson correlation, which fell on June 22, 1752 in the Gregorian calendar.

The Makemson correlation, it may be recalled,[235] was derived from astronomical considerations, the fundamental hypotheses being:

---

[235] Makemson 1946.

(a) that the dates at the head of the Dresden eclipse table, i.e.,

9.16.4.10. 8   12 Lamat   1 Muan
9.16.4.11. 3   1 Akbal   16 Muan
9.16.4.11.18   3 Eznab   11 Pax

represent observational records or predictions of two solar eclipses 30 days apart and a lunar eclipse halfway between them.

(b) That the epoch of the Venus ephemeris 9.9.9.16.0 1 Ahau 18 Kayab falls within 18 days of a heliacal rising of the planet. The margin of error, 18 days, was chosen in order to include the Goodman-Thompson correlation in the investigation.

From the basic premises 64 possible correlations between the Maya and Julian calendars were found. These were then tested for agreement with certain post-conquest criteria:

(a)   A year 12 Kan fell partly in 1553.

(b)   The Maya year commenced on July 16, 1553.

(c)   A Katun 13 Ahau ended between 1530 and 1540.

The Goodman-Thompson correlation met all these tests, as well as the astronomical ones; but there was a competitor, a new correlation which agreed in all respects except with regard to the formula July 16 = the year-bearer 12 Kan. This new contender could not be disregarded without further investigation, particularly as it agreed with the astronomical data somewhat more closely than the Goodman-Thompson equation. It made the total lunar eclipse of the Dresden tables visible in Central America on May 25, 495, whereas the lunar eclipse predicted by the Goodman-Thompson correlation took place on the opposite side of the globe. Moreover, the new correlation gave the extremely important result, in the opinion of an astronomer, that it made the four great festivals described by Landa fall near the times of the equinoxes and solstices.

An investigation of Landa's "typical year" brought me to the conclusion that the accepted formula

12 Kan 1 Pop = 1553 July 16 Julian

is based on a misunderstanding of Landa's own statements and that it has been written in at a subsequent date.

Landa says: ". . . it will be enough to say that the letter or character *with which their count of the days or calendar began, is called Hun Imix* [1 Imix], and it has no certain or fixed day on which it falls." [236]

Now I believe that Landa wrote down a list of the 365 Maya days beginning with 12 Kan 1 Pop opposite January 1. Justification for such an arrangement is found in his statement: ". . . and I shall give their calendar here *in no other way than according to the order of our own,* to which I shall join it, so that our letters (Dominical) and theirs (the tzolkin days), and our months and theirs, may be shown."

When he came to 1 Imix in his list of Maya days, Landa made a notation beside it, in keeping with his statement above, "Here begins the Calendar of the Indians." In a comparative list of days starting with January 1, *1 Imix falls beside July 17.*

Aguilar appears to have been the first Spanish writer to comment on the calendar after Landa. Bowditch [237] writes of him: "Doctor Don Pedro Sanchez de Aguilar was born in . . . Yucatan and received the degree of doctor in 1588. In 1613 he wrote 'Informe contra idolorum cultores,' which was published in Madrid in 1639. He went to Bolivia in 1619 to become dean of the cathedral of La Plata, and died there in 1648."

Aguilar declares in no uncertain terms that the Maya year began on July 17. Is it not probable that he interpreted Landa's notation "Here begins the Calendar of the Indians" as referring to July 17, instead of to 1 Imix, to which it was attached? From this faulty initial assumption, he then went on to associate 12 Kan 1 Pop, the New Year's day, with July 17. That Aguilar did not possess correct authentic information regarding the Maya calendar is corroborated by the fact that three times on a single page he mentions six supplementary days instead of five, calling them *caniculares,* "dog-days."

Aguilar's book followed Landa's by about 50 years. After another half century, Diego Lopez de Cogolludo set out to write his *Historia de Yucathan,* which was published in Madrid in 1688. Cogol-

[236] Tozzer 1941: 149.
[237] Bowditch 1910: 8.

ludo accepted Aguilar's interpretation of Landa to the effect that the
Maya year started on July 17, but he corrected the more obvious error of the *six* supplementary days to *five:*

"For this count they divided the year into 18 months, but commenced their new year in our July, on the 17th day. . . . The five
days which were required to complete the year of 365 days, they
called the 'nameless' days. . . . And those fearsome days were the
12th, 13th, 14th, 15th and 16th of our July."

Don Pio Perez, writing in 1843, reconstructed the Maya calendar according to information gathered from the Spanish and native
chronicles. He accepted Aguilar's equation January 12 = 1 Yax,
but by interpolating only five epagomenal days, he arrived at July
16, as the New Year's day 12 Kan 1 Pop. He was probably not the
first to make this modification, for the *uinal* list in the latter part of
the Book of Tizimin (page 38) begins the year on July 16. At the same
time, some investigator must have inserted the words in Landa's
Relacion which made the Maya year start on July 16.

Evidence that the Maya themselves had lost their original year-
beginning day so far as its relation to the Christian calendar is concerned, is seen in the following table:

Table 4

modern Maya New Year's days

Ixil	1939 March	12
Kanhobal	1932 March	14
Jacalteca	1927 March	16
Pokomchi	1914 December	28
Ixtlauacan	1854 May	1
Kekchi	1804 August	3
Quiche	1722 May	4
Cakchiquel	1688 January	31

These dates indicate that (a) the Maya calendar was never
"frozen" into the Christian calendar with the year beginning on
July 16 (or 26 Gregorian) as has sometimes been asserted; and that

(b) none of these can be traced back to a New Year's day on July 16 in 1553, if no leap year day has been intercalated.

In the authentic Tizimin chronicle, there are statements which strongly suggest that the year-count or more properly the month-count upon which the year depends, had been lost, in spite of the fact that the tzolkin and katun counts may have been kept up until the beginning of the 18th century. The first hint of difficulties with the year-bearer is found on page 26 of the manuscript:

"Ten will interpret the opening of the sealed katun of 10 Ahau (1673-1693). One looks at the face of Citbolon or at the face of the sky of Citbolon, one at the sun, one at the forests, one at the trees, to determine what kind of remedy the heavens will provide, to be written down [in the Book of the Katun] for future years. . . . The lords bind up their faces in pain because true men swelter in toil and hunger is their burden, and because of their bad conscience about protecting the people. . . . The lords hold their breath in the throat and make true their promise about setting Pop in order. It has become perverted by this time, a stain on the good name of our people. When the bearer of Katun 10 Ahau arrives, *there will be great sorrow among the lords on account of the year-bearer.*"

There seems to be no reason for doubting that the phrase "setting Pop in order" definitely refers to rectifying the month-count by fixing the date of 1 Pop, although some authorities assert that the words have no relation to the calendar. The passage is interesting for the light it throws on the responsibilities of the aristocracy toward the people.

Anxiety about the year-bearer appears again on page 28: "And no one is gallant enough to hear the news calmly when everyone is involved in the omens of Katun 4 Ahau. Likewise the pestilence will enter our houses. There is also reason for suspecting that even now the year-bearer will continue to be an important and grave problem of Ah Kin Chilam, when he teaches about the bearer of the katun."

In the description of the spurious katun of 24 years (instead of 20 tuns) in the latter part of the Tizimin manuscript which was probably added to the older manuscript in the latter part of the 18th century, we are told (page 33):

"Now, however, Ahau is subservient to the year-bearer of the south, 3 Cauac on the first of Pop, the year being 1752. The god Four is submerged on that very day, 4 Ahau."

My interpretation of this cryptic utterance is as follows: The sequence of year-bearers as well as that of the katun-ending days had been kept intact; but their connection with the Maya months and their positions in the Christian calendar were not known. Even the exact length of the katun had been lost from memory. The Maya scholar of the mid-eighteenth century who set out to reconstruct the ancient calendar had very little to proceed by. He knew that the Maya year-bearer of 1752 was 3 Cauac. He knew that the day of the katun was 4 Ahau. Since 4 Ahau follows immediately upon 3 Cauac, he made the erroneous deduction that the katun day fell on 4 Ahau 2 Pop, the year having entered on 3 Cauac 1 Pop. Thus 4 Ahau may be said to have been "subservient" to the year-bearer.

He deduced from Landa's *Relacion* or from one of Landa's imitators that the New Year's day fell on July 16, and this date for 1 Pop appears on page 38 in connection with the year-bearer 1 Kan. No allowance has been made for leap year days since 1553 or for the shift of ten days to the Gregorian count. He knew that Katun 4 Ahau, which he erroneously named for its *beginning* day, should be followed by a Katun 2 Ahau. Landa had attributed 20 years to each katun; but his calculations showed him that 20 years would not bring him to 2 Ahau as the new katun-beginning day. Going on from 20 years, instead of backward to 20 tuns, he finally arrived at 24 vague years as the correct interval between katun-day 4 Ahau and katun-day 2 Ahau.

The Makemson correlation makes the actual katun-ending day 4 Ahau 3 Kankin fall on June 22, 1752. This was the important day 13.0.0.0.0 which was discussed earlier, but by this time all understanding of the Long Count had long since disappeared. The day 4 Ahau 3 Kankin falls 261 days after 3 Cauac 2 Pop.

The Goodman-Thompson correlation makes the katun-day 4 Ahau coincide with the month day 3 Xul. By consulting the *Maya Date-finder*, constructed by Charles V. Imeson, one quickly finds that the katun-day 4 Ahau 3 Xul came in a year 7 Cauac and on the Long Count date 12.7.0.0.0. This was in the year 1756.

The ancient Book of Chilam Balam of Tizimin ends with the prophecy on page 33. How long an interval elapsed between the last entry on page 33 and the statement, "Now, however, Ahau is subservient to the year-bearer of the south" cannot be estimated. Here for the first time appears a pro-Christian bias, but it is only an interpolated paragraph, unrelated to what precedes or follows:

"There is one Jesus Christ, the very most correct count above all counts. Yes, and when they are all in order, He protects their backs from the pressure of the ancient Maya teachings in the land."

The very next sentence, on the other hand, again expresses deep concern over the loss of the year-bearer as well as a suspicion regarding the new 24-year katun:

"And when they count, they are deceived as to the year-bearers of the teachings, like an old wound breaking out afresh, when they teach the three counts of the deceptive katun."

In whose brain did the spurious katun originate? It is idle to speculate. Pio Perez adopted the 24-year katun with its four "nameless" years, in his own reconstruction of the Maya calendar, giving as his authority "various ancient documents," which were probably the Books of Chilam Balam.

The list of 365 Maya days which occupies the final twelve pages of the Book of Chilam Balam of Tizimin begins with

January 1 = 10 Oc.

Yax enters on January 12, in agreement with Aguilar's enumeration of the days. It corresponds with New Year's day 1 Pop on July 16 Julian. The year-bearer may be considered as 11 Cimi on 1 Pop or 12 Manik on 2 Pop. Manik was one of the year-bearers of the ancient calendar, but coincided with 0 Pop in the time of the inscriptions.

Curiously enough, two other days in the long list are designated "the first day of Pop." They are 7 Kan on April 25 and 6 Cauac on September 27. Kan and Cauac are among the year-bearers listed by Landa. It is possible that April 25 has some connection with the March dates of New Year's among the modern tribes of the Ixil, Kanhobal and Jacalteca as shown in Table 4. September 27 on the other hand is the New Year's day of 1736 according to the Makemson correlation.

There is one item of information in the Tizimin chronicle that can be cited in support of the Goodman-Thompson correlation, the well-known double date discovered by Martinez-Hernandez. It is found in the following paragraph:

Page 13: "My property and my hacienda are in the land called the district of Salamanca, in the section over against Chactemal, in the land division of Vaimil, where I established my grant in writing it may be on the 18th day of Zac, on 11 Chuen, on February 15 in the year 1544."

The date has been discussed in connection with the counting of the pebbles of the days of Katun 5 Ahau in Bakhalal, in 1614, and according to it the Maya priest who counted the katun days in 1614 must have been an extremely old man, assuming that he had attained his majority before he was granted title to land in 1544. At best, we must consider 1544 as very uncertain. In the Goodman-Thompson correlation, however, 11.16.4.6.5 5 Chicchan 13 Zac fell on February 15, 1544, and 11 Chuen 19 Zac arrived on February 21. The Makemson correlation makes 11 Chuen 19 Zac fall on June 20, 1543, on the Long Count date 12.9.7.17.11.

Since this double date is not in agreement with the calendar of the Tizimin, or with any other data of the first 33 pages, it does not possess much value as a single item of evidence against so much internally consistent calendrical data.

There are three other small items of interest which shed a little light on the Maya calendar. Two are found on page 5:

"Fierce warriors were among those who were doubtful of the outcome and they felt that further ceremonials were required to observe properly the festival of the katun [5 Ahau] when 5 Muluc [the year-bearer] came, at his taking office. Fruit was falling from the trees and the elder brothers collected it in great quantities to save what they could. When 5 Ahau arrived on his day within the year 5 Muluc, there was a crescent moon."

A glance at Tables 2 and 3 reveals that 5 Muluc fell on the following days in the two correlations under discussion:

Goodman-Thompson	Makemson
July 5, 1598	November 1, 1597

Nothing of value can be deduced from these circumstances since we do not know what kind of fruit was falling, or when the rainy season started in these years. The katun-day 5 Ahau occurred 91 days later. These dates, with the corresponding ages of the moon follow:

Goodman-Thompson	Makemson
October 4, 1598	January 31, 1598
Moon-age 14 days	Moon-age 4 days

Here the evidence is distinctly favorable to the new correlation, since there was a crescent moon on the day in question, whereas in the other case, the moon was nearly full.

The third observation involves one of the rare "double dates," and it equates April 19, 1629, to the last day of Yaxkin:

Page 39: "Now on April 19, 1629, there came a shaking and destruction as things were thrown together in heaps, the bundles of food falling violently to the ground in ruin. On the very last day of Yaxkin, the great manifestation of the earthquake finally relaxed its shaking."

If the Maya new year had been frozen at July 16 Julian the last day of Yaxkin would have arrived on December 2 Julian, or December 12, Gregorian. If the new year had been frozen at November 12 Julian, as given by the Makemson correlation for 1553, the last day of Yaxkin would arrive on March 30 Julian or April 9 Gregorian. Thus the new correlation comes closer to satisfying the conditions of this double date.

In conclusion it may be said, I think, that the details of the Maya calendar as set forth in the Tizimin manuscript agree to a remarkable extent with those given by the new 12.9.0.0.0 correlation, the one exception being the date in 1544. The only theory that can be made to fit the two separate lines of evidence is that there were two separate calendars. Both Goodman and Gates pointed out the inevitability of such a conclusion on the basis of all the evidence, if taken to be correct.

Bibliography
and
Index

Bibliography

BOWDITCH, CHARLES PICKERING
1910. *The Numeration, Calendar Systems and Astronomical Knowledge of the Mayas.* Cambridge.

COGOLLUDO, DIEGO LOPEZ
1688. *Historia de Yucatan.* Madrid.

GATES, WILLIAM E.
1932. *Excerpts from the Chumayel.* Maya Soc. Quart. I.
1938. *A Grammar of Maya.* Maya Soc. Pub. 13.

GOODMAN, J. T.
1897. *The Archaic Maya Calendar.* Biol. Cent.-Amer. Arch. Pt. 8. Appendix. London.

IMESON, CHARLES V.
The Maya Date Finder.

LA FARGE, OLIVER
1934. *Post-Columbian Dates and the Maya Correlation Problem.* Maya Research Vol. 1: 109-124.

LINCOLN, J. STEWARD
1942. *The Maya Calendar of the Ixil of Guatemala.* C.I.W. 528. Washington.

LOTHROP, S.K.
1930. *A Modern Survival of the Ancient Maya Calendar.* Proc. 23rd Internat. Cong. of Americanists.

MAKEMSON, MAUD W.
1943. *The Astronomical Tables of the Maya.* C.I.W. 546: 183-221. Washington.

1946. *The Maya Correlation Problem.* Pub. Vassar College Obs. No. 5. Poughkeepsie.

MAKEMSON, MAUD W. WITH EVANS, LOUISE HOWE

1948. *Christian Maya Prophecies from the Tizimin Manuscript.* S.W. Jl. of Anthrop., 4, No. 4, Albuquerque.

MORRIS, EARL H.

1931. *The Temple of the Warriors.* Scribner.

Motul Dictionary
     Photostat of manuscript in the John Carter Brown Library. Providence.

PEREZ, JUAN PIO

1898. *Coordination alfabetica de las voces del idioma Maya.* Merida.

ROYS, RALPH L.

1933. *The Book of Chilam Balam of Chumayel.* C.I.W. 438. Washington.

1949. *The Prophecies for the Maya Tuns or Years in the Books of Chilam Balam of Tizimin and Mani.* C.I.W. Pub. 585: 153-186. Washington.

SANCHEZ DE AGUILAR, PEDRO

1639. *Informe contra idolorum cultores del Obispado de Yucatan.* Madrid. 3rd ed. Merida. 1937.

SATTERTHWAITE, LINTON, JR.

1947. *Concepts and Structures of Maya Calendrical Arithmetics.* Joint Pub. No. 3. Mus. of U. of Penn. and Phila. Anthrop. Soc. Philadelphia.

SPINDEN, HERBERT J.

1924. *The Reduction of Maya Dates.* Peabody Mus. Pap. 6, No. 4. Cambridge.

THOMPSON, J. ERIC

1935. *Maya Chronology. The Correlation Question.* C.I.W. Pub. 456, 51-104. Washington.

TOZZER, ALFRED M.

1921. *A Maya Grammar.* Peabody Mus. Pap. 9. Cambridge.

1941. *Landa's Relacion de las cosas de Yucatan.* Peabody Mus. Pap. 18. Cambridge.

Index